Expletives Deleted
Selected Writings

Expletives Deleted
Selected Writings

ANGELA CARTER

Chatto & Windus

LONDON

Published in 1992 by
Chatto & Windus Ltd
20 Vauxhall Bridge Road
London SW1V 2SA

A CIP catalogue record for this book is
available from the British Library.

ISBN 0 7011 3999 4

Printed in Great Britain by
Mackays of Chatham plc,
Chatham, Kent

Despite our best efforts we were unable to trace
two of the writers whose letters are included
in this book on pp 83–84, but we would
like to thank them both.

Contents

Introduction I

TELL ME A STORY 7

1. Milorad Pavic: *Dictionary of the Khazars* 9
2. Milorad Pavic: *Landscape Painted with Tea* 17
3. *Irish Folk Tales, Arab Folktales* 20
4. Danilo Kis: *The Encyclopedia of the Dead* 24
5. John Berger: *Pig Earth* 27
6. John Berger: *Once in Europa* 30
7. The German Legends of the Brothers Grimm 33
8. Georges Bataille: *Story of the Eye* 37
9. William Burroughs: *The Western Lands* 39
10. William Burroughs: *Ah Pook is Here* 42
11. J. G. Ballard: *Empire of the Sun* 44
12. Walter de la Mare: *Memoirs of a Midget* 51
13. The Alchemy of the Word 67

TOMATO WOMAN 75

14. *An Omelette and a Glass of Wine* and other Dishes 77
15. Redcliffe Salaman: *The History and Social Influence of the Potato* 85
16. *Food in Vogue* 90
17. Elizabeth David: *English Bread and Yeast Cookery* 94

18. Patience Gray: *Honey from a Weed*   100

HOME   107

19. Hanif Kureishi: *The Buddha of Suburbia*   109
20. Ian Jack: *Before the Oil Ran Out* and others   112
21. Michael Moorcock: *Mother London*   116
22. Iain Sinclair: *Downriver*   119

AMERIKA   129

23. Robert Coover: *A Night at the Movies*   131
24. Hollywood   135
25. Edmund White: *The Beautiful Room is Empty*   139
26. Paul Theroux: *My Secret History*   143
27. Gilbert Hernandez: *Duck Feet*   146
28. Louise Erdrich: *The Beet Queen*   151
29. Grace Paley: *The Little Disturbances of Man* and *Enormous Changes at the Last Minute*   155

LA PETITE DIFFERENCE   159

30. Charlotte Brontë: *Jane Eyre*   161
31. David Kunzle: *Fashion and Fetishisms*   173
32. Christina Stead   177
33. Phyllis Rose: *Jazz Cleopatra*   193
34. Murasaki Shikibu: *The Tale of Genji*   196
35. Eric Rhode: *On Birth and Madness*   200

Envoi: Bloomsday   207

Notes   214

Index   220

Introduction

I am known in my circle as notoriously foul-mouthed. It's a familiar paradox – the soft-spoken, middle-aged English gentlewoman who swears like a trooper when roused. I blame my father, who was neither English nor a gentleman but Scottish and a journalist, who bequeathed me bad language and a taste for the print, so that his daughter, for the last fifteen-odd years, has been writing book reviews and then conscientiously blue-pencilling out her first gut reactions – 'bloody awful', 'fucking dire' – in order to give a more balanced and objective overview.

My father kept a shelf of Penguin classics in translation by his bed. Homer, Thucydides, Apuleius. My mother preferred Boswell, Pepys – she adored gossip, especially antique gossip, but she mistrusted fiction because she believed fiction gave one an unrealistic view of the world. Once she caught me reading a novel and chastised me: 'Never let me catch you doing that again, remember what happened to Emma Bovary.' Both my parents had left school at fifteen, they were among the last generation of men and women whose minds were furnished out of curiosity about the printed word.

In the medieval morality play of *Everyman*, Knowledge says: 'Everyman, I will go with thee and be thy guide, In thy most need to go by thy side.' The old Everyman editions used to print this on the inner covers, it was their motto. (The revived Everyman editions happily use the same motto.) I remember another slogan: 'A good book is the precious life blood of a great master', or words to that effect. We sat at meals with our open books. My mother liked to read cookery books between meals, especially during the period of food rationing. We were the only family in my class at school who didn't have a television set. They got one at last, when my father retired, ostensibly so that he could watch the news; things went downhill, after that.

Although I grew up with books and have spent a good deal of my adult life among them, make my living out of writing them and very much enjoy writing about them, I can contemplate with equanimity the science-fiction future world that every day approaches more closely, in which information and narrative pleasure are transmitted electronically and books are a quaint, antiquarian, minority taste. Not in *my* time, anyway, I say to myself. And, anyway, a book is simply the container of an idea – like a bottle; what is inside the book is what matters. Even so, I admit to having a fetishistic attitude to books, to their touch, their smell. All the same, human beings told each other stories, instructed one another in the names of things, speculated about the meaning of it all (and came to few if any conclusions), discussed the habits of animals, composed recipes, before there was such a thing even as writing and will doubtless continue to do so because the *really* important thing is narrative.

All books, even cookery books and car-maintenance manuals, consist of narratives. Narrative is written in language but it is composed, if you follow me, in time. All writers are inventing a kind of imitation time when they invent the time in which a story unfolds, and they are playing a complicated game with *our* time, the reader's time, the time it takes to read a story. A good writer can make you believe time stands still.

Yet the end of all stories, even if the writer forebears to mention it, is death, which is where our time stops short. Sheherezade knew this, which is why she kept on spinning another story out of the bowels of the last one, never coming to a point where she could say: 'This is the end.' Because it *would* have been. We travel along the thread of narrative like high-wire artistes. That is our life.

But there is more to it than that. The Balinese embark on a marathon session of reading aloud after they have prepared a corpse for burial. They read stories from collections of popular tales without stopping, twenty-four hours a day, for days at a time, in order to keep out the demons:

Introduction

Demons possess souls during the vulnerable period immediately after a death, but stories keep them out. Like Chinese boxes or English hedges, the stories contain tales within tales, so that as you enter one you run into another, passing from plot to plot every time you turn a corner, until at last you reach the core of the narrative space, which corresponds to the place occupied by the corpse within the inner courtyard of the household. Demons cannot penetrate this space because they cannot turn corners. They beat their heads helplessly against the narrative maze that the readers have built, and so reading provides a kind of defence fortification . . . It creates a wall of words, which operates like the jamming of radio broadcast. It does not amuse, instruct, improve or help to while away the time: by the imbrication of narrative and the cacophony of sound, it protects souls.[1]

And that is quite enough about the importance of narrative and ought to explain why the largest section of this book is devoted to pieces of writing about storytelling in its purest form, that is, to invented stories, and the strategies writers have devised to cheat the inevitability of closure, to chase away the demons, to keep them away for good.

Don't think I don't like real novels, though, the kind of novel in which people drink tea and commit adultery – I *do* like novels! I do! In spite of my mother's warning. Although, if a comic charlady obtrudes upon the action of a real novel, I will fling the novel against the wall amidst a flood of obscenities because the presence of such a character as a comic charlady tells me more than I wish to know about the way her creator sees the world.

Because all fiction, all writing of any kind, in fact, exists on a number of different levels. 'Never trust the teller, trust the tale,' said D. H. Lawrence, and he was right, even if he did not want this to happen to *his* tales. If you read the tale carefully, the tale tells you more than the writer knows, often much more than they wanted to give away. The tale tells you, in all innocence, what its writer thinks is important, who she or he thinks is important and, above all, why. Call it the sub-text.

I don't really think that writers, even great writers, are prophets, or sages, or Messiah-like figures; writing is a lonely, sedentary occupation and a touch of megalomania can be comforting around five on a November afternoon when you haven't seen anybody all day. But one or two of the people I'm writing about, here, have aspirations in the Messianic direction and I'm all for pretension; besides, I'm *glad* that Iain Sinclair did his bit to bring about the resignation of Margaret Thatcher. But, rather than the gift of prophecy, it seems to me that the times *shine through* certain writers, so that we think they see more clearly than we do, whereas in reality they are making *us* see more clearly. Calling such writers seers, or prophets, is a form of shorthand. I suppose I'd include John Berger and William Burroughs in this category, probably J. G. Ballard, certainly Christina Stead.

Otherwise, I like to write about writers who give me pleasure. Pleasure has always had a bad press in Britain. I'm all for pleasure, too. I wish there was more of it around. I also like to argue. There is also a strong irascibility factor in some of these pieces. A day without an argument is like an egg without salt.

I've divided up this mass of evidence of fifteen years writing about books into sections according to various enthusiasms. Storytelling, yes. Food and the semiotics of food. My country, this messy, post-imperialist Britain, which is not the country of my childhood in Atlee's austere, dignified egalitarian Forties, nor yet of my young womanhood in the ecstatic Sixties but something much more raucous and sinister. And there is also Amerika. Note I have adopted Kafka's spelling for the title of this section.

Like most Europeans of my generation, I have North America in my bloodstream. It started with the food parcels we used to receive just after the war, with the sticky American candies all over nuts and the cans of peaches, each half-peach as round, firm, golden, and ersatz as (had I but known it then) a silicone breast. I remember, possibly a trick of memory but even so, copies of *Glamour* and *Mademoiselle* and *Seventeen* thrown in as makeweights that showed me a world, as pastel-coloured and two-dimensional as a *Loony Tunes* cartoon, where people with good teeth on permanent exhibition in wide smiles ate inexplicable food, hamburgers, hot-dogs, French fries, and there were teenagers, bobby-sox, saddle Oxfords.

It was the bright, simple world of the post-War Eisenhower Utopia and I didn't encounter it again until Pop Art, when I realised it had been a vicious fake all the time.

But it was the movies that administered America to me intravenously, as they did to the entire generation that remembers 1968 with such love. It seemed to me, when I first started going to the cinema intensively in the late Fifties, that Hollywood had colonised the imagination of the entire world and was turning us all into Americans. I resented it, it fascinated me.

It still does – that giant, tragic drama of American history, the superspectacle of the twentieth century, the nation that invented itself and continually reinvents itself through its art. I've lived in the Mid-West, with its pastoral simplicity and the endless promise of the land, and in upstate New York, on the upper reaches of the most beautiful river in the world, the Hudson, and other places, too, though less passionately, and I think of the United States with awe and sadness, that the country has never, ever quite reneged on the beautiful promise inscribed on the Statue of Liberty . . . and yet has fucked so much up.

So there is an American section. And since my life has been most significantly shaped by my gender, there is a section titled 'La Petite Différence'. I spent a good many years being told what I ought to think, and how I ought to behave, and how I ought to write, even, because I was a woman and men thought they had the right to tell me how to feel, but then I stopped listening to them and tried to figure it out for myself but they didn't stop talking, oh, dear no. So I started answering back. How simple, not to say simplistic, this all sounds; and yet it is true.

I've ended the book with a little piece about James Joyce, in Dublin, because for any writer in the English language, the twentieth century starts on 16 June 1904, Bloomsday, and shows no sign of ending yet.

The pieces aren't arranged chronologically because I didn't start reviewing seriously until I was thirty-five years old and fully grown up; my tastes were pretty much formed, I knew what I liked although every now and then something new would astonish me and still does. But there is a consistency of taste, if not chronology. I haven't changed much, over the years. I use less adjectives, now, and have a kinder heart, perhaps.

My thanks to the literary editors who commissioned these reviews or, in some cases, acceded to my requests for commissions to review books they themselves might not have thought of: Karl Miller, Tony Gould, Blake Morrison, Waldemar

Januscek, Tim Radford, above all Bill Webb. Thanks to Susannah Clapp. My dear friend, Carmen Callil, thought this collection was a good idea, and found me Mark Bell, my amanuensis, without whom this book could not have been assembled. My thanks, above all, to the staff of the Foulis Gallery, the Brompton Hospital, London, also without whom . . .

For more than three years, Salman Rushdie, Britain's most remarkable writer, has suffered the archaic and cruel penalty of a death sentence, passed on him for writing and publishing a book. All those who work in the same profession are affected by his dreadful predicament, whether they know it or not. Its reverberations upon the freedoms and responsibilities of writers are endless. Perhaps writing *is* a matter of life and death. All good fortune, Salman.

TELL ME A STORY

Death is the sanction of everything the storyteller can tell. He
has borrowed his authority from death.

Walter Benjamin

Milorad Pavic: *Dictionary of the Khazars*

According to Apuleius, Pleasure is the daughter of Cupid and Psyche – of Love and the Soul, that is, a sufficiently elevated pedigree, one would have thought. Yet the British still put up a strong resistance to the idea that pleasurability might be a valid criterion in the response to literature, just as we remain dubious about the value of the 'decorative' in the visual arts. When Graham Greene made 'entertainment' a separate category from the hard stuff in his production, he rammed home the point: the difference was a moral one, a difference between reading to pass the time pleasurably – that is, trivially – and reading *to some purpose*.

The 'great tradition' does not brook even the possibility of libidinal gratification between the pages as an end in itself, and F. R. Leavis's 'eat up your broccoli' approach to fiction emphasises this junkfood/wholefood dichotomy. If reading a novel – for the eighteenth-century reader, the most frivolous of diversions – did not, by the middle of the twentieth century, make you a better person in some way, then you might as well flush the offending volume down the toilet, which was by far the best place for the undigested excreta of dubious nourishment.

The Yugoslav writer Milorad Pavic's *Dictionary of the Khazars* is an exercise in a certain kind of erudite frivolity that does not do you good *as such*, but offers the cerebral pleasure of the recognition of patterning afforded by formalism, a profusion of language games, some rude mirth. In culinary terms, the book is neither tofuburger nor Big Mac, but a Chinese banquet, a multiplicity of short narratives and prose fragments at which we are invited, not to take our fill, but to snack as freely or as meagrely as we please on a wide variety of small portions of sharply flavoured delicacies, mixing and matching many different taste sensations. In other words, it is not like a novel by Penelope Lively. It will not set you up; nor will it tell you how to live. That is not what it is for.

The mother-type of these feast-like compilations is *The Arabian Nights Entertainment* – note the word 'entertainment'. That shambolic anthology of literary fairytales linked by an exiguous narrative was originally, and still is, related to the folktale of peasant communities and its particular improvisatory yet regulated systems of narrative. The whole of *Dictionary of the Khazars* is a kind of legendary history, and some of the individual entries have considerable affinities to the folktale ('The Tale of Petkutin and Kalina' in the section called 'The Red Book', for example): but, I suspect, not so much the influence of an oral tradition – though that's still possible in Yugoslavia – as the influence of an aesthetic owing a good deal to Vladimir Propp's *Morphology of the Folk-Tale*, first published in Russia in 1928.

Propp's thesis is that the traditional fairytale is not composed, but built up out of discrete narrative blocks that can be pulled down again and reassembled in different ways to make any number of other stories, or can be used for any number of other stories in combination with other narrative blocks. That is partly why there is no place for, nor possibility of, inwardness in the traditional tale, nor of characterisation in any three-dimensional way. If the European novel of the nineteenth and twentieth centuries is closely related to gossip, to narrative arising out of conflicted character, then the folktale survives, in our advanced, industrialised, society, in the anecdote. Gossip would say: 'You know the daughter of that bloke at the "Dog and Duck"? Well . . . ' An anecdote might begin: 'There was this publican's daughter, see . . . ' In our culture, the folktale survives in the saloon bar.

A traditional storyteller does not make things up afresh, except now and then, if the need arises. Instead, he or she selects, according to mood, whim and cultural background, the narrative segments that feel right at the time from a store acquired from a career of listening, and reassembles them in attractive, and sometimes new, ways. And that's how formalism was born. (Italo Calvino, the most exquisite of contemporary formalists, is also, it should be remembered, editor of the classic collection of Italian fairytales.)

Pavic advises the reader to behave exactly like a traditional storyteller and construct his or her own story out of the ample material he has made available. The main difference is, Pavic has made all this material up by himself. 'No chronology is observed here, nor is one necessary. Hence, each reader will put together the book for himself, as in a game of dominoes or cards.' The book is an exercise, not in creative writing, but in creative reading. The reader can, says Pavic, rearrange the book 'in an infinite number of ways, like a Rubic cube'.

Pavic positively invites you to join in, as if opening his imagination to the public. 'It is an open book,' he says in the preliminary notes, 'and when it is shut it can be added to: just as it has its own former and present lexicographer, so it can acquire new writers, compilers, continuers.'

In a US review, Robert Coover suggested that computer hackers might make *Dictionary of the Khazars* their own as a prototype hypertext, unpaginated, non-sequential, that can be entered anywhere by anybody. This looks forward to a Utopian, high-tech version of the oral tradition where machines do all the work whilst men and women unite in joyous and creative human pastimes. It is a prospect to make William Morris's mind reel, publishers quail.

But who are, or were, the Khazars? 'An autonomous and powerful tribe, a warlike and nomadic people who appeared from the East at an unknown date, driven by a scorching silence, and who, from the seventh to the tenth century, settled in the land between two seas, the Caspian and the Black.' As a nation, the Khazars no longer exist, and ceased to do so during the tenth century after 'their conversion from their original faith, unknown to us today, to one (again, it is not known which) of three known religions of the past and present – Judaism, Islam or Christianity.'

The *Dictionary* purports to be, with some additions, the reprint of an edition of a book published by the Pole, Joannes Daubmannus, in 1691, which was 'divided into three dictionaries: a separate glossary of Moslem sources on the Khazar question, an alphabetised list of materials drawn from Hebrew writings and tales, and a third dictionary compiled on the basis of Christian accounts of the Khazar question'. So the same characters and events are usually seen three times, each from the perspective of a different history and set of cultural traditions, and may be followed through the three books *cross-wise*, if you wish. The 'ancient' texts are organised according to the antiquarian interests of the seventeenth century. As in *The Arabian Nights*, an exiguous narrative set in the present day is interwoven throughout the three volumes of the dictionary and provides some sort of climax.

The most obvious immediate inspiration for this 'plot' is surely a certain Volume XLVI of the *Anglo-American Cyclopaedia* (New York, 1917), itself a 'literal but delinquent reprint of the *Encyclopaedia Britannica* of 1902', in which Bioy Cesares and Jorge Luis Borges discovered the first recorded reference to the land of Uqbar. But instead of, like Borges, writing a story about a fake reference book that invades the real world, Pavic has set to and compiled the book itself, a book that contains a whole lost world, with its heroes, its rituals, its deaths, its mysteries, and especially its theological disputations, providing a plausible-enough-sounding apparatus of scholarly references that involve a series of implicit jokes about theories of authenticity just as the skewed versions of characters such as Princess Ateh, recurring three times, involve implicit jokes about cultural relativity.

Unless, of course, these aren't jokes at all. Yugoslavia is a federation of states with extraordinarily diverse cultural histories that came together as a nation almost by accident in 1918, with a sizeable Moslem population, to boot. This idea of a tripartite version of an imaginary history ought to appeal to the British, since the United Kingdom is also a union of principalities with extraordinarily diverse cultural histories, and a significant Moslem minority, too.

There is a blatant quality of fakery about the *Dictionary*. One imagines Pavic gleefully setting to with a Black and Decker drill, inserting artificial worm-holes into his synthetic oak beams. This fakery, this purposely antiqued and distressed surface, is what makes Pavic's book look so post-modern as to be almost parodically fashionable, the perfect type of those Euro-bestsellers such as Patrick Suskind's *Perfume* and Umberto Eco's *Name of the Rose* that seem, to some British critics, to spring from an EEC conspiracy to thwart exports of genuine, wholesome, straightforward British fiction the same way French farmers block the entry of English lamb. However, Yugoslavia is not a member of the Common Market and the British have developed a nervous tendency to label anything 'post-modern' that doesn't have a beginning, a middle, and an end in that order.

In Yugoslavia, according to Martin Seymour-Smith, 'except for a few years after Tito came to power in 1945, Modernism has flourished almost, if not quite, as it wished' (*Guide to World Literature*, edition of 1985). *Dictionary of the Khazars* fulfils, almost too richly, all Wallace Steven's prescriptions in 'Notes towards a Supreme Fiction':

> it must be abstract
> it must change
> it must give pleasure.

Most of the time, Pavic speaks in the language of romantic modernism – that is, surrealism. Al Bakri, the Spaniard, dies 'dreaming of salty female breasts in a gravy of saliva and tooth-ache'. The Princess Ateh composes a prayer: 'On our ship, my father, the crew swarms like ants: I cleaned it this morning with my hair and they crawl up the clean mast and strip the green sails like sweet vine leaves into their anthills.' A man, a certain Dr Ismail Suk, waking, blinks, 'with eyes hairy as testicles'.

Dr Suk is the hero of a section called 'The Story of the Egg and the Violin Bow' that boasts all the inscrutability of surrealist narrative plus a quality of what one can only call the 'mercantile fantastic' reminiscent of the short stories of Bruno Schulz, with their bizarre and ominous shops and shopkeepers. 'The shop was empty except for a hen nestled in a cap in the corner. She cocked one eye at Dr Suk and saw everything edible in him.' The Polish woman who will murder Dr Suk is called Dr Dorothea Schulz.

In fact, there is a strong sense of pastiche everywhere, most engagingly in the collection of Islamic sources on the Khazar question, although the poem in question purports to have been written by the Khazar princess Ateh. It is a piece of spoof Kafka. A woman travelling to a distant school to take a test is subjected to bureaucratic misinformation and then told: 'you can't reach the school today. And that means not ever. Because the school will no longer exist as of tomorrow. You have missed your life's destination . . . '

But this is a revisionist version of Kafka. Once her destination is withheld from her, the traveller searches for the significance of her journey in the journey itself – and finds it in one luminous memory, of a table with food and wine. 'On the table by the food a candle with a drop of flame on the top; next to it the Holy Book and the month of Jemaz-ul-Aker flowing through it.' A happy ending!

There is the casual acceptance of the marvellous common to both surrealism and the folktale: 'Ibn Ashkany was himself a very deft player. There exists a written record of his fingering for a song, so we know that he used more than ten fingers to play his instruments.' (In fact, Satan used this name for a time, and we learn how he played the lute with both his fingers and the tip of his tail.) A band of Greek merchants are 'so hirsute that the hair on their chests had a part like the hair on their heads'.

But the sense of the marvellous is most often created simply by the manipulation of language: 'Avram Brankovich cuts a striking figure. He has a broad chest the size of a cage for large birds or a small beast.' One way and another, the task of Pavic's translator, Christina Privicevic-Zoric, must have been awesome, for among the Khazars we are living in a world of words *as such*. The vanished world of the Khazars is constructed solely out of words. A dictionary itself is a book in which words provide the plot. The Khazars are nothing if not people of the Book, dithering as they did between the three great faiths, the sacred texts of Christianity, Islam, and Judaism. One of the copies of the 1691 edition of the *Dictionary*, we are told, was printed with a poisoned ink: 'The reader would die on the ninth page at the words *Verbum caro factum est.* ("The Word became Flesh.")' Almost certainly, something metaphysical is going on.

The Khazars indefatigably enter that most metaphysical of states, dreaming. 'A woman was sitting by her fire, her kettle of broth babbling like bursting boils. Children were standing in line with their plates and dogs, waiting. She ladled out the broth to the children and animals and immediately Masudi knew that she was portioning out dreams from the kettle.'

The Dream Hunters are a set of Khazar priests. 'They could read other people's dreams, live and make themselves at home in them . . .' That is the Christian version. The Moslem Dictionary is more forthcoming: 'If all human dreams could be assembled together, they would form a huge man, a human being the size of a continent. This would not be just any man, it would be Adam Ruhani, the heavenly Adam, man's angel ancestor, of whom the imams speak.'

The book of Hebrew sources is most explicit:

> The Khazars saw letters in people's dreams, and in them they looked for primordial man, for Adam Cadmon, who was both man and woman and born before eternity. They believed that to every person belongs one letter of the alphabet, that each of these letters constitutes part of Adam Cadmon's body on earth, and that these letters converge in people's dreams and come to life in Adam's body.

(I am not sure that Pavic thinks of Freud when he thinks of dreams.)

So we can construct our primal ancestor out of the elements of our dreams, out of the elements of the *Dictionary*, just as Propp thought that if one found sufficient narrative elements and combined them in the right order, one would be able to retell the very first story of all – 'it would be possible to construct the archetype of the fairy tale not only schematically . . . but concretely as well.'

Please do not run away with the idea that this is a difficult book, although it is flamboyantly and intentionally confusing. I first came across the *Dictionary of the Khazars* in the following manner. Last summer, on the beach of a rather down-market Italian resort, I was staying, for reasons I won't bore you with, at the best hotel. Under a beach umbrella there was a wonderfully extrovert French businessman and his wife, who originally hailed from Yorkshire ('I was passing through Paris thirty-five years ago and I'm still passing through'). He was recovering from a bypass operation; under the sun-tan oil his chest was ravelled. They first attracted my attention in the hotel restaurant because they ordered everything flambé. She, in a white jump-suit printed with huge orange flowers, danced on the beach with my little boy. Meanwhile her husband was reading *Dictionary of the Khazars*. It had just been published in France, it was his holiday book. He kept reading bits aloud to her: 'Kyr Avram is sometimes wont to say, "A woman without a behind is like a village without a church!"' 'I'm all right, then,' she said. He was laughing so much

I feared for his scars. At dinner, they read bits to the waiter as he flambéd their steaks.

I thought that if this wonderful man and woman were enjoying the book so much, then so would I. In fact, perhaps the best way of tackling it *is* to read bits aloud, to treat it like a game. In his *New York Times* review, Coover suggested that, if marketed as a board game, it might soon outsell 'Dungeons and Dragons', which is probably true. It is a book to play with, to open up and take things out of, a box of delights and a box of tricks. It is a novel without any sense of closure, the product of a vast generosity of the imagination – user-friendly, you could say, and an invitation to invent for yourself.

The book, by the way, comes in two editions, a male one and a female one, differing by 17 lines, perhaps because the scribe, Father Theoctist Nikolsky, avers that 'masculine and feminine stories cannot have the same ending.' Why not? But the gender difference between the editions is not crucial, in spite of the warning on the jacket, although the very concept is the only point in the book where Pavic's invention nearly founders under an access of sheer cuteness.

(1989)

Milorad Pavic: *Landscape Painted with Tea*

Central to the argument of this frisky but intellectually gripping work of fiction is the idea of two oppositional human types – the idiorrhythmics, who are solitaries, each moving to his own rhythm of life, unique, separate; and the cenobites, the *solidaries*, who join in brotherhood and live in common. And a person must be either the one or the other. Never both.

This is a classic either/or situation. Obviously, you can't be both existentially alone and warmly part of a fraternity at the same time. 'A man with a heart full of silence and a man with a heart full of quiet cannot be alike,' opines the narrator of *Landscape Painted with Tea* in one of the frequent aphorisms that adorn the text. The book twists and turns about this contradiction and various resolutions to it.

Although *Landscape Painted with Tea* is narrated in the third person from a traditionally omiscient and god-like point of view, the novel is constructed to let its reader in on the action at every opportunity, by a variety of means. If the text is a constant, then the ways of reading it are not. Pavic's reader is invited, via the formal device of a crossword puzzle and its clues, to read the book 'not in order of succession and across (as the river flows) but *down*, as the rain falls'.

This produces an effect of intentional randomness not unlike that of some of Calvino's writing – like that of the marvellous *Castle of Crossed Destinies*, for example, which based its constellation of stories on the various ways in which the cards in the Tarot pack fell. But Pavic isn't interested in a new way of writing. He is interested in a new way of *reading*, because 'any new way of reading that goes against the matrix of time, which pulls us towards death, is a futile but honest effort to resist this inexorability of one's fate'.

The traditional novel, like the traditional anecdote, begins and goes on until it ends. Like life. Pavic wants more than that. He wants to disrupt time, to challenge death.

And why not, dammit. It's filthy work but somebody's got to do it. Kingsley Amis isn't going to try.

Pavic sets out to seduce the reader into the text. There is even a blank page at the end of the book where the reader can write out the denouement he or she has worked out by themselves. Pavic veers crazily between a particularly Balkan brand of cute surrealism ('I hear the birds' voices knitting endless socks and gloves with a thousand fingers') and the kind of high seriousness that can concern itself with the nature of narrative, with what it is and what it does. Sometimes, in his concern to massage the reader pleasurably into a rapt contemplation of what constitutes the act of reading, he can come a cropper. Most of the time, though, he contrives to discuss this question and also give pleasure, no mean feat.

You can't be an idiorrhythmic and a cenobite at the same time, but you *can* change over from one to the other. Think of Yoan Siropoulos; he was born and died a Greek but, in between, 'entered a different time, where different waters flowed', in which he became Yovan Siropulov, the Bulgarian. His story is a miniature version of the bizarre epic of the lives of the book's major figure, the Yugoslav architect, Atanas Svilar, who converts himself into the Russian mathematician, Atanas Fyodorovish Razin, and, after numerous adventures, emigrates to the USA.

There seems to be a complicated political sub-text going on beneath the rich palimpsest of stories and counter-stories that provide the material for Pavic's crossword clues. The architect, Svilar/Razin draws, again and again, the plans of the grand summer villa of Josip Broz Tito, 'general secretary of the Yugoslav Communist Party and president of the republic', finally building himself a replica of this palace in the USA. Since irony is Pavic's medium, it is hard for the non-Yugoslav reader to tell precisely what is going on, here. The central dichotomy between the idiorrhythmics and the cenobites has, of course, its own political resonance.

You need to take *Landscape Painted with Tea* slowly. You need to chew it for a long time, like certain kinds of peasant bread. It will reward you with constant shocks of pleasure. There is its pervasive lyricism: 'the moonlight . . . was the kind you enter from the dark, like a room . . . ' The aphorisms are frequent, always witty, sometimes with witty little teeth: 'Nobody can be masculine every day, not even God.' There are incidental stories whose characters have the radiant two-dimensionality of fairytale, like the man who wears two wrist-watches and tells his lover: 'This silver watch measures your time and this gold one mine. I wear them together, so that I can always know what time you have.'

It is the architect Razin who paints the landscapes in various kinds of tea, fruit teas, tisanes, Darjeeling (the champagne of teas), green tea, every shade and variation of colour executed in tea. But very early on in the book, a traveller recounts how he became a painter by accident after his wife 'wrote her signature in the snow, steering his penis like a fountain pen, and for a while the signature steamed like tea, and then became perfectly legible'. (Soon she was drawing pictures using the same method.) Landscapes Painted with Pee? Would this be a joke in Serbo-Croat?

(1991)

· 3 ·

Irish Folk Tales, Arab Folktales

Thomas Gray surely did not mean to be patronising when he referred to the 'mute, inglorious Milton' who might have been slumbering in the country churchyard. But if he indeed meant 'mute' metaphorically rather than physically, then it is difficult to imagine even an illiterate Milton refraining from discourse. Surely a ploughboy Milton would have made a lot of noise; and even if only other members of the rural proletariat heard him, that does not mean he would have been silent.

Few poets have been so intellectually well-armed as the real Milton, yet the antique glamour of the blind singer still clings to him, so that one thinks of him in the same breath as Homer, who, according to tradition, was also blind, and created epics too, and yet was almost certainly not illiterate but simply pre-literate – that is, could not have been literate even had he wished to be so. Language exists before its own written form. The voice is the first instrument of literature; narrative precedes text.

These first two plump handsome volumes in the projected Penguin Folklore Library transform oral narrative into texts, so that the tales will survive the voices of their narrators. Inea Bush-naq notes: 'It is a wistful moment when interest in recording an oral tradition wakens.' It means that the culture of the illiterate, that is, the poor, is no longer being taken for granted. Sometimes it means that it has started to die. As the voices fall silent, one by one, so we lose irreplaceable parts of our past.

Robert Darnton, the historian, says (in his essay, 'Peasants Tell Tales: the Meaning of Mother Goose') that folktales 'provide a rare opportunity to make contact with the illiterate masses who have disappeared into the past without leaving a trace.' This is rather an apocalyptic way of putting it. We may not know much about the lives of those 'illiterate masses' but most of us are directly descended from them, and we retain, if we have lost everything else from the oral tradition, a complicated folklore of family.

Besides, a flourishing illiterate culture has always wonderfully nourished the productions of the literati. Henry Glassie reminds us in his introduction to *Irish Folk Tales* that James Joyce named *Finnegans Wake* after a Dublin street song, even borrowed the plot.

But Ireland is a special case. In the last years of the nineteenth century, Yeats and Synge and Lady Gregory went out on purpose to listen to country storytellers, to strive consciously to reach out to those who had slipped through the huge holes in the net of history down which the common people vanish – to reconstruct from the mouths of the poor the basis for an authentically Irish literature, a project that bore abundant fruit. (It is interesting to read, in Inea Bushnaq's book, that there is 'a lively folklore department in the university at Bir Zeit,' on the debated West Bank, and an increasing interest is the collection and preservation of Palestinian culture.)

The stories assembled by Henry Glassie include some from those collections made by Yeats and his friends nearly a century ago, some from other nineteenth-century collections, others recorded far more recently by the editor himself and by other collectors currently working in Ireland, a nation which no longer contains a significant proportion of illiterates, but is, folklorically, far from a worked-out seam.

An American academic who has made the English language folklore of Ireland his special study, he is scrupulous about notes and sources; his bibliography is enormous and comprehensive; his *Irish Folk Tales* is both scholarly reference book and a pleasure to browse in – but the spare fluidity of the language of his informants has not rubbed off on him, alas.

He is grievously afflicted with fine writing ('Pure darkness welcomes the winds that skim off the ocean', etc.), and embarrassingly lyrical about his informants. 'They call him eccentric . . . they call him a saint,' he says of one. What does his informant call Henry Glassie?

But here are stories about Finn MacCumhail and the Fenians, as Jeremiah Curtain noted them down in Donegal in 1887; stories about St Finbar, and St Brigit, and St Kevin who made apples grow on a willow tree; stories about true folk heroes – Robert Burns, Daniel O'Connell. Yes, indeed; here is an Irish Cinderella (in which the three sisters are called, Fair, Brown, and Trembling). And a giant who opines of a visitor: 'I think you large of one mouthful and small of two mouthfuls.'

There are also some moving examples of legendary history. For example, how Cromwell possessed a black Bible that was so big 'it would take a horse to draw it'. When his servant opened up this Bible on the sly, lots of little men came out of it and ran around until the servant cried: 'Off ye go in the name of the Divell!'

The circumstances of life in these stories are universally harsh and the happy endings few and far between. A good breakfast is a pot full of boiled turnips. Drink is a curse. A man named George Armstrong went to Australia but all he came back with was thruppence and when he got home again he weighed so little his mother put him in a basket and kept him by the fire.

Inea Bushnaq's tales from Libya, Iraq, Morocco, Algeria, Syria – from all over the Arab world – reflect a different kind of life, one full of delicious smells and sights and sounds, fresh coffee, baking bread, rosewater and incense, flowers, embroidery, cloth of gold, apricots, figs. The Iraqi Cinderella wears golden clogs and a pearl comb in her hair. The people might be poor but the imagination is lavish.

The Arab countries have in common a language and a religion, Islam, and a still predominantly peasant culture in which story-telling as pastime and entertainment has survived in good order rather longer than it has in the advanced industrialised countries, although, as Inea Bushnaq says, television may well deal the *coup de grâce* with amazing speed.

Her method is quite different from Henry Glassie's: she has compiled an anthology from a variety of text materials, splicing some together and has selected stories 'most likely to interest the English reader'. It would be nice to know what criteria she used in picking them out.

She provides a vast amount of cultural background in a series of introductions to different sections of the collections, with their mouth-watering titles – Djinn, Ghouls and Afreets, Tales Told in Houses Made of Hair (that is, the goat-hair tents of the Bedouin), Beasts that Roam the Earth, and Birds that Fly with Wings. But this is not a scholarly collection so much as a triumphant, shining, glorious labour of love.

Perhaps Inea Bushnaq is more cavalier with her sources than a professional folklorist because she has heard many of the stories herself when she was a child and truly feels that they belong to her for just that moment of the telling, when the storyteller makes the story his or her own, the fleeting gift of the storyteller.

The stories invent a world of marvels – flying carpets, girls from whose mouths fall lilies and jasmine each time they speak, a boy whose ears are so sharp he can hear the dew fall. The cry goes out: 'A calamity and a scandal! The king's new queen has given birth to a puppy dog and a water jug!' A green bird spells out the stark terror of family life: 'My father's wife, she took my life. My father ate me for his dinner.' And once upon a time, there was a woman called Rice Pudding . . .

(1987)

· 4 ·

Danilo Kis: *The Encyclopedia of the Dead*

The scrupulously intelligent stories in *The Encyclopedia of the Dead* are fiction, but also, in an important way, *about* fiction. Implicit in the book is the question that all fiction raises by its very existence: what is real and what is not – and *how can we tell the difference*? In a story called 'The Legend of the Sleepers', Danilo Kis, a Yugoslav writer living in Paris, puts it this way: 'Oh, who can divide dream from reality, day from night, night from dawn, memory from illusion?'

The question is clearly rhetorical, and Mr Kis's apparatus of postscript and notes gives shape, purpose and an edgy, more documentary dimension to his storytelling. Mr Kis himself tells us that the stories are all about death – the one truly inescapable reality. Even if one of the legendary sleepers of Ephesus in 'The Legend of the Sleepers' may be dreaming his own death, death is the universal end of all our personal histories. The title story, 'The Encyclopedia of the Dead', reminds us of that.

This great encyclopedia is housed, we are told, in the Royal Library in Stockholm. Its many volumes contain complete biographies of everyone who ever lived. There is only one qualification for entry: nobody gets in who is featured in any other reference book. It is a memorial for those without memorials. A woman looks up her father's entry; the plain details of an ordinary life, meals eaten, hobbies, work, final diagnosis, are very moving.

And then the woman wakes; it was a dream. Yet in the dream she had made a drawing; awake she recreates it, and the drawing exactly resembles the fatal cancer that killed her father. This fusion of book, dream, and the world irresistibly recalls the fiction of

Borges; but Mr Kis is more haunted, less antic than the Argentine master, and his notes contain fewer jokes.

In his notes, Mr Kis introduces a further twist: he tells us that the encyclopedia might not be real, but the dream was – dreamed by a certain M., 'to whom the story is dedicated'. And he tells us that if the encyclopedia does not exist yet, work on an analogue has begun, and 'the Genealogical Society of the Church of the Latter Day Saints' is, at this present time, compiling just such a comprehensive reference book, filing away on microfilm details of everybody who ever lived, as far as can be researched, so that the Mormons can retrace their family trees and retroactively baptise their ancestors.

Truth is always stranger than fiction, because the human imagination is finite while the world is not, and Mr Kis seems to be ambivalent about making things up from scratch.

Indeed, he almost seems to apologise for the story, 'Red Stamps With Lenin's Picture', because it is 'pure fiction', about a literary love affair. He quotes Nabokov sympathetically: 'I never could understand what was the good of thinking up books or penning things that had not really happened in some way or other.' Not for Mr Kis art for art's sake, but for truth's sake.

Everywhere in these stories the correspondence among what is real, what might be real, and the mediation of the written word between these conditions, reverberates on many levels. In the superb 'Book of Kings and Fools', Mr Kis investigates the morality of the written word itself.

In this story, the central character is itself a book, titled 'The Conspiracy, or The Roots of the Disintegration of European Society'. We are told that the existence of the book was first hinted at as a rumour in an article in a St Petersburg newspaper in 1906, the time of the Jewish pogroms. This rumour concerned a document 'demonstrating the existence of a worldwide conspiracy against Christianity, the Tsar and the status quo'.

No sooner is it rumoured than the book appears, incorporated into a hysterical text by a fanatically mystic Orthodox priest. (And here I may have glimpsed one, only one, possible glitch in what reads like a seamlessly perfect translation by Michael Henry Heim: 'The local Red Cross Chapter volunteered to publish this book', it says here. But I can't see the International Red Cross doing any such thing. Perhaps the culprits were the Rosicrucians?)

'The Conspiracy', as the book is called, offers universal explanations, always popular. In Germany, it seeds the mind of 'a then unknown (as yet unknown) amateur painter'. It makes a deep impression on 'an anonymous Georgian seminary student who was *yet to be heard from*'. Soon it finds its way into the delirious paranoia of human practice. It is the obscene triumph of the antibook – a forged text designed to destroy.

Mr Kis scrupulously instructs us as to the nature of the reality constructed by the book's most zealous readers – the reality of the death camps, a reality beyond the power of the human mind easily to imagine.

In his essential postscript, Mr Kis tells us that his intention was 'to summarize the true and fantastic – "unbelievably fantastic" – story of how *The Protocols of the Elders of Zion* came into existence'. The story began as an essay, but in researching the obscure history of that anti-Semitic forgery whose construction is one of the greatest of all crimes against humanity, there came a point where Mr Kis 'started imagining the events as they *might have happened*'. Then he moved into fiction; the fable is no less powerful than fact.

Books don't really have lives of their own. They are only as important as the ideas inside them. The book, as we know it, took shape with the invention of the printing press in the fifteenth century; it was the tool of the dissemination of humanism but can, just as easily, spread the antithesis of humanism. 'In point of fact,' says Danilo Kis, 'sacred books, and the cannonized works of master thinkers, are like a snake's venom: they are a source of morality and iniquity, grace and transgression.' He is wise, grave, clever, and complex. His is a book on the side of the angels.

(1989)

John Berger: *Pig Earth*

In a formal sense, *Pig Earth* is innovatory. John Berger uses three kinds of writing – fiction, poetry, and exposition – to precipitate in the reader a precise awareness of a specific kind of life, that of a contemporary French peasant community in the Alps.

This community is the village in which Berger himself lives. Though he does not invoke his own presence as an actor in any of the stories, the section of exposition titled 'An Explanation' relates his work as a writer, a professional storyteller, to the storytelling and gossip that makes life in the village what he calls a 'living portrait of itself', a continuous narrative that 'confirms the existence of the village'.

Pig Earth is devoted to the imaginative exploration of a way of life rooted in what Berger calls a 'culture of survival', as opposed to the 'culture of progress' which is the urban imperative of all classes. He is, in part, attempting to crystallise and define this 'culture of survival' at the very time when it may not, in fact, survive.

The three kinds of writing in *Pig Earth* fit together to make a three-dimensional picture of a village which is also artistically three-dimensional. That is to say, the heightened lyricism of the brief poems illuminates the straightforward verismo of the stories in a way which recalls Hardy's dry observation – how Farmer Oak was not, as the sophisticate might think, insensible to the beauties of nature.

The polemical nature of the two sections, 'An Explanation' and 'Historical Afterword', informs the physical landscape and the landscape of labour through which the reader has travelled in the course of the book with a sense of urgency that removes *Pig Earth* altogether from the genre of bourgeois pastoral, which is the consolatory celebration of a fictive 'rusticity'.

Berger says: 'Nobody can reasonably argue for the preservation and maintenance of the traditional peasant way of life. To do so is to argue that peasants should continue to be exploited, and that they should lead lives in which the burden of physical work is often devastating and always oppressive.' But his culminating assertion is that the elimination of the peasantry is the final act in the destruction of the experiential reservoir of the past, so that it can no longer be part of the totality of the present. This destruction Berger sees as the 'historic role of capitalism itself, a role unforeseen by Adam Smith or Marx'.

Once history is destroyed, all energy may be concentrated on what is about to occur, the future, which, as every grammarian knows, does not exist; though the old man who, in the story, 'The Value of Money', plants apple trees he will not live to see bear fruit, *can* prepare for a hypothetical future because he has certain knowledge of the past.

The 'Afterword' gives a depth of focus to the stories which precede it. Some are spare, lucid accounts of events – the slaughter of a cow, the birth of a calf, the mating of a goat on a snowy night, genre scenes in which men and women engage with domestic beasts on terms of familiarity and respect. Another, more evolved story is organised around a pig-killing, a feast, and the death of the grandfather who is a boy's 'authority about everything which was mysterious'; this culture is carnivorous and patriarchal. And the community is growing old.

Here, youth and, in some sense, hope exist as memory; the sons of Marcel, the orchard planter, won't work the farm when he's gone. Young people mostly leave the village. A certain elegaic tone is inescapable and the longest and strangest story, 'The Three Lives of Lucie Cabrol', takes its narrator finally among the dead. This story, with its fierce dwarf heroine and its hero who has returned to the village to die, is the only one that seems to carry a burden of allegory.

Tiny Lucie, nicknamed the Cocadrille out of love and hate, despised, half crazy, scours the mountains for berries, mushrooms, herbs that she sells in the city, is murdered for her savings, comes back to haunt the man who rejected her in favour of the spurious lure of America, and convinces him at last of her inextinguishable love and the presence of the good neighbours, the dead.

Pig Earth is only the first part of a larger work, in which Berger intends to examine still further the meaning and consequence of the threat of the elimination of this reservoir of human experience.

(1979)

· 6 ·

John Berger: *Once in Europa*

Soon, nostalgia will be another name for Europe. These stories of European country life in the late twentieth century are permeated with a sense of loss. We know that, even as we read them, the world they describe is crumbling away. They are stories about the final divorce of human beings from the land, as great a change as, perhaps greater than, the transition from Stone Age to Bronze Age, yet one that has been accomplished within the lifetime of the old people who still hope to die in the houses where they were born, to which their children will never return.

Not that the deserted village is a phenomenon unique to the late twentieth century. Throughout history, plague, famine, and changes in agricultural practice have periodically emptied the countryside. What *is* unprecedented is what could be called the *deruralisation* of the countryside, as the multinational agribusiness industry renders subsistence farming in general and the small farmer in particular permanently redundant. Then everywhere that is not part of a city becomes in effect a giant suburb, dependent for all its services on the urban areas. This has already happened in parts of the USA and in much of Britain. In Europe, it is happening at dizzying speed.

There is a time limit on the timeless, eternal world of the peasant. The villages do not stay deserted for long. They become tourist resorts. Conurbations of weekend cottages. The land becomes so much scenery, no longer the site of labour, reduced to pure decoration.

John Berger approaches this enormous theme with infinite delicacy, through the experience of some of the men and women of the region of the Alps where he himself lives. He is often present, a reticent witness, in these stories, which are remarkable for their quality of visionary intimacy, a sense of the sacred quality of everyday things that recalls the interiors of Vermeer. And also for their intense respect for people, their *seriousness*.

Berger says that these are love stories, and 'Boris is Buying Horses' is, amongst other things, a study of obsession, but they are just as much stories about loneliness, that savage passion, as if love and loneliness are aspects of the same thing.

In the first story, 'The Accordion Player', the central figure, left alone to work his remote farm after his mother's death, finds himself suddenly weeping for the loss of the past, and also for the loss of the future. 'He wept for the farm where there were no children.' For what woman would marry a peasant farmer, these days? Marry toil that remains ceaseless and an isolation that increases in direct relation to mechanisation, as farming requires fewer and fewer workers? In the old days, the whole village turned out to help with the hay harvest. In summer, everybody adjourned to the high pastures, to graze the cows. What used to be celebrations are now lonely chores. 'In the Time of the Cosmonauts' puts this very graphically: 'A number of years ago when the Russian, Gagarin, the first man in space, was circling the earth, every one of the twenty scattered chalets at Peniel housed, each summer, cattle and women and men. So many cattle that there was only just enough grass to go round.' Twenty-five years later, only an old man and a girl are there, and 'there was so much grass they could let their animals graze night and day'.

As it happens, this girl, Danielle, might have married a peasant farmer, if one had asked her. But the mountains, in the concrete person of the old man, filthy, almost demonic, almost heroic, offer themselves to her in such a primitive and atavistic manner that, terrified, she runs away.

Even so, little that is primitive and atavistic remains in these upland farms, where now the mating season heralds the visit to the eager cows not of the bull but of the inseminator. The most primitive and atavistic thing in the mountains is a man-made horror, the manganese plant in the title story, 'Once in Europa'.

A small family farm, home of the woman who tells the story, is flung down like a gauntlet in the face of insensate industrialisation; the plant surrounds it. The plants kill her lover; it has

31

crippled the man whom she later marries. During the course of her life, its noxious fumes lay waste to the valley in which she lives.

Yet there is an infernal grandeur about the manganese plant and the devastation it wreaks. Only nature itself could be more destructive. Can't one bolt of lightning kill a whole flock of sheep? There is no such grandeur about the slow erosion of the farming communities as they are encroached upon by the banality which is our century's particular gift to civilisation. In 'Boris is Buying Horses', a woman seduces a farmer in order to gain possession of his house, which she and her husband proceed to run as a souvenir shop. This is a glimpse of a future in which the Alps have become a giant theme park.

Once in Europa is about history at work in daily life. This is the second volume of Berger's projected trilogy about twentieth-century peasant life, which has the general title *Into Their Labours*. It is Berger's genius – and I don't use the word lightly – to reveal to us how the process of history affects people we come to know as friends, so that we suffer with them, grieve for them, hope for them, realise that we, too, are part of the same process.

The final story in the book, 'Play Something For Me', takes a young farmer on a day trip to Venice, where he makes love to a shop assistant during a *festa de l'unita*, which is a good urban substitute for a village festival. She urges him to leave his cows and come and work in the oil refineries at Mestri. Perhaps he will. Like the eponymous accordion player of the first story, he is a music maker. 'The accordion was made for life on this earth, the left hand marking the bass and the heart-beats, the arms and shoulders labouring to make breath, and the right hand fingering for hopes!' These are not pessimistic stories, although often they will make you cry.

(1989)

The German Legends of the Brothers Grimm

Unlike the Grimms' collection of fairytales, without which no home is complete, their collection of German legends has never been translated into English before. What is the difference between a fairytale and a legend? The Grimms themselves scrupulously differentiate in their own Foreword to the first German edition of 1816. A fairytale, they say, can 'find its home anywhere', it belongs to the timeless, international zone of poetry; but the legend – ah! the legend, securely attached to a specific place, often a specific date, is the folk spirit recreating its own history. Is distilled essence of folk spirit. Is, in short, essentially, gloriously and unpollutedly *German*. 'Nothing is as edifying or as likely to bring more joy than the products of the Fatherland.' H'm.

Ironically, Donald Ward's scholarly notes on individual legends suggest that many of the German legends aren't so very German, after all – wild hunts, mermen, headless horsemen, dwarfs and giants distribute themselves throughout Europe and, indeed, the world with a grand disregard for frontiers.

Volume One is composed of odd, fragmentary bits and pieces of pseudo-history and folk belief taken, mostly, directly from the mouths of the German folk themselves. It is a feast of snacks. The very inconsequentiality is enchanting. 'There is a bridge outside of Haxthusen-Hofe near Paderborn. Beneath it lives a poor soul who sneezes from time to time.' Who? Why? You can almost see the Grimms' informant shrug. Who knows? Just take my word for it.

Early nineteenth-century Germany was rife with such spooks;

many of them seem to have fallen out of a household tale, folk motifs in search of a narrative. What of the ghostly girl, carrying a bunch of keys, often seen washing herself in a certain spring? And another girl, with long, golden hair, who frequents the mountainside on which she was burned to death – what *can* they be up to?

The answer, usually, is nothing. Neither numinous nor ominous, they possess only the existential validity of being there, part of the imaginative furniture of the place, ubiquitous and homely as the village idiot.

Sometimes the legends are uncanny just because they are so enigmatic:

> Once a man was riding through a forest late in the evening when he saw two children sitting next to each other. He admonished them to go home and not to tarry any longer. But the two began laughing loudly. The man rode on and after a while he encountered the same two children, who began laughing again.

The pointlessness of it is the whole point; it is a free-form apparition, awaiting a random injection of significance, or the formal shaping of the storyteller's craft.

I wonder if the method of the collectors differed when they were out after *real* pseudo-history, serious German essence rather than frivolous invented narrative? How much did they themselves want their informants actually to believe in the things the informants were relating? The almost lunatic precision of dating and locating material – 'in 1398 . . . near Eisenach, in Thuringia . . . '; 'In 1519, just before the plague killed many people in the city of Hof . . . ' – gives a specious appearance of authenticity to many a tall tale, though, indeed, some of these references come from old books to back up the memories of old people. All the same, these legends occupy a curious grey area between fact and fiction.

There are anecdotes, old-wives tales, tales of saints and miracles, marvellous lies designed to test the gullibility of the listener – most of them designed to be neither believed nor disbelieved, designed to court no more positive response than 'Well, fancy that!' It is a loose-jointed, easy-going way of decorating the real world with imaginative detail. As Lévi-Strauss says about such benign and cheering superstitions, they make the world 'more tasty'. It was a tasty old world that the Grimms found, all right.

Mermen are just the same as we are except for their green teeth. The edges of the petticoats of water-pixies are always sopping wet. The devil, a constant visitor, lends his name to inauspicious tracts of land like the Devil's Dance Floor, and the Devil's Pillow, a boulder on which the very mark of his ear may still be seen. Dwarfs borrow pots and pans for their weddings. Fairies borrow human midwives for their lyings-in.

Some narratives start out like true fairytales, only to collapse in grand anti-climax, pricked balloons from which the magic suddenly leaks out. A young man releases a dwarf from a spell but no good fortune accrues; he can't get rid of the dwarf, an unwelcome lodger, thereafter. A girl sees another dwarf pouring water in front of a house; shortly afterwards, the house is saved from fire. Some time later, the dwarf is out with his watering-can again; and what happens this time? A big fat nothing happens, this time.

Often the very magical matter of the fairytale comes down to earth with a bump in these matter-of-fact renditions of wonderful occurrences. The anti-hero makes his appearance. A poor girl who, like the Fairy Melusine, is a snake from the waist down, must be kissed three times by a chaste youth to regain her natural shape. But the lad from our village dared kiss her only twice! 'Each time, in great anticipation for the unhoped-for miracle, the maiden made such dreadful gestures that he feared she was going to tear him to pieces. He, therefore, did not dare kiss her for the third time, and instead departed in haste.' Departed, in fact, to forthwith lose his virtue to an 'impure woman' and, with it, all his fairytale eligibility for the task of rescue.

Some of the legends are, in fact, shaggy-dog stories. The boy in Freiburg in 1545, for instance, who was cursed to remain standing up. Eventually his feet wore grooves in the floor. Because he was standing near the stove he got in everybody's way, so they picked him up and stowed him away in corners. At last they all got bored with him and covered him up with a cloth.

Amongst many other such delights may be found the true stories of the Pied Piper of Hamelin and of Bishop Hatt and the

Rats. There is a delicious little giant girl who scoops up plough, horses, ploughmen, and all in her apron and takes them home to play with: 'Oh, Father, it's such a marvellous toy!'

Volume Two is a very different kettle of fish, a collection of heroic legends very few of which come from the living traditions of real people. The Grimms say these stories could be called Legends of Teutonic Tribes and Royal Families and, here, they are as much concerned with myth-making as with folklore. They embrace the historic with disturbing enthusiasm: ' . . . it is . . . a noble attribute of people . . . any people . . . when both the dawn and the dusk of their day in history consists of legends.' The relation between the rise of folklore studies and that of modern nationalism is an interesting one; there are things here that uncomfortably tease the mind.

To quote King Dagobert who, while he lay on his deathbed, said to his dogs: 'No company is so good, that one cannot take leave of it.'

(1981)

· 8 ·

Georges Bataille: *Story of the Eye*

There's a photograph – among the surrealist souvenirs – of the poet, Benjamin Peret, insulting a priest. One lesson of Georges Bataille's erotic novella, *Story of the Eye*, is that French intellectuals are made of sterner stuff than we are.

We think blasphemy is silly. They are exhilarated by it. Bataille's hero and heroine end up doing a lot more to a priest than just insulting him. The fine European tradition of anti-clericalism is central to the preoccupations of this grand old surrealist fellow-traveller and sexual *philosophe*. It underpins Bataille's theory of active sexuality as the assertion of human freedom against the laws of church and state. There can be few texts that illustrate so precisely the cultural differences between the Roman Catholic and the Protestant sensibility.

Bataille puts pornography squarely in the service of blasphemy. Transgression, outrage, sacrilege, liberation of the senses through erotic frenzy, and the symbolic murder of God. This is a scenario alien to the secular heritage of Protestant humanism. It confirms the free-thinker's darkest fears about the nauseating madness inherent in Judaeo-Christianity itself. One can understand why Susan Sontag – whose worthy but dull essay, 'The Pornographic Imagination', is appended – refrains from commenting on the climax of *Story of the Eye*, where a priest is enticed into lapping up his own urine from a sacramental chalice. Sontag is concerned to define what kind of literature pornography might be; she doesn't notice that *Story of the Eye* is didactically lewd.

After the hapless cleric has drained the cup to its dregs of marinated Host, the polymorphously perverse heroine, Simone, orgiastically strangles him, gouges out his eye and pops it into her vagina, which she has already used as a repository for eggs, both raw and cooked, and the testicles of a bull. Roland Barthes, in *his* essay in the buxom appendix to the brief tale, points out the complex circularity of the dominant imagery of eye, egg, testicle. No content man, he; his whimsical formalism is too disingenuous by half. *Story of the Eye* was first published in France in 1928; two years later, French fascists smashed up the cinema in which Buñuel and Dali's *L'Age d'Or* was celebrating erotic blasphemy. Bataille was dicing with death and *Story of the Eye* is about fucking as existential affirmation against death, who is also God. (Unless Bataille's own blind, paralysed father – syphilis, naturally – is God; he materialises horribly in an afterword.)

Now Simone, her lover, and an onanistic English milord set sail to America. They won't be able to raise Susan Sontag's eyebrows, whatever they get up to there; but since they crew their boat with black sailors, no doubt these guerrillas of the libido will think up a few stunts that will get up everybody else's noses.

That English milord, the non-participatory entrepreneur of obscene spectacles, is an unkind cut. The French have always thought we are sexually weirder than we have ever thought them, which is saying something. This has to do with the relativity of the notion of the sense of sin; and to do, too, with the way the metaphysics of *Story of the Eye* evaporate in the translation (by Joachim Neurgroschel), just as the crystalline rhetoric of Bataille's incomparable prose muddies in English. Nevertheless, this marvellous, scatological fairytale about the omnipotence of desire, as Barthes says, 'between the banal and the absurd' still enlightens.

(1979)

· 9 ·

William Burroughs: *The Western Lands*

Since William S. Burroughs relocated from New York City to Lawrence, Kansas, the town blasted by IBMs in the antinuke TV spectacular, 'The Day After', he has evidently perfected a final loathing for the instruments of mass death and – 'no job too dirty for a fucking scientist' – their perpetrators.

Pointless to head for the hills, these days: 'What hills? Geiger counters click to countdown. Decaying lead spells out the last syllable of recorded time. Orgone balked at the post. Christ bled. Time ran out. Radiation has won at a half-life.'

The densely impacted mass of cultural references here – Macbeth, the Western, Reich, Dr Faustus, pulp science fiction – isn't an isolated example of *The Western Lands*' intense awareness of literature and of itself as literature, suggesting that perhaps one of the things going on, here, is an elegaic farewell to all that. The peremptory demand on which the novel ends, 'Hurry up, please. It's time', is a straight quote from 'The Wasteland', reminiscent also of Cyril Connolly's remark about closing time in the gardens of the West.

Unless Burroughs is practising some complicated double irony (and I wouldn't put it past him), the West of Connolly's usage has nothing to do with the Old West of Burrough's obsession, site of his last novel, *The Place of Dead Roads*, which was second in the trilogy of which *Cities of the Red Night* was first and this the last. The 'Western Lands' of Burroughs' title are, mythologically speaking, where the dead live. That is, the place beyond death.

Essentially we are talking about immortality, the immortality promised by the poet to Mr W. H., which is no longer compatible

39

with the weapons that cause 'Total Death. Soul Death'. 'Well, that's what art is all about, isn't it? All creative thought, actually. A bid for immortality.' Who is talking about immortality? William Seward Hall, for one, old man and blocked writer, who decides to 'write his way out of death' just as old novelists, like Scott, wrote themselves out of debt.

But, both in and out of this transparent disguise, Burroughs is talking about immortality, too. *The Western Lands* is structured according to an internal logic derived from an idiosyncratic reading of Egyptian myth; immortality, in its most concrete form, greatly concerned Egyptians.

In spite of a series of discontinuous story lines featuring a variety of heroes, the book often resembles a nineteenth-century commonplace book. The most urgent personal reflections are juxtaposed with jokes, satires, quotations, essays in fake anthropology, parody, pastiche, and passages of Burroughs' unique infective delirium – piss, shit, offal, disembowellings. This is slapstick reinterpreted by Sade.

Cats of all kinds weave in and out of the text; Burroughs has clearly taken to them in a big way in his old age and seems torn between a fear they will betray him into sentimentality and a resigned acceptance that a man can't be ironic *all* the time.

The method is eclectic and discrete and it is important, and essential, because Burroughs is doing something peculiar with the reader's time. He's stopping it. Or, rather, stop-starting it. Taking it out of the reader's hands, anyway, which is where we tend to assume it ought to be.

He'll give you a paragraph, a page, even three or four pages at a time, of narrative like a railway down which the reader, as if having boarded a train, travels from somewhere to somewhere else according to an already existing timetable. Then – the track vanishes. The train vanishes. And you find you don't have any clothes on, either. While all that's left of the engine driver is a disappearing grin.

This constant derailment of the reader happens again and again, shattering the sense of cause and effect, whilst all the time one is reassured in the most affectingly disingenuous manner: 'How can any danger come from an old man cuddling his cats?'

You cannot hurry Burroughs, or skim, or read him for the story. He likes to take his time and to disrupt *your* time in such a way that you cannot be carried along by this narrative. Each time it tips you out, you have to stand and think about it; you yourself are being rendered as discontinuous as the text.

In fact, Burroughs' project is to make time stand still for a while, one which is more frequently that of religion than of literature and there are ways in which Burroughs' work indeed resembles that of another William, the Blake of the self-crafted mythology of the Prophetic Books, although it must be said that Burroughs is much funnier.

He is also the only living American writer of whom one can say with confidence he will be read with the same shock of terror and pleasure in a hundred years' time, or read at all, in fact, should there be anybody left to read.

(1988)

William Burroughs: *Ah Pook is Here*

Ah Pook is Here is an apocalypse. Ah Pook is the Mayan death deity. John Stanley Hart, a young American student of immorality, searches the jungle for the lost Mayan codices that contain Ah Pook's secrets of fear and death. But, when he finds them, he reads them 'as one who reads Moby Dick to find out about whaling and to hell with Ahab'. For Hart is addicted to a personal immortality predicated on the mortality of others, 'gooks, niggers, human dogs, stinking *humans*'.

The arcane secrets of fear and death are utilised to make a world safe for John Stanley Hart to live (forever) in. 'Is this terrible knowledge now computerised and vested in the hands of far-sighted Americans in the State Department and the CIA?' Burroughs is often so outrageously upfront about his moral indignation it is possible, I think wrongly, to dismiss it as a cheap effect.

But a fugue of deathless mutant boys precipitate a bizarrely ecstatic finale that looks like it's been choreographed by Hieronymous Bosch. 'A boy whipped with a transparent fish sprouts wings . . . Flying fox boy soars above a burning tree.' Wild boys lyrically ejaculate robins and blue birds. Nobody, it turns out, can Hire Death as a company cop. Or not for long.

This is by no means an adequate summary of the only hitherto unpublished text in this little garden of Burroughs. *Ah Pook is Here* is infinitely more thematically complex, more uncomfortable and replete with far more deadpan black humour than I have begun to suggest. But you can't easily fillet the meaning out of Burroughs' work because he is against succinct verbal exposition, which he sees as a sinister form of thought control. What he likes to do is hit you with an image and let the image act for itself.

No wonder, then, all these pieces reflect his interest in scripts composed of signs and hieroglyphs. *Ah Pook is Here* was originally intended as a picture-book based on the Mayan codices. The second piece, 'The Book of Breething', actually turns into pictures. In the third piece, 'The Electronic Revolution', Burroughs talks approvingly about Chinese, 'a script derived from hieroglyphs . . . [and therefore] more closely related to the objects and areas described'.

Elsewhere, he defines words as 'moving pictures'. The dialectic between the concrete and the discrete in Burroughs, between the solidity of the image and the arbitrariness of sequence, is what makes his own prose *move*, makes it kinetic, gives it, in spite of its obsession with death, mind-death, soul-death, death-in-life, its superabundant life.

(1979)

· II ·

J. G. Ballard: *Empire of the Sun*

J. G. Ballard says he's an optimist, which, given his penchant for apocalypses, initially seems unlikely but is nevertheless reassuring. He convinces me Reagan won't start World War III because he's too gaga to locate the whereabouts of the red button. Since, back in the Sixties, Ballard was the only sane person in the entire Western world who predicted the ex-movie actor would one day rise to the dizzying heights of the Presidency, maybe Ballard-the-prophet will hit target on this one too. Cross fingers.

It was in a story titled 'Why I Want To Fuck Ronald Reagan', written, Ballard thinks, in 1966, that he foretold Reagan would run for the White House and that 'the profound anality of the Presidential contender may be expected to dominate the US in the coming years'.

Not that he presented it as a prophecy exactly, or that 'Why I Want To Fuck Ronald Reagan' is a short story on the terms of V. S. Pritchett or William Trevor. It is a piece of fiction, a set of ferocious images, a fragment of Swiftian satire, and it subsequently formed part of a book called *The Atrocity Exhibition*, published in 1970, which is one of the important works of British fiction produced in those exploding years.

I read 'Why I Want To Fuck Ronald Reagan' to a class of English Literature majors at a liberal East Coast college in one of the four states in the Union that stayed with Jimmy Carter that November day in 1980 when a British science-fiction writer's mad notion came true. They laughed until they cried, except those who vice versa'd, and then they demanded: 'Who is this man? He is one of your great writers! Why haven't we heard of him before?'

Perhaps it was just because they *were* Eng. Lit. majors that they hadn't heard of him before. He was certainly big stuff in the semiotics department already. Besides, Ballard doesn't like to think of himself as a 'literary man'. He bridles and huffs at the very thought. He is an imagery and ideas man, surreal, troubling – 'sensitive and enigmatic', *The Times Literary Supplement* once characterised his work, making him sound like Denton Welch, for God's sake. He is *not* a fine-writing man:

> I see myself primarily as an imaginative writer, and the imaginative writer isn't primarily concerned with his own medium. The fact that I express myself in a prose narrative is in a sense incidental – if I'd had a different facility, it could have been painting. It's the images I produce, and the ideas enshrined in the images that are the key things – their translation into words is the least important part of the enterprise.

In spite of that, Ballard is one of those rare beings who talk in grammatically correct sentences. His fiction has been characterised by restless and brilliant formal innovation, highly stylised, extreme and shocking violence, pitch-black humour . . . all the post-modernist characteristics. But you are still less likely to find Ballard on the shelf next to Barth and Barthelme and Coover than you are to find him filed along with Bug-Eyed Monster. After the publication of his new novel, *Empire of the Sun*, however, he will be among the bestsellers.

But up until now, Ballard has lived – very happily; he's not one of those sf writers who grumble about being ghettoised – in the privileged seclusion of genre. That is, as a science-fiction writer, he's been able on occasion to be as adventurous with narrative as he may be; to refer to Hans Bellmer or Max Ernst or Alfred Jarry as often as he feels the need without anybody putting him down for pretension. In fact, to carry on with all the freedoms of the 'experimental' writer who has an intelligent and sympathetically critical audience ever eager to find out what he has been up to, this time.

The price of all this? Even if he is greatly admired by Kathy

Acker, has been a massive influence on performance art, and an inspiration to musicians and painters, Ballard is rarely, if ever, mentioned in the same breath, or even the same paragraph, as such peers as Anthony Powell or Iris Murdoch. Fans such as Kingsley Amis and Anthony Burgess praise Ballard to the skies but they themselves are classified differently, as, God help us, 'serious writers' in comparison.

This is a price Ballard has been happy, nay, positively ecstatic to pay. He has fans at the very top end of the market, and fans in the pulps. The mainstream parts around him, leaving his feet comfortably dry. It has been thus ever since the delirious days of Michael Moorcock's magazine, *New Worlds*, twenty years ago, when science fiction started to excavate a whole new era – inner space, i.e. the unconscious – and joined hands with surrealism.

Ballard was attracted to science fiction in the early days because, when he arrived in Britain from China, where he was born, after the war was over and as a stranger with a strange, cold eye, he found that the reality of British society seriously overstretched the traditional resources of British naturalistic fiction:

> I wanted a revolutionary fiction; I wanted the recognition
> of the whole domain of the unconscious, something British
> naturalistic fiction never attempted. I wanted a fiction of
> the imagination which would tell us the truth about our-
> selves. I wanted the future, not the past – I wanted the
> future of the next five minutes.

One of the results of this desire was that Ballard became the great chronicler of the new, technological Britain. A man prone to thrust himself into the grip of obsessions – 'I *am* my obsessions!' – he grew increasingly obsessed by the aspects of our landscape those of us who grew up with the culturally programmed notion of Britain as a 'green and pleasant land' conspire to ignore. Motor-ways. High rises.

There eventually ensued novels of pure technological nightmare – *Crash!*, *High Rise*, *The Concrete Island*. These were the vinyl and broken glass, sex 'n' violence novels, describing a landscape of desolation and disquiet similar to that of the novels of William Burroughs; the fame they brought was of a kind distinctly parallel to the norm of the world o' books. Burgess and Kingsley Amis could go on admiring him in comfort, free from the suspicion he might creep up behind them and pinch their laurels, even if the younger Amis, as big a fan as his father, showed signs of picking up a trick or two from his hero.

Ballard's thirty-odd-year career as a cult classic is, however, about to come to an end. He has, in his mid-fifties, produced what they call a 'breakthrough' novel. No doubt the 'literary men' (and women) will now treat Ballard as the sf writer who came in from the cold. Who finally put away childish things, man-powered flight, landscapes of flesh, the erotic geometry of the car crash, things like that, and wrote the Big Novel they always knew he'd got in him.

Yet *Empire of the Sun*, which is indeed a Big Novel, is manifestly the product of the same unique sensibility as his last major novel, *The Unlimited Dream Company* (1979), and has a great deal in common with it. They share the theme of death and resurrection, the earlier one in a radiant, visionary mode, the later one as delirious obsession. But *Empire of the Sun* is a recreation of the recent past, not a myth of the near future, and the well-loved Ballardian leitmotifs, confinement, escape, flight, have the gritty three-dimensionality of real experience. The novel is even about a kind of apocalypse, the destruction of the British community in Shanghai by the Japanese.

All the same, the chapters have titles that recall those of earlier Ballard short stories: 'The Drained Swimming Pool', 'The Open-Air Cinema', 'The Fallen Airman'. It is a shock to find so much of the recurrent, hypnotic imagery of J. G. Ballard moored to the soil of an authentic city, at an authentic date in real time – Shanghai, as the European residents of that city of salesmen are engulfed ineluctably in war. It was the place of Ballard's childhood.

Empire of the Sun is, very notably, a novel about the fragility of the human body, and the dreadful spillability of that body's essential juices, shit, piss, blood, pus. It is also about the resilience of children; and about the difficulty experienced by the British in adjusting to changing circumstances. More specifically, it is about one child's war, and hence an investigation of twentieth-century warfare, in which non-combatants such as children and also the old, the weak, the sick increasingly fare worst. It is about one child's war in a prison camp, and how he came to feel at home there.

There has, notes Ballard, been surprisingly little fiction about the war in the Far East, perhaps because the British lost it. No, he hasn't read J. G. Farrell's *The Singapore Grip*, which is an account of the fall of Singapore. 'Was Farrell there?' Ballard asked sharply. He obviously doesn't trust book-based research in this area. A note at the front of *Empire of the Sun* says the novel 'draws on my experiences in Shanghai, China, during the Second World War, and in Lunghua C.A.C. (Civilian Assembly Centre) where I was interned from 1942–45'. The strange, cold eye which Ballard turned on Britain when he first came here was evidently trained to look on, unflinching, in Lunghua.

He says:

> I always intended to write a novel about China and the war, but I put it off because I always had more urgent things to do, in fiction. Then, two or three years ago, I realised if I didn't write the China book soon, I would never do so. Memory would fade, apart from anything else. It took a very long time, 20 years or so, to forget the events that took place in Shanghai and it took a very long time to remember them, again . . . I don't just mean to bring them to mind, but to flesh them out, to remythologise them.

Jim, 'my young hero', misses his Scripture exam because the Japanese attack Shanghai; at first that missed exam seems the most important thing. Although he mislays his parents early on, it is a long time before he finally surrenders his school cap and blazer. This well-brought-up boy goes to the Cathedral School. His father's house in Amherst Avenue has a swimming pool (soon to be drained) and nine servants. Jim has the sense of security only privilege can bring.

He is too young to be surprised when he finds the servants gone and the house deserted. He is on his own; it is an adventure. Trying to surrender to the Japanese is more of a problem. They don't really want any more prisoners, but the camp, for all its privations, offers more safety than the dangerous chaos of the city, where a thief will cut off your arm for the sake of a watch, kill you for your shoes, where there is no food left, where the water is full of cholera. Where privilege has evaporated.

Once in the camp, Jim adjusts quickly. Too young to feel nostalgia, he focuses his memory forward. Soon he will be reunited with his parents! One day. Soon. Until then, he lives in the present. He scavenges. He runs errands. He keeps himself busy. He sneaks and wheedles extra sweet potatoes. If his ingratiating smile drives the Japanese guards into paroxysms of fury and all the other children are afraid of him, he is free from self-pity, sustained by the very business of living, and his dreams are nourished by contraband copies of *Readers Digest* scrounged from American prisoners.

Jimmy Ballard lived in Lunghua Camp; he lived in the very hut that his young hero inhabits. The entire context of the novel is true, but Jim's adventures are invention. The book is by no means autobiographical. Ballard was with his parents and his sister in the camp and he knows that children, particularly when they are with their parents, can witness appalling events and feel no fear.

It was a peculiar life for the business community in Shanghai, before the war, after the war, even during the war – until the crunch came and internment began.

'Like my young hero,' Ballard says,

> one witnessed, on a daily basis, the most appalling events – starvation, disease, brutality – but through the window of a chauffeur-driven car. So that one was very, very close to the terrible brutalities inflicted on the Chinese by the Japanese, who surrounded Shanghai, and by the Chinese themselves on one another, but one could do nothing about it. And one wasn't directly involved. And, in a way, writing the book may be an attempt to go back and put emotion in.

Only at the end of the novel, reunited with his parents, about to leave China forever, does Jim, now sixteen, a child no longer, see that Shanghai is now and always was a 'terrible city'; and these, the last words of the novel, restore to the adjective 'terrible' all its original force. The last image of the novel is the haunting one of the paper flowers that decorate the coffins the Chinese, too poor to afford burial, launch into the sea, the drowned flowers that come back to the city, along with the corpses.

Empire of the Sun is a rich, complex, heartrending novel, in characteristically Ballardian prose – a prose with a curiously metallic quality, cold as steel, that makes the imagery shine out, as he wants it to, with the hallucinatory clarity of that of naive painters. The image of those paper flowers decorating the corpses, not of the Chinese dead, but of British sailors dying in the Yangtze River; the mask of flies on the face of the dead airman; the silvery shapes of the American bombers Jim sees from the corner of his eye when he is sick with fever, that are the emissaries of death.

It is easy to think of *Empire of the Sun* as the logical culmination of a career, the book towards which Ballard has been working all his life. Since he is far too young to retire, to think that would be an error. The novel has the look of a significant change of direction for Ballard, yet its appearance of naturalism is only superficial – it is, once again, a triumph of the imagination. The imaginative recreation of that 'terrible city' and the resurrection of its teeming population of dead are to do with the notions of transformation that have always informed his work.

It is hard to imagine – top that! – what he will do next. But, then, it always has been. Meanwhile, here is the fruit of that obsessiveness Ballard so much admires, the obsessive single-mindedness of, as he puts it, 'long-incarcerated mental patients who remain totally faithful to their few obsessions throughout their long lives, the sort of dedication shown by Japanese soldiers hiding out in the jungle for 30-odd-years . . . ' The obsessive pursuit of his own imagery to its origins has brought us this riveting and sombre and, yes, funny (humour blacker than black, this time) and humane novel, that is the kind of novel we used to think we no longer had the energy to write, that Ballard was writing all the time.

(1984)

· 12 ·

Walter de la Mare: *Memoirs of a Midget*

Memoirs of a Midget presents itself as the first-person account of the early life, in particular the tempestuous twentieth year in the life, of a Victorian gentlewoman who has the misfortune to be, although pretty and perfectly formed, of diminutive size. This year includes death, passionate infatuation, some months as a lion of high society, suicide, and attempted suicide. It ends in temporary madness. This summary gives the impression of melodrama yet *Memoirs of a Midget* seduces by its gentle charm and elegant prose. It may be read with a great deal of simple enjoyment and then it sticks like a splinter in the mind.

Miss M.'s fictional autobiography is introduced with the nineteenth-century imitation-documentary device of an editor's preliminary note. Here the reader learns something of Miss M.'s life after the end of her own narrative, and of her – not death, but vanishing. She has, she explains to her housekeeper in a note, been 'called away'. Called away, perhaps, to a happy land where all are the same size as she, where she is not a stranger in a world designed for clumsy giants with sensibilities of a cruel clumsiness to match.

For Miss M. is always a stranger in *this* world. She, literally, does not fit in. The novel is a haunting, elegiac, misanthropic, occasionally perverse study of estrangement and isolation. Miss M. herself describes her predicament: 'Double-minded creature that I was and ever shall be; now puffed up with arrogance at the differences between myself and gross, common-sized humanity; now stupidly sensitive to the pangs to which by reason of these differences I have to submit.' She may stand as some sort of metaphor for the romantic idea of the artist as perennial stranger, as scapegoat and outcast – the artist, indeed, as perpetual adolescent, with the adolescent's painful sense of his own uniqueness when alone and his own inadequacy when in company. In some ways, the novel is about making friends with loneliness, which is not quite the same thing as growing up. And, of course, it is impossible for Miss M. to grow up.

The narrative is imbued with that romantic melancholy which was de la Mare's speciality in both prose and poetry. The novel has all the enigmatic virtues of repression; what is concealed or disguised speaks more eloquently than what is expressed.

Walter de la Mare evaded some of the more perilous reefs of literary criticism in his lifetime by simply casting a spell of charm over his readers. He also liked to suggest elements of religious allegory, which is as good as putting up a 'No Trespassers' sign. Kenneth Hopkins, in a British Council pamphlet on de la Mare published in 1953, entirely abandons discussion of *Memoirs of a Midget*, claiming that 'the work is its own interpretation'. The adjectives, 'beloved' and 'magical' were frequently applied to de la Mare's work; his poetry for children, in particular *Peacock Pie* and his anthology, *Come Hither*, remain beloved cornerstones of the middle-class nursery. Nevertheless, the middle-class nursery is a rapidly dwindling constituency and his reputation as poet and writer for adults has softly and silently vanished away since his death in 1956.

Yet, in 1948, Faber issued a *Tribute to Walter de la Mare on his Seventy Fifth Birthday*, which contained contributions from J. B. Priestley, Vita Sackville-West, Dover Wilson, J. Middleton Murry, Laurence Whistler, John Masefield, C. Day Lewis, Lord David Cecil, and, among others, not Uncle Tom Cobley but Marie Stopes, of all people. De la Mare was the court magician to the literary establishment and, at least after his middle age, enjoyed the pleasantest but most evanescent kind of fame, which is that during your own lifetime.

It seems unlikely his reputation as a poet will revive. His fiction is another matter. His output of novels and stories is uneven, his range limited, but *Memoirs of a Midget* is a novel that clearly set out with the intention of being unique and, in fact, is so; lucid, enigmatic, and violent with the terrible violence that leaves behind no physical trace.

Walter de la Mare: *Memoirs of a Midget*

Memoirs of a Midget was first published in 1921; it was not the work of a young man. De la Mare was born in 1873 and, in his fiction, remained most at home, as most of us do, in the imaginative world of his youth and early middle age. Victoria is still on the throne of Miss M.'s England, a queen who, as Miss M. notes, is not *that* much taller than herself. The novel was instantly successful, brought de la Mare a vastly increased readership and drew from its admirers curious tributes in the shape of teeny-tiny objects, miniature Shakespeares, and so on, suitable for the use of Miss M. Russell Brain (*Tea with Walter de la Mare*, Faber, 1953) describes a cabinet full of these wee gifts in the writer's home.

These gifts tell us something important about de la Mare's readership; it was particularly susceptible to the literary conjuring trick because it wanted to believe in magic. The writer seduced his readers, not only into believing in the objective reality of Miss M. but also into forming a sympathetic identification with her little, anguished, nostalgic, backward-looking figure, lost in a world she has not made. Perhaps she was an appropriate heroine for the English middle-class in the aftermath of the First World War; she is both irreproachable, lovable, and, as an object for identification, blessedly oblique.

At the time of the publication of *Memoirs of a Midget*, de la Mare had been earning his living as a man of letters for thirteen years; was an established poet in the Georgian style, in which he remained; a critic (*Rupert Brooke and the Intellectual Imagination*, 1919); and had published several novels, the most significant of which are a death-haunted book for children, *The Three Royal Monkeys* (1910), and *The Return* (also in 1910).

The Return is about the demonic possession of a dull suburban householder by the perturbed spirit of an eighteenth-century French rake and suicide. It is extraordinary, given such a plot, that so little should happen in the novel. Like *Memoirs of a Midget* it is about estrangement. The hero spends the novel in a state of intense alienation from himself, partly because the revenant boasts an infinitely more complex and attractive personality than its host; and, indeed, it is a notion to make the mind reel – that of Dagwood Bumstead possessed by, say, Casanova. No wonder de la Mare scares himself. It is as if, having invented the idea of demonic possession as a blessing in disguise, de la Mare shies away, terrified, from the consequences, perhaps because he knew he wanted to make evil attractive, but not *all that* attractive. It is a problem he faces again, and deals with more successfully, in the character of Fanny Bowater in *Memoirs of a Midget*, where he seems more at home with the idea that a sexually manipulative woman is inherently evil.

The Return is not a good novel. It is blown out with windy mystification and can hardly have satisfied de la Mare himself since he spent the next decade concentrating on poetry and short stories. He perfected his use of language until his prose is music as plangent as that of Vaughan Williams or Arthur Butterworth, composers with whom he shares an interest in the English lyric. Some of these short stories, 'The Almond Tree' and 'In the Forest', for example, achieve a high gloss of technical perfection that deflects attention from the cruelty of the content, which in both these stories is the brutal innocence of children.

Later stories retain this high surface sheen upon an internal tension of terror, often a psychological terrorism, as in the remarkable 'At First Sight', from a collection aptly titled *On the Edge* (1930). Here a young man's family drive an unsuitable girlfriend to suicide. But all is done gently, gently, over the teacups. This young man suffers from a startling affliction; he is physically incapable of raising his head, of looking up, without suffering intense pain, so his sight is confined to a limited, half-moon-shaped segment of the ground before him. This circumscribed, painful, but intense vision is somewhat similar to de la Mare's own.

These stories are 'tales' in the nineteenth-century sense, highly structured artefacts with beginnings, middles, and ends and a schematic coherence of imagery, not those fragments of epiphanic experience which is the type of the twentieth-century short story. He sternly eschewed modernism, with the result that his fiction has more in common with that of, say, Borges, especially in its studied 'literariness', than with his own contemporaries who are, of course, the great moderns – Joyce, Lawrence, Kafka. I can find no evidence that de la Mare liked, or even read, these writers. Here the analogy with the hero of 'At First Sight' is almost distressing.

Even, or especially, in his most adult and cruellest writing, he shares some qualities with certain Victorian writing for children – George MacDonald's *The Princess and the Goblin* and Christina

Rossetti's *Goblin Market* come to mind – in which the latent content diverges so markedly from the superficial text that their self-designation as 'fairytales' seems to function as a screen, or cover, designed to disarm the reader.

De la Mare is a master of *mise-en-scène*. He is one of the great fictional architects and interior designers; he builds enchanting houses for his characters and furnishes them with a sure eye for those details of personality that are expressed through everyday objects. His ability to evoke mood and atmosphere, especially that of the English countryside in its aspect of literary pastoral, are related to this talent for *mise-en-scène*. The countryside often functions as a backdrop that partakes in the action, as the gardens do in *Memoirs of a Midget*. This quality of romantic evocation, of soft reverie as scenery, combined with the solid, conventional, middle-class milieu in which his most horrible stories take place, both domesticates, normalizes, the terror at their heart, and gives it a further edge.

He has a tremendous and, as if self-protective, enthusiasm for cosiness. There is scarcely a novel or a short story of his that does not involve an elaborate tea-time; tea, that uniquely English meal, that unnecessary collation at which no stimulants – neither alcohol nor meat – are served, that comforting repast of which to partake is as good as a second childhood. However, at certain of his tea parties – especially the one in 'At First Sight', and at several of Miss M.'s own – the cosiness only augments the tortures that are taking place, until the very crockery takes on the aspect of the apparatus of despair and it chinks like the chains of prisoners.

Nevertheless, this deliberate, cosy homeliness sometimes deflects the thrust of his imagination, an imagination which is permitted to operate only without reference to any theories of the unconscious.

This is important. De la Mare constantly invokes the 'imagination' but he does not mean imagination in the sense of the ability to envisage the material transformation of the real world, which is what the graffitistes of May 1968 meant when they wrote, 'Let the imagination seize power', on the walls of Paris. No. For de la Mare, the imagination is a lovely margin, a privileged privacy in the mind – 'that secret chamber of the mind we call the imagination', as Miss M. herself puts it. To read de la Mare's imaginative prose is to begin to understand some of the reasons for the tremendous resistance the English literary establishment put up against Freud, that invader of the last privacy.

This is an imagination that has censored itself before the dream has even begun. It is, of course, all traces of sexuality that must be excised especially rigorously. As Kenneth Hopkins says in his British Council pamphlet: 'if his [de la Mare's] characters kiss, he seldom tells.' This process of censorship means that the imagery arrives on the page in disguise and then, lest even the disguise give too much away, the writer must revise the structure which contains the disguised imagery, while the material world recedes ever further away until it is itself perceived as unreality. 'Death and affliction, even Hell itself, She turns to favour and to prettiness'; that offensive epitaph on the mad Ophelia could be applied to Miss M.'s narrative, did not de la Mare's imagination, perhaps because of the extraordinarily narrow range in which he permitted it to operate, retain its own sinister integrity.

In this theory of the imagination, the 'inner life' is all that is important but, although de la Mare was a great admirer of William Blake, he could scarcely have concurred with him that 'All deities reside within the human breast'. The 'inner life' is perceived as though it was a gift from outside, as though the imagination is the seat of visitations from another, lovelier world, from, in fact, that Other World which forms the title for the scrapbooks of poetry assembled by the anagrammatic Nahum Tarune in the fictional introduction to de la Mare's anthology, Come Hither.

It goes without saying that de la Mare's idea of the poet as somebody with a special delivery service from one of those spirits who, in Plato, operate like celestial telegraph boys, speeding messages from the Other World of real forms to this world of shadows, is directly at variance with the idea of the poet as privileged, drunken lecher which directly superseded it; both represent a mystification of the role of poet. Nevertheless, there is a suggestion it is one such spiritual messenger from the Other World who calls Miss M. away at the last, strengthening her possible role as metaphoric artist.

De la Mare's homespun neo-Platonism, filtered through Shelley, Coleridge, and the seventeenth-century neo-Platonists such as Traherne and Vaughan of whom he was particularly fond, gives him enormous confidence in the idea of the imagination as a thing-in-itself, an immaterial portion of the anatomy for which, in a profound sense, the possessor is not responsible. The possessor witnesses the work of the imagination but is not engaged with it. From this conviction comes the consolatory remoteness of his fiction from human practice, even when his characters are engaged in the most mundane tasks, like travelling in railway trains or eating breakfast; all seems as if frozen in time. There is a distance between the writer and the thing, feeling, or sensation he describes that removes it from everyday human actuality. In addition, literary devices, like saying of the taste of a fruit, 'I can taste it on my tongue now . . . ', do nothing at all to reproduce the sensuous actuality of eating a nectarine. If you have ever eaten a nectarine, however, perhaps it will make you remember.

De la Mare's prose is evocative, never voluptuous, and it depends on a complicity of association with the reader for it to work as he intends. This community of association depends on a response of glad recognition to certain words – 'old-fashioned' is one. It always means good things in de la Mare. So does 'reclusive' and, with the implication of a deprecating smile, 'bookish'. And to live in a remote house in the country with a large garden is to be half way towards a state of grace.

A common set of literary associations is important, too. Sir Walter Pollacke recognises Miss M. as a kindred spirit when he hears her recite the anonymous sixteenth-century poem, 'Tom a Bedlam': 'The moon's my constant mistress, And the lovely owl my marrow . . . ' Conversely, when Fanny Bowater quotes Henry Vaughan in a tone of facetious mockery, it is a sign of the blackness of her soul. To have a small, choice library in which Sir Thomas Browne and the metaphysical poets are well represented, with access to a good second-hand bookshop in a nearby country town takes one a little further towards bliss.

All this inevitably raises the question of social class. De la Mare's fiction most usually moves within a very narrow band of English society, characterised by phrases like 'a modest fortune', 'a small private income', 'comfortable circumstances' . . . sufficient to enable one to pick up the odd first-edition Herrick. In *Memoirs of a Midget* he manifests a kind of snobbery not unlike Jane Austen's, in which the aristocracy, typified by Mrs Monnerie, 'Lord B.'s sister', is, like the Crawfords in *Mansfield Park*, cynical, corrupt, and vicious, while the lower-middle and working class – Miss M.'s landlady, Mrs Bowater, and her nursemaid,

Pollie – are good-hearted stereotypes whose fictional execution uses techniques of physical idiosyncrasy derived from Dickens. (Jane Austen, of course, simply doesn't mention the lower classes.)

The rigid Procrustean bed of the middle class is that on which his fictions, these nightmares of bourgeois unease, are dreamed.

There is a caricature by Max Beerbohm of de la Mare staring fixedly across a fireplace at a grim, black-clad old lady sitting unresponsive in an armchair opposite: 'Mr W. de la Mare gaining inspiration for an eerie and lovely story.' It is one of the most perceptive, and wittily unkind, criticisms of de la Mare that could be made. Let his fancy meander whence it pleases, may his antennae be never so sensitive to messages from the Other World, there is a nanny inside him slapping his hand when it wanders to the forbidden parts of his mind.

However, repression produces its own severe beauties. Out of this terrified narrowness, this dedicated provincialism of the spirit, emerges a handful of pieces of prose with the most vivid and unsettling intensity, work which disquietingly resembles some of that which the surrealists were producing in France at the same period, operating from a rather different theory of the imagination. Indeed, it would be possible to make a claim for *Memoirs of a Midget* as the one true and only successful English surrealist novel, even though de la Mare would have hotly denied it. That he didn't know what he was doing, of course, only makes it more surrealist; and more baleful.

And I should say that Miss M. herself, in her tiny, bizarre perfection, irresistibly reminds me of a painting by Magritte of a nude man whose sex is symbolised by a miniature naked woman standing upright at the top of his thigh.

Miss M.'s size, in fact, is nowhere given with precision. It seems to vary according to de la Mare's whim. At five or six years old, she is small enough to sit on the lid of a jar of pomatum on her father's dressing table; she feeds butterflies from her own hand. This suggests a smallness which is physically impossible. Later, when she learns to read: 'My usual method with a common-sized book was to prop it towards the middle of the table and then seat myself at the edge. The page finished, I would walk across and turn over a fresh leaf.' This method has not much changed by the time she is twenty, except now she sprawls between the pages. At that age, she still has difficulty in descending staircases and, at her twenty-first birthday, can run down the centre of a dining-room table while, a few weeks later, she can travel comfortably in a disused bird-cage. However, earlier that year, on holiday, driving a goat-cart, she is disguised as a ten-year-old and though a grown woman the size of a ten-year-old child would be distinctly on the smallish side, she would scarcely be a midget; Jeffrey Hudson, the court dwarf of Charles I, was forced to retire when he reached the dizzy height of three feet nine inches.

Miss M.'s actual size, therefore, is not within the realm of physiological dimension; it is the physical manifestation of an enormous *difference*.

The midget child is a sort of changeling. Her mother treats her as a 'tragic playmate' rather than a daughter, and her father, affectionately embarrassed by her existence, effectively abandons his paternal role and makes no financial provision for her on his death. She is an anomaly. For their own sakes as well as hers they keep their daughter isolated from the world and their deaths leave her vulnerably inexperienced, besides newly poor.

Yet Miss M.'s childhood is itself a magic garden, in which, like Andrew Marvell in *his* garden, she is alone and hence in paradise. Almost all of *Memoirs of a Midget* takes place in Kent, the 'garden of England', and, as it happens, de la Mare's own home county; and Miss M. is most herself in a garden. When she is accompanied it is scarcely ever by more than one person. These country gardens, far from the habitations of common humanity, are almost always a little neglected, the 'wild gardens' of the English romantic imagination, nature neither dominated by man nor dominating him by its ferocity, but existing with him in a harmonious equality. The paradisial garden of childhood is that of Stonecote, her parents' house, to which, after the vicissitudes of her twentieth year, she will return and into which, taking only 'a garden hat and cape', she eventually, according to her editor, disappears, possibly accompanied by a Platonic angel.

But the garden of Stonecote is also where Miss M. first learns the stark and irrevocable fact of mortality, when, as a child, she encounters there a dead mole:

Holding my breath, with a stick I slowly edged it up in

the dust and surveyed the white heaving nest of maggots in its belly with a peculiar and absorbed recognition. 'Ah ha!' a voice cried within me, 'so this is what is in wait; this is how things are;' and I stooped with lips drawn back over my teeth to examine the stinking mystery more closely.

It is a mole, a blind creature that lives in the earth, who conveys the existence of a 'stinking mystery' in this world. Without the power of inward vision, the mole exists only in its corruptible envelope of flesh.

After her father's death and the expulsion from this primal Eden where Miss M. has been an infant Eve without an Adam, she takes a room with the very grim and black-clad woman from Beerbohm's drawing, the stern, kind, and irretrievably 'literary' Mrs Bowater, a mother or nanny surrogate. Here, Miss M. meets, not Adam, but Lilith. Fanny is Mrs Bowater's daughter . . . 'her voice – it was as if it had run about in my blood and made my eyes shine'. Fanny, who is lower class in spite of her beauty and cleverness, works as a teacher; she arrives home for Christmas, she is cognate with ice, snow, cold. Miss M.'s most passionate meeting with her takes place on a freezing, ecstatic night when they go star-gazing together, in the wild garden of the abandoned house of Wanderslore nearby.

This garden, untenanted, uncared for, is the garden of revelation. In this same wild place she meets the dwarf she calls Mr. Anon, who falls in love with her. In this same garden, Miss M. will later think of killing herself. In *Memoirs of a Midget* gardens function in the rich literary tradition that starts with the Book of Genesis, places of privilege outside everyday experience in which may occur the transition from innocence to knowledge. In yet another garden, that of the country house of her patroness, Mrs Monnerie, Miss M. conducts her last, fatal interview with Fanny, when Fanny announces her intention of destroying her.

Miss M.'s sado-masochistic relation with Fanny is central to the novel. Fanny, typical of the *femme fatale*, enslaves through humiliation. She writes her supplicant letters addressed to 'Dear Midgetina', and Miss M. replies signing herself with the same name, so that Leslie Fiedler (in a discussion of the novel in *Freaks: Myths and Images of the Secret Self*, New York, 1978) thinks

'Midgetina' is Miss M.'s given name. But it sounds more like a nickname callously bestowed and gratefully received – she is grateful for any attention from Fanny. For Miss M.'s anonymity is exceedingly important to de la Mare, I think.

Fanny's indifference is irresistible: 'I might have been a pet animal for all the heed she paid to my caress.' Later, Fanny will turn on Miss M. after a final declaration of love: 'Do you really suppose that to be loved is a new experience for me; that I'm not smeared with it wherever I go?' She is *la belle dame sans merci* in person, the cruel dominatrix of Swinburne and Pater, a *fin de siècle* vamp disguised as a landlady's daughter. Or, rather, step-daughter, for Fanny is a changeling, too; unknown to her, Mrs Bowater is her father's second wife. No blood of common humanity runs in Fanny's veins. She reminds Miss M. of mermaids and, sometimes, of snakes. She drives a love-sick curate to cut his throat for love of her. She is woman as sexual threat.

Fanny forces Miss M. to see herself as a freak, an aberration, an unnatural object. She promises ironically: 'Midgetina, if ever I *do* have a baby, I will anoint its little backbone with the grease of moles, bats and dormice, to make it like you,' quoting an ancient recipe for the commercial manufacture of dwarf beggars and entertainers, as if Miss M. had herself been made, not born. The account of Miss M.'s enslavement by Fanny burns with pain, although Fanny is far too motivelessly malign for any form of naturalist fiction; she is simply, emblematically, a *femme fatale*, or, perhaps, a bad angel.

When Fanny accidentally meets Miss M.'s friend and would-be lover, her casual description of him – 'a ghastly gloating little dwarfish creature' – makes Miss M. see how Mr Anon must look to *other people*, and so wrecks her own idea of him.

This question of the definition of identity recurs throughout the novel. Miss M. describes Fanny's charm: 'she's so *herselfish*, you know'; Fanny is powerful because she knows who she is. But Fanny uses all her power to define Miss M. as a deviant: 'Why was it that of all people only Fanny could so shrink me up like this into my body?' This problem is not altogether resolved; on the last page of her narrative, Miss M. says: 'We *cannot* see ourselves as others see us, but that is no excuse for not wearing spectacles.' Yet the last words of the novel are a plea to her editor, to whom she dedicates her memoirs, to 'take me seriously', that is, to see her as she sees herself. This unresolved existential plea – to be allowed to be herself, although she is not sure what that self is – is left hanging in the air. The suggestion is that Miss M. exists, like Bishop Berkeley's tree, because the eye of God sees her.

In another night interview between Fanny and Miss M. in the garden at Wanderslore, Fanny says: 'There was once a philosopher called Plato, my dear. He poisoned Man's soul.' With that, Fanny declares herself the eternal enemy; she has denied idealism. And something very odd happens here; Fanny goes off, leaving Miss M. calling helplessly after her, 'I love you'. They have been, apparently, quite alone. Then up out of nowhere pops the 'gloating, dwarfish creature', Mr Anon himself, to murmur to Miss M. how 'they' – that is, other people – 'have neither love nor pity'. She runs away from his importunity as Fanny has run away from hers; but this is only one of several places in the text where Miss M., believing herself alone in the garden, discovers Mr Anon is there, beside her. At last she decides he has been watching her secretly since she first discovered Wanderslore, just as the eye of God, in her nursery lesson book, *The Observing Eye*, watches over everything.

Although Mr Anon's corporality is affirmed throughout the book – he even takes tea with the emphatically 'real' Mrs Bowater – he has certain purely metaphysical qualities, not least the ability to appear whenever Miss M. needs him. He is her good, her guardian angel, the spiritual pole to Fanny.

But Miss M. is bewildered. Mr Anon's ugliness is that of the flesh alone, yet it is sufficient to repel her; Fanny's beauty is only an outward show, yet Miss M. finds her compulsively attractive. Poor Miss M., the psyche fluttering in between. 'And still he [Mr Anon] maintained . . . that he knew mankind better than I, that to fall into their ways and follow their opinions was to deafen my ears, and seal up my eyes, and lose my very self.'

Miss M. *does* fall into the ways of mankind for a season, however; indeed, not 'a season' but 'the Season'. She is collected by rich, aristocratic, corrupt, easily bored Mrs Monnerie to add to an assortment of 'the world's smaller rarities' in her London mansion. Miss M.'s stay in London is the most straightforward part of the novel, with a degree of satiric snap and bite oddly reminiscent of parts of Balzac's *Lost Illusions*. She is not by any means the first young person from the provinces to go to hell at the dinner tables of the gentry. 'What a little self-conscious donkey I became, shrilly hee-hawing away; the centre of a simpering throng plying me with flattery.'

Miss M. brings her own doom upon herself by introducing Fanny into this artificial paradise, where the only garden is that of the square outside, an arid, over-cultivated town garden where only 'piebald plane-trees and poisonous laburnums' grow. Fanny immediately seizes her chance and usurps Miss M.'s position as court favourite; she will marry unscrupulously for money and entertain herself by leading the *haute monde* a dance in preference to disrupting a vicarage tea party.

The climax of the London sequence is Miss M.'s twenty-first birthday party, with its cake decorated with replicas of twenty-one famous female dwarves, a fiesta of bad taste which is only exceeded by the dinner menu composed entirely of the minute, culminating in a dish of nightingales' tongues, on which Miss M. gags. Enough is enough. So Midgetina comes of age, in an orgy of humiliation, drunkenly making a spectacle of herself. 'Sauve qui peut!' she cries to Fanny, intent at last on rescuing her from damnation, calling out the name of a book Fanny once gave her as a satiric jest, Jeremy Taylor's *Holy Living and Holy Dying*, and passing out.

Banished to Mrs Monnerie's country house, Miss M. now exhibits herself in a circus in order to earn the money to buy her freedom. She paints her face and pads her bust and bottom; the disguise appears to her to be 'monstrous'. She takes on, in other words, the appurtenances of the flesh, and those of the flesh of a mature woman, at that. It is sufficient indirectly to cause Mr Anon's death.

This raises some interesting questions about the central spiritual conflict for which the dreamy beauty of the novel is a disguise. For, even if Mr Anon *is* Miss M.'s Good Angel and her rejection of him in favour of Fanny brings her near to losing her soul, why should she marry him, when she has no wish to do so, simply because they are a match in size? Not only is de la Mare quite definite about Miss M.'s not wanting to marry Mr Anon – 'not even love's ashes were in my heart' – but he scrupulously documents her absolute revulsion from physical contact. She flinches from all human touch except that of her childhood nursemaid.

Miss M. seems as alienated from sexuality as she is from all other aspects of the human condition, and if her passion for Fanny suggests it is only heterosexual contact from which she is alienated, de la Mare feels himself free to describe her emotional enslavement by Fanny because the idea this might have a sexual element has been censored out from the start. Although Miss M. declares repeatedly that she is in love with Fanny, the reader is not officially invited by de la Mare to consider this might have anything to do with her rejection of the advances of Mr Anon. The conflict is played out in terms of pure spirit.

And, at the circus, when she is in her erotic disguise, it is as if the spectacle of Miss M. suddenly transformed from visible spirit (she is slight, fair, pale) to palpable if simulated rosy flesh is too much for Mr Anon, who is, as ever, watching her. He refuses to allow her to degrade herself still further and takes her place in the circus ring on an unruly pony for the last parade, suffering a fatal injury while doing so. Miss M., therefore, out in the world on her own for the first time, tremulously experimenting with the appearance of sexuality, and, indeed, of work, too – for this circus turn is the first time she has attempted to earn her own living – actually loses her soul; and has to undergo an ordeal in the same neglected garden of Wanderslore where she used to meet both Fanny and Mr Anon before she can start out again on the path to regeneration, the return home.

This ordeal concludes with a balked attempt to poison herself with the fruit of the deadly nightshade, with 'forbidden fruit'.

This is not the first time she has been tempted by forbidden fruit. In the secure garden of childhood, she has 'reached up and plucked from their rank-smelling bush' a few blackcurrants very similar in appearance to the 'black, gleaming' poison berries on which, in her extremity, she gazes 'as though, from childhood up, they had been my one greed and desire'. But, desire them as she may, she cannot eat them; she seems physically incapable of doing so. She picks one, its 'bitter juices' jet out upon her, and then, overcome, she flings 'the vile thing' down. The fruit remains forbidden. Whatever taboo it represents remains unbroken, and the breaking of this taboo involves the 'stinking mystery' of mortality, anyway.

So the central core of the novel remains mysterious to itself; we never penetrate the real nature of the 'stinking mystery' in the garden, represented by the rotting carcase of the mole. Miss M. will remain a stranger in this world. She will not even learn to rejoice in her estrangement, although at last she rejoices in her solitude. But that is not the same thing.

The image of forbidden fruit has all the more potency because Miss M. customarily subsists on a fructarian diet. She drinks milk, nibbles biscuits but partakes freely only of cherries, slices of apple, strawberries, nectarines. Her diet is similar to that of the heroes of de la Mare's metaphysical novel for children, *The Three Royal Monkeys*, who promise their mother never to taste blood, to climb trees, or to grow a tail; their diet is a sign of their spiritual ascendancy over the other apes and Miss M. marks the beginnings of her own spiritual erosion in London when a doctor puts her on a strengthening diet of white meat. She starts to put on weight and that seems to her also a sign of degeneration; there is an interesting touch of the anorexic about Miss M. revealed in her choice of words to describe her padded circus costume: 'monstrous mummery'. This is connected with an odd little episode during her life at Mrs Bowater's, when she buries a blood-stained nightdress in a rabbit hole in the Wanderslore garden, just as young girls sometimes attempt to hide the evidence of their menses. (Miss M. tells us that this blood, however, comes from a scratch.) Mr Anon later returns this nightdress; nothing, nothing whatever, can be hidden from him. No wonder he annoys her.

After she throws down the forbidden fruit, untasted, she suffers a period of derangement and hallucination. We know in advance from her editor's preface that sufficient private means are stumped up somehow to buy back for her her father's house, and there she lives on, in seclusion, with Fanny's mother to wait on her. We leave Miss M.'s life in the same state of purposeless rustic gentility as it began but we already know she will be 'called away', by, it is implied, that spiritual messenger from the Other World, perhaps the beautiful stranger she saw in the audience in the circus tent. And yet the mystery of her departure seems arbitrary and forlorn.

De la Mare has certainly equipped the novel with hermetic meaning, yet this does not, finally, seem to console even the writer. The metaphysical sub-text seems to me a decoy; he offers a key to a door behind which is only another door. The novel remains dark, teasing, a system of riddles, leaving a memory of pain, a construct of remarkable intellectual precision and scrupulous dovetailing of imagery, finally as circular as hopelessness.

Something awful is looking out of the windows of the novel, just as it looks out of Fanny's eyes in Miss M.'s startling description of her: 'a beautiful body with that sometimes awful Something looking out of its windows.' De la Mare himself found this image sufficiently striking to use a version of it again in his own Introduction to the 1938 Everyman edition of a selection of his stories, essays, and poems:

> Feelings as well as thoughts may be expressed in symbols; and every character in a story is not only a 'chink', a peephole in the dark cottage from which his maker looks out at the world, but is also in some degree representative of himself, if a self in disguise.

All fiction, as Balzac said, is symbolic autobiography. Miss M.'s 'M' may stand, simply, for midget, or Midgetina; or, Metaphor. Or, Myself.

(1982)

· 13 ·

The Alchemy of the Word

Surrealism celebrated wonder, the capacity for seeing the world as if for the first time which, in its purest state, is the prerogative of children and madmen, but more than that, it celebrated wonder itself as an essential means of perception. Yet not a naive wonder. The surrealists did not live in naive times. A premonition of the imminent end of the world is always a shot in the arm for the arts; if the world has, in fact, just ended, what then? The 1914–18 war was, in many respects, for France and Germany, indeed the end of the world. The Zurich Dadas celebrated the end of the world, and of art with it. However, the Russian Revolution of 1917 suggested the end of one world might mark the commencement of another world, one in which human beings themselves might take possession not only of their own lives but also of their own means of expressing the reality of that life, i.e. art. It is possible for the true optimist to view the end of the world with sang-froid. What is so great about all this crap? Might there be something better? Surrealism's undercurrent of joy, of delight, springs from its faith in humankind's ability to recreate itself; the conviction that struggle *can* bring something better.

Any discussion of surrealism must, first of all, acknowledge that it was never a school of art, or of literature, as such. The surrealist painters and poets were not in the least interested in formal art or literature, and if they started to show signs of becoming so, Andre Breton, the supreme arbitrator, kicked them out of the group. It was the irreducible psychological element that makes a wonder out of the commonplace, the imagination itself, that obsessed them. As for art, anyone can make it; so they

67

made art, out of word and image, though their techniques were haphazard and idiosyncratic, and it must be said that some of them were better at it than others, though an unfair proportion of them all had that ability to light the blue touchpaper of the imagination and then retire, which a more élitist culture than the one at whose service the surrealists placed their work, or play, would have called genius.

Surrealism was not an artistic movement but a theory of knowledge that developed a political ideology of its own accord. Its art came out of the practice of a number of men and women who formulated and committed themselves to this theory of knowledge, some for a few years, some for their whole lives. They were practitioners and theoreticians at the same time. A poet, Andre Breton, wrote the Surrealist Manifesto; a film-maker and a punk painter, Luis Buñuel and Salvador Dali, made the two most comprehensive surrealist visual statements, *Un Chien Andalou* and *L'Age d'Or*, though Dali later recanted on the whole thing. Buñuel never recanted, kept turning them out, the greatest poet of the cinema and of love, who used the camera like a machine-gun, the dialectic like a *coup de grâce*.

However, surrealist theory is derived from a synthesis of Freud and Hegel that only those without a specialist knowledge of either psychoanalysis or philosophy might have dared to undertake. Over the surrealists, or, rather, around them lie the long shadows of Plato, amongst whom they moved as if they were made of flesh. The immediate literary avatars are easier to assimilate: Baudelaire, Lautreamont, Rimbaud, Alfred Jarry. The surrealists soon incorporated Marx, yet, with digestions like so many boa constrictors, were greedy for occult phenomena and utilised a poetic methodology based on analogy and inspiration, the free play of the unconscious, tangling with the French Communist Party – losing Louis Aragon and Paul Eluard to it. Most of the painters found themselves prize exhibits in the Hitlerian gallery of decadent art. The poetry, especially that of Eluard, with its themes of freedom and love, was used as propaganda in the French Resistance.

Like most philosophical systems put together by artists – like neo-Platonism itself – surrealism was intellectually shaky, but, artistically speaking, the shakier the intellectual structure, the better art it produces. (Christianity has produced some perfectly respectable painting, even poetry.) The British could never take its philosophic pretensions seriously; none of the surrealists knew any maths, and besides, they kept dragging sex and politics into everything, including the relations between men and women and the individual and the state, where every good Briton knows sex and politics have no right to be. Nevertheless, surrealist art is, in the deepest sense, philosophical – that is, art created in the terms of certain premisses about reality; and also an art that is itself a series of adventures in, or propositions and expositions of, this surrealist philosophy.

It was also a way of life; of living on the edge of the senses; of perpetual outrage and scandal, the destruction of the churches, of the prisons, of the armies, of the brothels. Such power they ascribed to words and images. A poem is a wound; a poem is a weapon:

> It has been said that it is not our right but our duty to start with words and their relations in order to study the world scientifically. It should be added that this duty is that of living itself, not in the fashion of those who bear death within them, and who are already blind walls, or vacuums, but by uniting with the universe, with the universe in movement, in process.
>
> Poetry will become flesh and blood only when it is reciprocal. This reciprocity is entirely a function of the equality of happiness among mankind. And equality of happiness will bear happiness to a height of which we can as yet have only a faint notion.
>
> (Paul Eluard)

Surrealism posits poetry as a possible mode, possibly the primary mode, of being. Surrealism was the latest, perhaps the final, explosion of romantic humanism in Western Europe. It demanded the liberation of the human spirit as both the ends and the means of art.

Surrealism = *permanent revelation*
Surrealism = *permanent revolution*

So it didn't work out. Those surrealists who are not dead are

69

very old and some are very rich, which wasn't on the original
agenda. Since poetry has to pay its dues at the custom-house of
translation, it rarely travels, and, besides, the nature of outrage is
not the same at all places and at all times. The Dadas are more
fashionable at the moment, since we live in nihilistic times. Surrealist romanticism is at the opposite pole from classical modernism, but then, the surrealists would never have given Pound or
Eliot house room on strictly moral grounds. A Mussolini fan? A
high Tory? They'd have moved, noisily but with dignity, to
another café. You don't *have* to collaborate, you know. *La lutte
continue*. It continues because it has to. This world is all we have.

It is this world, there is no other but a world transformed by
imagination and desire. You could say it is the dream made flesh.

Freud's *The Interpretation of Dreams* was a key book. When we
dream, we are all poets. Everywhere, the surrealists left their
visiting cards: 'Parents! Tell your children your dreams.' The
Bureau of Surrealist Enquiries was opened at 15 rue de Grenelle,
Paris, in October 1924. 'The Bureau of Surrealist Enquiries is
engaged in collecting, by every appropriate means, communications relevant to the diverse forms which the unconscious
activity of the mind is likely to take.' The general public were
invited to visit the Bureau to confide their rarest dreams, to debate
morality, to allow the staff to judge the quality of those striking
coincidences that revealed the arbitrary, irrational, magical corre-
spondences of life.

Antonin Artaud fired off letters to the chancellors of the European universities: 'Gentlemen: In the narrow tank which you call
"Thought", the rays of the spirit rot like old straw.' To the Pope:
'In the name of Family and Fatherland, you urge the sale of souls,
the unrestricted grinding of bodies.' And to the Dalai Lama:
'Teach us, Lama, material levitation of the body and how we can
be held no longer by the earth.' Note the touch of oriental mystic-
ism creeping into the last missive. A bit more of that kind of
thing and Andre Breton, the Pope of surrealism, its theoretician,
propagandist, and mage, expelled him from the group. Like many
libertarians, Breton had, in action, a marked authoritarian streak.
Artaud vanished from this world into that of madness.

In 1922 Max Ernst had already painted a group portrait: 'At
the Rendezvous of Friends.' The friends were the poets Rene
Crevel, Louis Aragon, Philippe Soupoult, Paul Eluard, Robert

Desnos, Andre Breton, and Benjamin Peret; Dostoievsky had also arrived. Jean Arp, like Ernst a former Dada, was a poet as well as a sculptor; Giorgio de Chirico and Ernst himself are primarily painters, even if Ernst is the most literary of all painters and de Chirico wrote an enigmatic novel, *Hebdomeros*, that begins in the middle of one sentence and ends in the middle of another. The surrealist freemasonry encompassed all kinds of art because it saw all kinds of art as manifestations of the same phenomena.

The term 'surrealism' was coined by Guillaume Appollinaire in the preface to his play, *Les Mamelles de Tiresias*, to describe the human ability to create the unnatural. Man's first surreal act, he opined, was the creation of the wheel. The wheel imitates the physical function of motion but creates a form entirely independent of forms known to exist in nature. It was a product entirely of the imagination.

At the première of *Les Mamelles de Tiresias*, at the Conservatoire Maubel, on 24 June 1917, the young Andre Breton observed an acquaintance in the audience; this young man had come to the theatre with a revolver in his hand, and excited by the scandal of the performance, was threatening to fire into the audience. This Jacques Vache, a Baudelairean dandy, exercised a far greater influence over surrealism than his exiguous life would suggest; ten years later, Breton would write in the *Second Manifesto of Surrealism*: 'the simplest surrealist act consists of going out into the street revolver in hand and firing at random into the crowd as often as possible.' Fifty years later, Buñuel filmed just such a random assassin in *The Phantom of Liberty*. A judge condemns the man to death and he walks into the street, free. Girls cluster round him for his autograph.

Put together your own set of connections between these events.

Vache wrote to Breton: 'Art is nonsense.'

In 1917, at the home of the ubiquitous Appollinaire, poet, art critic, modernist, Breton found issues of a magazine from Zurich, *Dada*. Which confirmed his intuition that, if art was nonsense – then nonsense might be art.

When Tzara arrived in Paris two years later, he, Breton, and friends organised a series of provocation-performances similar to those he had staged in Zurich; announcing a poem, Tzara would read from a newspaper, accompanied by bells and rattles. Breton would chew matches. Others screamed, caterwauled, or counted the number of pearls in the necklaces of ladies in the audience. But Breton could not keep up the pace for long. Nihilism can never be an end in itself.

Surrealism was born out of the row between Andre Breton and Tristan Tzara. It was the creative negation of destruction.

The young poets, the friends, who assembled around Breton concerned themselves with a direct relation to the unconscious: then ensued the period of automatic writing, of trance, of the recitals of dreams. Robert Desnos was so good at tranced pronouncements they thought he was faking it. A photograph of him, tranced, published in Breton's novel, *Najda*, in 1928, oddly prefigures the face of a man near death. It was by this photograph that a Czech student, working in the German concentration camp where Desnos lay dying of typhus, recognised him at the end of the Second World War.

What did these young people do with themselves when they were not engaged in the revolutionary act of sleep? For a start, they played games.

They played: the question game, in which you make a reply without knowing the question.

For example: Raymond Queneau: 'Who is Benjamin Peret?'

Marcel Noll: 'A zoo in revolt, a jungle, a liberty.'

They played: *l'un dans l'autre*, a thing described in terms of an analogy.

For example: George Goldfayn describes an armchair as if it were a hedgehog. 'I am a very small garden armchair whose springs pierce the leather cover under which I draw back by feet whenever someone comes near.'

(This kind of exquisite whimsy is the only thing the British have ever found tolerable about the whole damn crew.)

They drew analogical portraits; they collaborated on portraits; they invented animals, the flora and fauna of dream; they compiled manifestos, put together magazines, quarrelled, demonstrated, shocked the bourgeoisie. There is a beautiful photograph I have seen of Benjamin Peret snapped in the act of insulting a priest.

The surrealists also fell in love. Love, passionate, heterosexual love, together with freedom, from which it is inextricable, was their greatest source of inspiration; their women live vividly on the page at second hand. Gala, who left Eluard for Dali. Elsa

Triolet (for whom, and Communism, Aragon left surrealism). Youki Desnos. The three wives of Breton – he transferred his passion *en bloc* to each in turn. The surrealists were not good with women. That is why, although I thought they were wonderful, I had to give them up in the end. They were, with a few patronised exceptions, all men and they told me that I was the source of all mystery, beauty, and otherness, because I was a woman – and I knew that was not true. I knew I wanted my fair share of the imagination, too. Not an excessive amount, mind; I wasn't greedy. Just an equal share in the right to vision.

When I realised that surrealist art did not recognise I had my own rights to liberty and love and vision as an autonomous being, not as a projected image, I got bored with it and wandered away.

But the old juices can still run, as in the mouths of Pavlov's dogs, when I hear the old, incendiary slogans, when I hear that most important of all surrealist principles: 'The marvellous alone is beautiful' (*First Manifesto of Surrealism*, 1924).

Surrealist beauty is convulsive. That is, you *feel* it, you don't see it – it exists as an excitation of the nerves. The experience of the beautiful is, like the experience of desire, an abandonment to vertigo, yet the beautiful does not exist *as such*. What do exist are images or objects that are enigmatic, marvellous, erotic – or juxtapositions of objects, or people, or ideas, that arbitrarily extend our notion of the connections it is possible to make. In this way, the beautiful is put at the service of liberty.

An aesthetic of the eye at the tips of the fingers; of the preternaturally heightened senses of the dreamer. They liked William Blake; and they liked Lewis Carroll; and they liked Bishop Berkeley. Leonora Carrington was British and wrote, still writes, prim, strange, surrealist fictions but the movement never travelled across the Channel, not even in the Thirties, just as women never took it over. Breton died in 1966, securely ensconced as one of France's greatest modern writers.

So does the struggle continue?

Why not. Give me one good reason. Even if the struggle has changed its terms.

(1978)

TOMATO WOMAN

To eat is to fuck.

Claude Lévi-Strauss

· 14 ·

An Omelette and a Glass of Wine
and other Dishes

'Be modern – worship food,' exhorts the cover of *The Official Foodie Handbook*. One of the ironies resulting from the North/ South dichotomy of our planet is the appearance of this odd little book, a *vademecum* to a widespread and unashamed cult of conspicuous gluttony in the advanced industrialised countries, at just the time when Ethiopia is struck by a widely publicised famine, and the rest of Africa is suffering a less widely publicised one. Not Africa alone, of course, is chronically hungry all the time and acutely hungry some of the time: at a conservative estimate, eight hundred million people in the world live in constant fear of starvation. Under the circumstances, it might indeed make good twentieth-century sense to worship food, but punters of 'foodism' (as Ann Barr and Paul Levy jokily dub this phenomenon) are evidently not about to drop to their knees because they are starving.

'Foodies', according to Barr and Levy, are 'children of the consumer boom' who consider 'food to be an art, on a level with painting or drama'. It is the 'art' bit that takes their oral fetishism out of the moral scenario in which there is an implicit reprimand to greed in the constantly televised spectacle of the gaunt peasants who have trudged miles across drought-devastated terrain to score their scant half-crust. ('That bread alone was worth the journey,' they probably remark, just as Elizabeth David says of a trip to an out-of-the-way eatery in France.) Art has a morality of its own, and the aesthetics of cooking and eating aspire, in 'foodism', towards the heights of food-for-food's sake. Therefore the Third World can go suck its fist.

The Official Foodie Handbook is in the same format as, and it comes from the same firm that brought out, *The Official Sloane Ranger Handbook*. That is to say, it is 'a *Harpers & Queen* Publication', which means it springs from the loins of the magazine that most consistently monitors the lifestyle of new British affluence. These 'official handbooks' are interesting as a genre. The idea has been taken up with enthusiasm by *Harpers & Queen*, but the original appears to be *The Official Preppy Handbook*, published in the USA in the early days of the first Reagan Presidency. This slim volume was a lighthearted checklist of the attributes of the North American upper middle class, so lighthearted it gave the impression it did not have a heart at all. The entire tone was most carefully judged: a mixture of contempt for and condescension towards the objects of its scrutiny, a tone which contrived to reassure the socially aspiring that emulation of their betters was a game that might legitimately be played hard just *because* it could not be taken seriously, so that snobbery involved no moral compromise.

The book was an ill-disguised celebration of the snobbery it affected to mock and, under its thinly ironic surface, was nothing more nor less than an etiquette manual for a class newly emergent under Reaganomics. It instructed the *nouveaux riches* in the habits and manners of the *vieux riches* so that they could pass undetected amongst them. It sold like hot cakes.

The British version duly appeared on the stands a year or so later, tailored to the only slightly different demands of a youth newly gilded by Thatcherism. *The Official Foodie Handbook* mentions two fresh additions to the genre in the USA: *The Yuppie Handbook* ('the state-of-the-art manual for Young Urban Professionals') and *The Official Young Aspiring Professionals Fast-Track Handbook*. There seems to be no precise equivalent for the Young Aspiring Professional in Thatcher's Britain: the Tory Trade Unionist (or TUTU) might fill the bill in some ways, but not in others. The Yuppie is, presumably, driven by an ambition he or she now has the confidence to reveal nakedly, an ambition to go *one better* than the *vieux riches*. In Britain, it is never possible to go one better than the *vieux riches*, who always own everything anyway. *Harpers & Queen*, the self-appointed arbiter of these matters this side of the herring-pond, identifies the strivers peremptorily as Noovos, or Noovs. There is something a touch

Yellowplush Papers about all this, but there you go. It would seem that *The Official Foodie Handbook* is an attempt to exploit the nearest British equivalent to the Yuppie market, for, according to the arbiters, food is a cornerstone of this hysterical new snobbery.

Very special economic circumstances, reminiscent of those of the decline of the Roman Empire and also of the heyday of Edwardian England as described by Jack London in *People of the Abyss*, establish gluttony as the mark of a class on the rise. *The Official Foodie Handbook* notes: 'It takes several things to support a Foodie culture: high-class shops, fast transport bringing fresh produce from the land, enlightened well-paid eater-outers who will support the whole expensive edifice, lower-paid workers to make the food. Suddenly they are all present.'

Piggery triumphant has invaded even the pages of the *Guardian*, hitherto synonymous with non-conformist sobriety. Instead of its previous modest column of recipes and restaurant reviews, the paper now boasts an entire page devoted to food and wine once a week: more space than it gives to movies, as much as it customarily gives to books. Piggery has spawned a glossy bimonthly, *A la Carte*, a gastronomic *Penthouse* devoted to glamour photography, the subject of which is not the female body imaged as if it were good enough to eat, but food photographed according to the conventions of the pin-up. (Barr and Levy, ever quick with a quip, dub this kind of thing 'gastro-porn'.) The colour plates are of awesome voluptuousness. Oh, that coconut kirsch roulade in the first issue! If, as Lévi-Strauss once opined, 'to eat is to fuck', then that coconut kirsch roulade is just asking for it. Even if the *true* foodie knows there is something not quite . . . about a coconut kirsch roulade as a concept. It is just a bit . . . just a bit *Streatham*. Its vowels are subtly wrong. It is probably related to a Black Forest gâteau.

A la Carte is an over-eager social climber and is bound to give the game away. 'Do you know the difference between a good Brie and a bad one? One made in a factory or on a farm? If *you* don't, your guests might.' Then you will be universally shunned and nobody will attend your dinner parties ever again. This mincing and finicking obsession with food opens up whole new areas of potential social shame. No wonder the British find it irresistible. Indeed, in Britain an enlightened interest in food has always been the mark of the kind of person who uses turns of phrase such as 'an enlightened interest in food'. If a certain kind of upper-class British cookery represents the staff's revenge upon its masters, an enthusiasm for the table, the grape, and the stove itself is a characteristic of the deviant sub-section of the British bourgeoisie that has always gone in for the arts with the diligent enthusiasm of (as they would put it) 'the amateur in the true sense of the word'. This class is more than adequately represented by Mrs Elizabeth David.

In *An Omelette and a Glass of Wine*, a collection of her journalism dating back to the Fifties, there is an article describing the serendipitous nature of provisioning in London just after the war. Mrs David remembers how 'one of my sisters turned up from Vienna with a hare which she claimed had been caught by hand outside the State Opera House.' A whole world is contained within that sentence, which could be the first line of a certain kind of novel and sums up an entire way of life. It is no surprise to discover that Mrs David admires the novels of Sybille Bedford, nor that she was a friend of Norman Douglas. It *is* a little surprising that she has never turned her acclaimed prose style to fiction, but has always restricted herself to culinary matters, if in the widest sense, taking aboard aspects of history, geography, and literature. Her books, like her journalism, are larded with quotations, from recherché antique cookery books to Virginia Woolf, Montaigne, Walter Scott. Her approach is not in the least like the gastronomic dandyism of the 'food-for-food's sake' crowd; she is holistic about it. She is obviously a truly civilised person and, for her, knowing how to eat and to prepare good food is not an end in itself, but as much a part of civilisation as is the sensuous appreciation of poetry, art, or music. In the value system of the person who is 'civilised' in this way, the word carries the same connotation as 'moral' does in the value system of Dr F. R. Leavis.

Mrs David's journalism consists of discursive meditations upon food and foreign parts, but, in the course of *An Omelette and a Glass of Wine*, one learns a discreet but enticing amount about her private life, enough to appreciate that her deftness with the pans is not a sign of domesticity but of worldliness. She is obviously the kind of woman before whom waiters grovel when she arrives alone at a restaurant. One imagines her to be one of those tall, cool, elegant blondes who make foreigners come over all funny, and it is plain that she is the kind of Englishwoman who, like the heroines of Nancy Mitford, only fully come to life Abroad. Her recipes are meticulous, authentic, and reliable, and have formed the basic repertoire not only of a thousand British late twentieth-century dinner parties but also of a goodly number of restaurants up and down these islands. She has been the conduit whereby French provincial cooking and French country cooking, of a kind which in France is being replaced by pizzas and hamburgers, may be raptly savoured in rural England.

The eponymous 'Chez Panisse' of the *Chez Panisse Menu Cookbook* is directly inspired by Mrs David, who now spans the globe. The cook-proprietor of 'Chez Panisse', Alice Waters, says in her Introduction: 'I bought Elizabeth David's *French Country Cooking* and I cooked everything in it, from beginning to end. I admired her aesthetics of food and wanted a restaurant that had the same feeling as the pictures on the covers of her books.' It seems an unusual desire, to create a restaurant that looks like a book-jacket, and most of the cooks from whom Mrs David originally acquired her recipes would think it even more unusual to learn to cook from a book instead of from Mum. But all this must spring naturally from the kind of second-order experience that lies behind the cult of food. Alice Waters is a girl from New Jersey who earned her culinary stripes by resolutely cooking her way through a compendium of French recipes assembled by an Englishwoman, using ingredients from Northern California and serving them up to the me-generation in a restaurant named after an old movie. The result is a Franco-Californian cuisine of almost ludicrous refinement, in which the simplest item is turned into an object of mystification. A ripe melon, for example, is sought for as if it were a piece of the True Cross. Ms Waters applauds herself on serving one. 'Anyone could have chosen a perfect melon, but unfortunately most people don't take the time or make an effort to choose carefully and understand what that potentially sublime fruit should be.' She talks as if selecting a melon were an existential choice of a kind to leave Jean-Paul Sartre stumped.

Behind Ms Waters' wincingly exquisite cuisine lies some post-hippy Platonism to do with the real and the phoney. 'Depersonalised, assembly-line fast food may be "convenient" and "time-saving" but it deprives the senses and denies true nourishment,' she opines. Like anorexia nervosa, the neurotic condition in which young girls voluntarily starve themselves to death, the concept of 'true nourishment' can exist only in a society where hunger happens to other people. Ms Waters has clearly lost her marbles through too great a concern with grub, so much so that occasionally 'Alice Waters' sounds like a pseudonym for S. J. Perelman. 'I do think best while holding a tomato or a leg of lamb,' she confides. For a person of my generation, there is also the teasing question: could she be the Alice, and 'Chez Panisse' the *real* Alice's Restaurant, of the song by Arlo Guthrie? And if this is so, where did it all go wrong?

(1984)

This review provoked the following interesting correspondence.

SIR: It is better to think while holding a tomato or a leg of lamb than not to think at all, and Angela Carter (*LRB*, Vol. 7, no. 1) might have been wise to heed Alice Waters' advice. I thought I had been unlucky when motherhood got in the way of her perpetually forthcoming *LRB* notice of my *The British at Table 1940–1980* a year or so ago, but now I am not so sure. A woman capable of splashing blame for the Ethiopian famine on Elizabeth David is scarcely to be trusted with a baby's pusher, let alone a stabbing knife, and it would not have needed a very long session with the tomato to realise that victims of ecological disaster in Africa have more to fear from worshippers of power or money or both, in Downing Street and Addis Ababa, than from simpler souls like Paul Levy, whose god is their belly.

However, all these authors can look after themselves, and my own claim to a crumb of the action is as editor and for that matter initiator of the *Guardian*'s food and drink page, to which Angela Carter also alludes – forgetting perhaps that the paper has published weekly pieces on wine as well as on cookery and restaurants for many years past, and that her own debut as a contributor to it arose from an experience of waiting at table, *circa* 1967.

Just to set the record straight, food and drink does *not* occupy as much space in the paper as either movies or books, if you count related feature articles and interviews as well as straight criticism, and if you remember that the food page reviews Elizabeth David, for instance, leaving the book page to get on with Angela Carter. Not that I would think a reverse ratio between these different cultural topics disproportionate, whether in terms of pleasure or of public concern. And I know which of those two authors I would take to a desert island, too.

Christopher Driver

London N6.

SIR: I see small reason to entrust the review of three cookery books to Angela Carter (*LRB*, Vol. 7, no. 1): a woman who obviously has a Puritanical contempt for decently prepared food, and considers eating a rather nasty necessity for staying alive. She shoves aside her subject with a panegyric on the Ethiopian famine: a situation largely brought about by a Leftist government which recently spent fortunes on entertaining a Third World Conference in grand style. If she is a crusader, she should go down there and help fight the circumstances, which have more to do with the plight of the natives than with someone trying to make a proper salad in their own kitchen.

She derides those who consider that cooking can be an 'art', yet she is a novelist, and many a serious scholar would consider the reading and creating of fiction a frivolous pastime; it is, perhaps, a matter of degree. She takes exception to someone who goes on about selecting a melon carefully, and calls it 'genuinely decadent'. What actually is decadent is to take products which cost quite a lot and to turn them into something both disgusting to eat and bad for the health: a specialty both in England and Scotland, whether on British Rail or in working-class homes bulging with sausages and fat, or whether one messes it up all on one's own. She knows about 'fast food': let her stick to it, and spare the rest of us.

Peter Todd Mitchell

Sitges, Barcelona

SIR: Fascinating as it is to learn that Angela Carter considers herself morally superior to anyone interested in eating good food (except maybe Elizabeth David), I found the general tenor of her argument difficult to follow. She sneers at those of us who buy expensive foodstuffs while Ethiopians starve. Does she think *not* buying these things will bring about beneficial changes in that country's political turmoil? This suggests belief in some very strange conspiracies. Perhaps she only thinks self-righteous prig-gery a more appealing posture than self-indulgent piggery when confronting the woes of the world. But that kind of hauteur seems a bit rich coming from her, a novelist – what occupation could be more frivolous or useless in helping out the hungry . . . and with as much pretention as cookery to being an art? But I write to point out an error of suggestion (given that Ms Carter is free to imagine Elizabeth David's appearance and manner in any way she wants, even if a moment's research could have set that fantasy straight): Alice Waters is not Alice Brock, the Alice of Alice's Restaurant.

John Thorne

Boston, Massachusetts

· 15 ·

Redcliffe Salaman: *The History and Social Influence of the Potato*

Eighty-odd years ago, when my father was a little boy, he would ask: 'What's for dinner?' And my grandmother might reply: 'Potatoes and point'. That is, she would point to the hook in the rafters where the ham, if they'd had one, would have hung. Then they'd eat potatoes. This didn't happen often: the family was relatively prosperous petit bougeois and, besides, the coast of North East Scotland, where they lived, had never become as totally dependent on the potato for nourishment as other communities in Europe, most notably Ireland. Even so, it happened.

The trouble with the easily grown and plentifully cropping potato is that it is so good for you, especially if you eat it with the skin on. It contains carbohydrates, protein, minerals, and sufficient vitamin C to ensure that the general use of the potato amongst urbanised communities did much to abolish scurvy. Potatoes and milk, taken together, form an adequate if monotonous diet, provided the potatoes are eaten in sufficient quantities. If you add leeks, butter, and cream to your mess of milk and potatoes, it turns into *potage bonne femme* and if you then chill it (vichysoisse) you arrive at *haute cuisine*, but the indigent poor of Europe rarely aspired so high and the Irish of the nineteenth century were often forced to skip the milk. They also preferred to eat their potatoes only partially cooked ('wid be bones in 'em'): that way, they stayed longer in the belly.

Redcliffe Salaman's monumental book was first published in 1949, though it bears the mark of many long years in the making. A revised edition now appears with a new Introduction by J. G. Hawkes. This account of the causes and effects of European potato-eating is also a history of poverty and of the manner in which the potato, 'the root of misery', helped to confine the poor within their poverty. Salaman describes the process as it operated, with the most classical simplicity, in Ireland: 'by reducing the cost of living to the lowest possible limit, it caused the value of labour to fall to a corresponding level.' Marie Antoinette thought the flowers of the potato plant were so pretty she could not resist tucking them in her hair. This was a precise visual equivalent of saying: 'Let them eat cake,' an innocent, ignorant, provocative act.

The origins of the potato in its native South America are unimaginably ancient but, for Europe, it is a modern vegetable, uniquely suited to the economics of the modern period. It was brought from Peru in the sixteenth century by the Spanish Conquistadores who, says Salaman, 'immediately recognised its economic importance and at once relegated it as a food for slaves'. The tuber formed part of the booty of Spanish imperialism, a part with as far-reaching a significance as syphilis. How it got to Britain is a mystery. The legend that Raleigh brought it home from Virginia does not hold water: Raleigh never visited Virginia, where, in any case, the potato did not grow. Another legend persistently posits a shipwreck – a remnant of the Armada with potatoes amongst it stores foundering off the coast of Ireland, or Wales, or Lancashire, or all three.

It was a godless vegetable. It wasn't mentioned in the Bible. The Old Believers, who broke away from the Russian Orthodox Church in 1667, regarded potatoes, along with sugar and tobacco, as abominations. The Irish surrounded the planting and harvesting of their crops with ritual and superstition, with good cause, as it turned out. Planting traditionally took place on Good Friday. The new vegetable soon acquired a good deal of old folklore. At Epinal, in France: 'The woman who carries home the last sheaf, or the last basket of potatoes, is known throughout the year as the "corn" or "potato dog".' It must be the relative newness of the potato that makes the 'potato dog' seem a little incongruous; the potato is not a numinous vegetable. It is, literally, of the earth, earthy. One Spanish name is *turma de tierra*, that is, 'earth testicle', bringing to mind Max Miller's celebrated appearance with a couple of potatoes – 'King Edwards!' – at the Royal Command Variety Performance.

The potato became with great speed a staple food throughout Europe. It was greeted with especial enthusiasm in Ireland, where the moist climate is largely unsuited to the growing of wheat, and the people had been reduced to penury. The exemplary tragedy of the Great Hunger of 1845 and 1846 lies at the core of Salaman's book and he arrives at it step by dolorous step, tracing the entire history of the English in Ireland and the systematic destruction of the Irish economy and domestic agriculture until, by the early nineteenth century, there survived a peasant class more miserable than any other in Europe, 'a social order', as Salaman says, 'in which the distinction between the amenities of human life and those of the beasts of the field had become blurred'. In their turf cabins, the enormous families, six or seven children, eight or nine children – from the evidence Salaman amasses, the English were haunted by the spectre of Irish over-population – these feckless, ever-increasing, ragged families would gather round the cauldron hanging over the smoky peat fire, the interested cow or pig (should they be lucky enough to have one) looking on. Each, including the domestic animals, took his or her potato from the common pot. Salaman demands rhetorically: 'What pride could be taken in the home, or what call was there for ceremony, however elementary, to welcome a meal that was about to be shared with the pigs and the poultry and from the same cauldron?'

Potatoes excepted, it would have been an ambience in which Langland's Piers Plowman would have felt at home. It was one of Ireland's misfortunes that much of her rural population found themselves helplessly locked in the late Medieval period, as in a time-warp, whilst England was bustling busily through the nineteenth century. There was scarcely any coin circulating in those villages: what there was went on rent. Otherwise, no need for cash! The family potato plot provided all the food and the potato does not take much in the way of cultivation. Neither do boiled potatoes take much of the cook's time and attention. No washing-up, either. There was ample leisure. Indeed, some of Salaman's sources exhibit a sharp moral dismay that the poor should have it so easy. He quotes Sir Charles Trevelyan:

The Irish smallholder lives in a state of isolation, the type of which is to be sought for in the islands of the South Sea, rather than in the great civilised communities of the ancient world. A fortnight for planting, a week or ten days for digging, and another fortnight for turf-cutting, suffice for his subsistence; and during the rest of the year he is at leisure to follow his own inclinations, without even the safeguard of the intellectual tastes and legitimate objects of ambition which only imperfectly obviate the evils of leisure in the higher ranks of society.

One might almost think Sir Charles envied the Irish small-holder, so bitter is his resentment. Even Redcliffe Salaman himself, impregnably decent as he is, can see only a degraded peasantry sunk in sloth and intellectual darkness, locked in a hopeless symbiosis with the tuber. But, in spite of the most vicious inducements to abandon it, these peasants retained their impenetrable language, concealed within it a vast and continually refreshed tradition of oral poetry, and continued to make music of a beauty and complexity to be found nowhere else in Western Europe except Spain. They married young and sought to drive out the English by outnumbering them.

All the same, even if a way of life based exclusively upon the potato may be richer than Sir Charles Trevelyan suggests, when the root fails, all is lost. It is estimated that up to a million people died, either from starvation or from disease that came in the Famine's wake. Emigration, to the United States and also to Australia, that followed the Famine robbed Ireland of another million or so, and dowered those nations with a rich strain of ineradicable Anglophobia. To live habitually on the cheapest food is to leave yourself without resources – 'except', as Malthus said, 'in the bark of trees like the poor Swedes.'

The History and Social Influence of the Potato is an extraordinary book, like no other, a vast compendium of curious fact and passionately recounted social history that calls to mind an unexpected but completely satisfying fusion of *The Anatomy of Melancholy* and Fernand Braudel's *Capitalism and Material Life*. In its inflamatory humanitarianism, the book may now also stand as a monument to the sensibility of the period of welfare socialism voted in at the end of the Second World War: possibly the only time in the history of Britain (excepting 1649) when the great majority of British people actively demonstrated that they knew what was good for them, that potatoes were not sufficient fare.

Redcliffe Salaman: *The History and Social Influence of the Potato*

In an article in the current *Tatler*, Mrs Elizabeth David laments that Salaman did not include recipes: in fact, he includes several. This is one, for the soup served in Epping Workhouse in the last years of the eighteenth century: '4lbs pickled pork, 6 stones of shins and legs, 6lbs of skibling (meat waste), 28lbs of potatoes, 20lbs of Scotch oatmeal, 21lbs of salt, 1lb of whole pepper and 1/4lb of ground pepper, a dozen carrots and a handful of mint, to 56 gallons of water.' He notes: 'The Epping soup was designed on more generous lines than was usual in such cases.'

(1986)

· 16 ·

Food in Vogue

There's a smashing Erté on the cover of this luscious production, showing a woman dressed up as a carrot, though its point is by no means that Woman is only another edible, and an everyday, common or garden item of consumption, at that. Elsewhere, here, you can find her companions: an Erté onion woman, a celery woman, and a tomato woman, designs for George White's *Scandals* (New York, 1926). These costumes transform the most commonplace comestibles into something rich and strange via the medium of beautiful women.

To transform women themselves into food was evidently a favourite Twenties trick in stylish circles. There's an account of the Santa Claus Ball at the Kit-Kat:

> The characters will present a typical Christmas dinner. Lady Grant will be Plum Pudding, Mrs Redmond McGrath Red Wine, Lady Dunn White Wine, Lady Ashley, Lady Jean Dalrymple, Dorothy Bethell, Lady Scarsdale are all parts of the menu; while Lady Patricia Douglas is Mince Pie and Mrs McCorquodale, who is organising the pageant, is to be Champagne.

So, although all the recipes in this something more than cook-ery book are perfectly viable and many are splendid, one can't escape the feeling that *Food in Vogue* is not purely food. Not food as fuel, pure and simple, but food as an aspect of style.

At the front of the book is a photograph of a girl with an oyster shell in one hand, a fork in the other, and, wedged – to her unsurprise – firmly between her teeth, a pearl, presumably out of the oyster. It's a striking image but not so much a concrete sign as a diffuse suggestion of a total environment of high living.

One of the interesting things about the sixty-year trek through *Vogue* back-number cookery columns is the point at which the women to whom those columns were addressed actually began to cook themselves, instead of employing other people to do it for them.

The early decades boast occasional references to bachelor girls frying themselves bacon sandwiches, but not half so many references as there are to cooks, cocktail bars, and dinners in restaurants, itself a helpless response to the post-First World War shortage of staff.

In the Thirties, when *Vogue* prose reached an apotheosis of tinkling breathlessness, cookery for the upper classes was introduced as a witty eccentricity:

> Some of the most unlikely people are cooking. The Hon Mrs Reginald Fellowes has had a perfect little kitchen built next to her sitting-room and, if you think this is an idle gesture, consult some gourmet who has exclaimed his way through a dinner prepared by her own white hands.

But the contemporary tomato woman regards cooking as a stylish accomplishment and may look herself up in the index and find no less than ten ways to cook herself, including one recipe for tomato in horseradish-flavoured cream that is almost as stylish as a pheasant with gin and juniper from the Thirties, as elegant in its excess as Cole Porter. But tomatoes with horseradish, from the most recent pages of the magazine, is the sort of simple little thing that somebody who cooks every day might well do for best; pheasants with gin and juniper is the sort of one-off job that somebody who hardly ever cooks at all can spend a whole day of therapeutic endeavour on – especially when there is somebody to clear up the dirty dishes for her.

A recurring theme throughout the cookery columns is a curiously magical linking of recipes with famous names. As if something of the mana of ladies or gentlemen of wealth, birth, and distinction may be absorbed via the ingestion of dishes, or entire menus, synonymous with them. In the Sixties, Loelia, Duchess of Westminster, suggests Homard Frappé, White Devil (which turns out to be just devilled chicken, no skull beneath the skin), and apples in rum for a 'magic' Sunday dinner. Back in the Thirties, Lady Portalington and Lady Juliet Duff and Mrs Syrie Maugham contributed recipes that, though perfectly sound, are so amazingly boring – Scotch collops, apple tart, pancakes with haddock – it doesn't seem surprising that English upper-class tables had such a bad reputation, nor that *Vogue* made sporadic forays into continental high life for fresh fare, sometimes with disappointing results. The Comtesse Mercati had a chocolate cake that no one could duplicate without the recipe – 'and she can't remember the recipe.' Tough.

With the arrival of Elizabeth David and Robert Carrier in the Fifties and Sixties, the cult of the personality tended to centre itself round the cook as magus, rather than the inspired amateur as cook. Miss David's magistral hauteur and Carrier's transatlantic exuberance and professionalism – 'During this new series of articles on food, drink and entertaining, I am going to dispel the maze of myths that surround *haute cuisine*' – helped make cooking well a classy thing to do. And if the book ends with a flourish on Pamela Harlech's column titled, 'Seventies People and their Recipes' (Mrs Rupert Hambro's ginger soufflé, Anthony West's cucumber soup, Lady Elizabeth von Hofmannsthal's cabbage in cream) the upper classes clearly – by their fruits shall ye know them – spend a bit more time with the pots and pans than they did when top-flight cooks were ten a penny. This food has its own mana. It is magic because it is Good.

There is also, hereabouts, Arabella Boxer's recipe for wild green salad (sorrel, dandelion, watercress, and so on) which suggests that even after the collapse of absolutely everything, those of us dedicated to gracious living will still attack the weeds and roots and nuts and berries that may well form a staple diet with a bit of flair and verve. Cooking as dandyism.

Indeed, the most touching thing about these resurrected pages of early *Vogue*, their menus, their parties, their restaurants, their famous hostesses, and their table settings, is an absolute concentration on the frivolous that can, on occasion, aspire to the heroic. A wartime caption: 'On leave, he likes to dine against the sophisticated decor of Popote du Ritz. You in his favourite black, his favourite lace, feminine to the last flounce.' That'll show Hitler what we're made of.

And from the Thirties, the caption to a charming, minimal drawing by Cecil Beaton: 'Here you see a picnic in progress. The Marchioness of Queensberry and Miss Carley Robinson enjoy China tea out of a sprigged teapot and sit gossiping and watching the hovering butterflies.' Style as an end in itself; the exquisiteness, the rightness of that China tea, that sprigged teapot – so much glamour would vanish had it been a brown earthenware one with a woolly teacosy. And some of the heartless innocence of style, as well, of a leisured class that took its leisure as a right and not as a privilege.

As an informal history of the changing diet and social mores of the English upper-middle and aspiring upper-middle classes, *Food in Vogue* does very well, and even better if read as the concretisation of a consensus wish-fulfilment fantasy about the nature of stylish living. 'How One Lives from Day to Day . . . Dinner hour at the Savoy; Surveying the kitchens at the Ivy; Supper at Rules; the Jardin des Gourmets has a delightful atmosphere of French rusticity; Entering the Spanish Grill at the Dorchester.' How one lived from day to day in the Thirties, until, in December 1939. 'In Paris – Now – They shelter in the Ritz super-cellars in satin or wool pyjamas, hooded coats, warmly, gaily lined (Molyneux and Piguet) . . . ' (Students of linguistics will be interested to note the usage, 'one', omnipresent in *Vogue* copy of the Twenties and Thirties and now confined, almost exclusively, to the Royal Family.) It is the stuff of modern-day fairytale.

This lavishly illustrated book is also an informal history of English illustration over the last sixty years, flowering in the Forties, that heyday of English drawing: Keith Vaughan, John Minton, Edward Ardizzone, that beautifully agonised black and white with nostalgia already implicit in every line. Then the Sixties, and the rise of the photographer, Penn, Lester, Bookbinder, oh my, oh my. And with the Seventies, Tess Traeger's photographs that look exactly like oil paintings, Victorian oil paintings, at that; actual icons of nostalgia, images of a beautiful never-never land of fruit and beautiful children and flowers. This is the land where the tomato woman would like to live.

(1977)

Elizabeth David: *English Bread and Yeast Cookery*

My corner shop sells wrapped, sliced white loaves that, at a pinch, could poultice a wound. It also, sometimes, stocks twisted, unsliced bread with sesame seeds on top emanating from a Cypriot concern on the other side of London which can fool the unwary into thinking it is somehow a more authentic product than the Mother's Pride stuff, though authentic in *what* way I can't say. The corner shop also sells plastic bags of pitta, which is fine, though it looks a bit odd filled with butter and marmalade at breakfast. (Kebabs *a l'anglaise*.)

Five minutes walk away is one of those hot-bread outlets that sell poultices fresh from the oven. Seven minutes' walk away, virtually side by side, two shops stocking different varieties of those wholemeal breads that look hand-thrown, like studio pottery, and are fine if you have all your teeth. But, if not, then not. Perhaps the rise and rise of the poultice or factory-made loaf, which may easily be mumbled to a pap between gums, reflects the sorry state of the nation's dental health.

It is usually interpreted, however, as the result of a lack of moral fibre, as if moral fibre is somehow related to roughage in the diet. The British, the real bread lobby implies, are rapidly going, if they have not already gone, all soft, bland, and flabby, just like their staple food. The iron grip of the multinationals has squeezed all the goodness out of British bread, via the machinations of the giant miller-bakers, Allied Bakeries, Rank Hovis McDougall *et al.*, and the only way to fight back is to lob a homemade stone-ground wholemeal cob at them. (Which, in some cases, would indeed be a lethal missile.)

Elizabeth David: *English Bread and Yeast Cookery*

The real bread lobby has, of course, right, virtue, and healthy bowel movements on its side. On the whole, it is free from that paranoid nostalgia that afflicted Anthony Burgess, when he – I think it was he – laid squarely at the feet of the Welfare State the blame for the fact that Heinz baked beans no longer taste as tangy as they did when he was a boy.

The Welfare State it is, according to the formula of reactionary food fetishism, that has made us all soft and bland and flabby and that is why we dig into Mother's Pride and Wonderloaf and Sunblest with such enthusiasm. Behind this, is an ill-concealed and ugly plot – not so much to swell the coffers of the hippy wholefood entrepreneurs who concoct those loaves that either go straight through you or else stay with you, heavily on the chest, for days, nay, weeks, as to get women back where they belong. Up to their elbows in bread dough, engaged in that most arduous and everlasting of domestic chores, giving the family good, hearty, home-baked bread.

Oddly enough, in all of Europe, the British housewife is, historically, the only one of all who found herself burdened with this back-breaking and infinitely boring task, for watching bread dough rise is the next best thing to watching paint dry, activity reminiscent of some of those recorded in early Warhol movies. The average black-clad Italian, French, or Greek mama, if asked to make bread, has always tossed her head with a haughty sneer. What else are baker's for? For herself, she's got better things to do – the meat sauce, the *coq au vin*, the dolmas, and so on. Of course, it's always been more difficult, given British cuisine, for our housewives to get away with that excuse. Since we've got to have something to shine at, it turned out to be baked goods, didn't it?

And, oh God, in my misspent youth as a housewife, I, too, used to bake bread, in those hectic and desolating days just prior to the woman's movement, when middle-class women were supposed to be wonderful wives and mothers, gracious hostesses à *la* Miriam Stoppard, and do it all *beautifully*. I used to feel so womanly when I was baking my filthy bread. A positive ecstasy of false consciousness. I probably dealt the death blow to some local baker with a wood-fired brick-oven when I took away my custom, for in those days, there were old-fashioned bakers aplenty, no doubt then closing down on all sides under the twin onslaughts of the newly fashionable anorexia nervosa and all that compulsive home breadmaking.

However, even here, twenty years later, in south London, there are a couple of perfectly decent old-fashioned bakers within easy walking distance (both stocking that indescribable speciality, bread pudding). Even if southern England *is* heavily saturated with chain bakeries, good bakers are thick on the ground from Lincolnshire on to the north and Scottish bakers are wonderful. Obviously, lots of people just pick up a Wonderloaf at the corner shop or supermarket, perhaps even habitually: but I wonder whether they don't make a distinction between bread for sandwiches and bread for, as it were, eating. Certainly, sliced white comes into its own for the former use – basically, a wrapping for a sweet or savoury filling, akin to edible greaseproof paper.

Along with the notion that British factory-made bread is bad bread comes the one that all artisan-made bread is *good* bread. Although the recipe books of Tuscany are suspiciously full of handy hints for dealing with large quantities of stale bread, it is still impossible to resist a sigh of satisfaction when the waiter weighs down the paper tablecloth with the basket of rough-hewn bread chunks in the somnolent, shadowless heat of some Florentine lunch time . . . though, since the saltless, fatless bread of the region will, by then, have been out of the oven for some hours, it is now only good for carving into putti. Or dipping into the squat tumbler you have just filled with red wine from a straw-wrapped (or possibly, plastic-coated) bottle. And that's it! Pow! It hits you. The atavistic glamour of the continental holiday; the timeless, mythic resonance of the bread and the wine . . . for what good is a continental holiday unless it is jam-packed with resonances?

It always puzzles me that Christianity got off the ground, even to the limited extent that it did, in those parts of the globe where its central metaphor – the bread and the wine – were incomprehensible. A sacramental meal of shared rice and saké, the nearest Chinese equivalents to the Mediterranean staples, suggests a very anaemic Christ indeed.

Wheat bread, in fact, is not only a specifically European staff of life, but even a specifically Mediterranean one. Northern Europe tends towards black, rye bread and wheat bread took a long time to penetrate to the northernmost parts of even our own island, where all bakers still stock the traditional crisp, flat, unleavened oat cake in large quantities. (When the Scots first clapped eyes on grain, they knew immediately what to do with it; they distilled it. No wonder the Scots proved averse to the doctrine of transubstantiation. A deity with flesh of oat cakes and blood composed of volatile spirit makes the mind reel.)

Nevertheless, part of the fuss we make when we think our bread – our BREAD – has been tampered with must, surely, relate to the sacramental quality inherent in bread in our culture. Our bread, our daily bread, has been profaned with noxious additives. Although that bread is certainly no longer our 'daily bread' within the strict meaning of the prayer. In the sixteenth century, 'bread' meant 'food' just as 'rice' (*gohan*) in Japanese still means dinner. For most of us, in those days, food *was* bread – bread with, perhaps, a condiment of cheese, onion, or bacon grease to go with it, and maybe a chickweed salad on high days and holidays.

The menus of the Lambeth poor researched before the First World War by Maud Pember Reeves for her book, *Round About a Pound a Week*, feature bread heavily at all three daily meals. Two of those meals, breakfast and supper, are composed exclusively of bread plus a smear of margarine, jam, or sweetened condensed milk. The stunted, sickly, patently under-nourished, and often dying children described by Pember Reeves do not appear to have thrived particularly well on such a diet.

One should not, of course, ascribe to magic doses of Wonder-loaf and Mother's Pride the almost intolerable health, strength, and vitality of the children of Lambeth at this present time. How these kids keep it up on salt 'n' vinegar flavoured crisps, orange crush, and fish fingers indeed perplexes me. One can only conclude that a varied diet of junk food is, in the final analysis, considerably more nutritious than a diet of not very much food at all and most of it starch.

In a culinary sense, though not, I suspect, in an emotional one, bread has been secularised in postwar Britain. It has become a food, like any other, no longer to be taken in large quantities. There are other things to eat, even other carbohydrate foods – rice, pasta. Yams. One of the things Pember Reeves' housewives liked about bread was its portability – a child did not have to sit down to eat a hunch of bread and marge and that was convenient if you did not have sufficient chairs, or even a table, on or at which to sit. Most families, nowadays, do manage occasional communal sit-down meals. Most homes, today, boast knives and forks. We no longer live by bread alone.

When one does not live by bread alone on a varied and interesting diet, bread changes its function while retaining its symbolism. Ceasing to be the staff of life but ever redolent with its odour of sanctity – an odour the hot bread-poultice shops have exploited commercially to the hilt – bread turns into a mere accessory, the decorative margin to a meal, or else into the material for a small but inessential meal, that very 'afternoon tea' beloved of the English upper classes, with which they used to stuff their faces in that desert of oral gratification between their vast lunches and their gargantuan dinners.

It is no surprise, therefore, to find that Elizabeth David's vast and highly lauded tome, *English Bread and Yeast Cookery*, is jammed full of tea-time recipes – buns, tea cakes, fruit breads, and so on. For David, the high priestess of postwar English cookery, she who single-handed put an olive-wood chopping block into every aspiring home, to turn her attention to currant buns means that something is up.

English Bread and Yeast Cookery is a vademecum to the art of home baking. And I use the word, 'art', rather than 'craft', advisedly, since her recipes are intended for the artist baker in her studio kitchen rather than the artisan in the common workshop.

David, ever apt with the up-market quotation, certainly knows how to add that final touch of arty glamour to the business! She whisks away the last surviving touch of dirndl skirt and Fabian Society from the concept of the home-baked loaf when she quotes a description of Virginia Woolf kneading away like nobody's business.

Virginia Woolf? Yes. Although otherwise an indifferent cook, Virginia could certainly knock you up a lovely cottage loaf. You bet. This strikes me as just the sort of pretentiously frivolous and dilettantish thing a Bloomsbury *would* be good at – knowing how to do one, just one, fatuously complicated kitchen thing and doing that one thing well enough to put the cook's nose out of joint. 'I will come into the kitchen, Louie,' she said to this young employee of hers, 'and show you how to do it.'

This attitude of the dedicated hobbyist reveals the essential marginality of the activity. David manages to turn the honourable craft of the baker into a nice accomplishment for refined ladies. Bread is put in its place; it is a special kind of art-object.

Hers is, furthermore, the bitter-sweet bread of nostalgia, summoning up a bygone golden age of golden loaves, before Garfield Weston, of Allied Bakeries, the demon king in the real-bread scenario started buying up British bakeries in the Fifties and smirching with his filthy profane Canadian hands the grand old English loaf.

Although her book is full of quotations – Thomas Traherne, Keats, Chaucer – she does, however, let the heavy freight of symbolic significance borne by bread in our culture severely alone except, oddly enough, for a seventeenth-century French recipe for consecrated bread. This, she claims, sounds like brioche, which suggests it might have been used for a rather Firbankian mass. What *can* they have put in the chalice?

It is appropriate she leaves religion alone since *English Bread and Yeast Cookery* is already proving to be something like the holy book of the cult of the True Loaf, in which the metaphoric halo surrounding bread is turned back on itself, the loaf becomes not foodstuff nor symbol but fetish.

(1987)

· 18 ·

Patience Gray: *Honey from a Weed*

I bought my first cookery book in 1960, as part of my trousseau. It was called *Plats du Jour, or Foreign Food* by Patience Gray and Primrose Boyd, a Penguin paperback with a seductive pink jacket depicting a large family at table – evidently not a British family, for its members, shirt-sleeved, aproned, some of them children, were uncorking bottles, slicing bread, eagerly tucking their napkins under their chins, faces aglow with the certain knowledge their dinners would not disappoint, which was, in those days, extremely rare in this country.

My copy of *Plats du Jour* now gives forth a mellow smell of old paper; the pages are crisp, brown, and dry as Melba toast. But it has outlasted the husband for whose pleasure I bought it by some eighteen years, proof positive of the old saw, 'Kissin' don't last, cookin' do'. And now it is a historic object, a prototype of the late twentieth-century British cookery book, a book to browse in as much as to cook from, its prose as elegant as its plentiful line-drawings. And, oh, that easy, graceful cosmopolitanism! 'For anyone who has eaten a well-prepared Gulyas in one of the little restaurants on the Buda side of the Danube, overlooking the lantern-threaded bridges and the electric glitter of Pesth on a warm summer night before the war . . . ' The nascent genre infected an entire generation with wanderlust.

Patience Gray helped to instigate the concept of the cookery book as literary form – part recipes, part travel book, part self-revelation, part art-object. Now, some thirty years on, she has assembled what may be its culmination. *Honey from a Weed* is less a cookery book than a summing-up of the genre of the late modern British cookery book. It is a book like very few others, although it has some of the style of the seventeenth-century commonplace book, replete with recondite erudition and assembled on the principle of free association, as when Mrs Gray lists uses for goose fat. In a cassoulet. In soups. On bread. On toast. 'On your chest, rubbed in in winter. On leather boots, if they squeak. On your hands if they are chapped.'

Above all, it is a book about a particular sensibility – a unique and pungent one – that manifests itself most characteristically in the kitchen. That is what the genre is all about. M. F. K. Fisher had pioneered the culinary autobiographical novel in the US years before the Penguin school of cookery writers found its greatest star in Elizabeth David in the late Fifties and early Sixties. For these writers, and for Patience Gray, cookery is what the open road was to Cobbett or the natural history of Selbourne to Gilbert White. There is, however, a difference: these are women to whom food is not an end in itself but a way of opening up the world. And, indeed, they are all women: this is, at the highest level, a female form.

It is unique to Saxon culture, to my knowledge, that the ability to cook well is a sign of a woman of the world. Traditional plump home-bodies may deliver the goods in France and Spain and Italy, but in Britain and the US the classic cooks are awesomely sophisticated, aristocratically beautiful and often connected with the arts. Elizabeth David, friend of Norman Douglas, is eternalised in the lovely icon of John Ward's drawing, the epitome of chic in her companionable kitchen. M. F. K. Fisher is just as beautiful. Her most beloved husband was a painter, and her books are so instinct with upmarket bohemianism that it is no surprise to find her in a cameo role in the autobiography of the painter and photographer, Man Ray, in which a starring part is allotted to Lee Miller, the universal muse of the surrealists, who herself became a famous practitioner of gourmet cookery.

Patience Gray belongs to this nexus of cookery and the arts, although she has an earthy, hands-on approach to the real lives of the predominantly peasant communities in Southern Europe where she has chosen to live, and to the arts: she works in silver and gold, making jewellery, and lives with a stone-carver whom she calls the Sculptor (she is refreshingly free from irony). Her book recounts their wanderings during a shared life dominated by the Sculptor's quest for suitable stone. Glamorous as this way of life may seem, it is no easy option. Patience Gray's kitchens have been exceedingly sparsely equipped. The hand-pump over the marble sink of one particular Etruscan kitchen did not work: 'I got the water in a bucket and lowering it into the outdoor cistern had a marvellous view of the glittering Monte Sagra and the Apulian Alps on one side and on the other a view to the Tyrrhenian.'

This combination of material asceticism and passionate enthusiasm for the sensuality of the everyday is at the core of the tradition from which Mrs Gray springs, with its obvious affinities to the style of Bloomsbury, where it was a moral imperative that the beautiful should always take precedence over the comfortable. Though 'beautiful' is not quite the right word – it is a kind of authenticity which is invoked here, as though water is more authentic, more real, wetter, drawn from an open-air cistern than from a city tap.

The metaphysics of authenticity are a dangerous area. When Mrs Gray opines, 'Poverty rather than wealth gives the good things of life their true significance', it is tempting to suggest it is other people's poverty, always a source of the picturesque, that does that. Even if Mrs Gray and her companion live in exactly the same circumstances as their neighbours in the Greek islands or Southern Italy, and have just as little ready money, their relation to their circumstances is the result of the greatest of all luxuries, aesthetic choice. 'Poverty', here, is sloppy language – a rare example of it. Mrs Gray isn't talking about a pavement dweller in Calcutta, or a member of the long-term unemployed in an advanced, industrialised country; not about poverty as such, but about a way of life which has a dignity imposed upon it by its stoicism in the face of a nature on which it is entirely dependent. The Japanese created an entire aesthetic, and a moral philosophy, out of this stoicism and this intimate relation with natural forces; as soon as they had a bob or two in their pockets, of course, they binged on consumerism, but the hard core is still there.

Then again, Mrs Gray and her companion are not too perturbed about the absence of piped water. Her companion, when pressed, expresses a preference for shitting beneath a fig tree, rather than in a flush toilet. When workers recruited from Southern Italy moved into subsidised housing in Turin, people used to say: 'No use giving them baths, they'll only grow basil in them.' Mrs Gray would think that was an eminently sensible thing to do with a bath. After a couple of days of toting buckets, my own appreciation of any view would have waned, somewhat. But arduous circumstances never diminish Mrs Gray's rapt sense of wonder, and her book is dedicated to genuine austerity, an austerity reflected in many of the recipes she includes in her text. The section titled 'Fasting on Naxos' describes just that: 'The four weeks of the Advent fast and the six weeks of the Lenten one correspond with moments when on Naxos there was hardly anything to eat.'

She describes the harsh life of these Greek islanders without sentimentality, if with a degree of romantic awe, in a prose that will suddenly, effortlessly, fall into the very cadences of Sir Thomas Browne: 'In Homer's time, a King could go out to plough his land and build his bed of giant timbers.' Her prose is usually ravishing, sometimes breathtaking. The entire section titled 'Pasticceria and the Apulian Baroque' is composed according to the principles of the startling architectonics she describes:

> The city [Lecce] within the walls calls to mind the Bourbon Kings of Naples, who once a year ordered the construction of castle edifices made of stout edible materials – gigantic hams, cheeses, enormous mortadelle, and the fore and hindquarters of deer and Indian buffalo, in order then to gloat at the spectacle of the starving Neapolitans – admitted at the moment of completion – vociferously and violently vying with each other, to the accompaniment of martial music and gunpowder explosions, in their destruction.

The book moves among its venues at the whim of memory, according to no precise chronology. With Mrs Gray, we eat dried beans cooked a variety of ways in a variety of places. We eat potatoes and green beans boiled together, potatoes with alliums (the common name of the onion family) and olive oil, potatoes cooked in the oven with streaky bacon. Some of her recipes would certainly ease the plight of the long-term unemployed in advanced, industrialised countries because, even here, the ingredients cost so little. Then again, *Honey from a Weed* is a very expensive book. Such are the ironies of the politics of romantic austerity.

We make, with her, salads of hedgerow greens and boil up delicious weeds to eat hot with lemon juice – dandelions, comfrey, wood sorrel, field sorrel, wild fennel, fat hen, tassel hyacinth, purslane, field poppy. (When gathering your weeds, watch out for pesticides.) A meal may be made – *has* to be made – from whatever is to hand. M. F. K. Fisher's wolf ('How to cook a wolf', included in *The Art of Eating*) was metaphorical. Patience Gray 'met a number of people around Carrara not at all averse to cooking a fox', and tells you how to make fox *alla cacciatore* (with garlic, wine, and tomatoes). 'Exactly the same method can be applied to a badger . . . '

A connoisseur of free food, she waxes lyrical on snails, especially the *Helix operta*, oval in shape, golden brown in colour, 'with a beautiful logarithmic spiral structure'. Surely, of all the creatures we eat, we are most brutal to snails. *Helix operta* is dug out of the earth where he has been peacefully enjoying his summer sleep, cracked like an egg, and eaten raw, presumably alive. Or boiled in oil. Or roasted in the hot ashes of a wood fire. In Catalonia, vineyard snails are laid out in rows on a bed of straw. 'The straw is set alight and the snails are retrieved from the ashes by jabbing them with sharply pointed sticks.' If God is a snail, Bosch's depictions of Hell are going to look like a vicarage tea-party.

Mrs Gray does not conceal the fact that the traditional communities she describes are now in the process of violent change. Her twenty years of wandering the limestone margins of the Mediterranean have coincided with the breakdown of ancient forms of village life:

> It sometimes seems as if I have been rescuing a few strands
> from a former and more diligent way of life, now being
> eroded by an entirely new set of values. As with students
> of music who record old songs which are no longer sung,
> soon some of the things I record will also have vanished.

This is partly what makes her book so valuable, and gives it an elegiac quality that sometimes recalls the recent work of a writer, John Berger, with whom she might seem to have little else in common except a respect for philosophical anarchism: Berger's majestic stories of peasant life, *Pig Earth*, invoke the awesome severities and orgiastic celebrations of a past as recent as yesterday and already as remote as the Flood.

The point is, dammit, that they *did* have, as Iago griped about Othello, a daily beauty in their lives that makes ours ugly. In one of the stories in *Pig Earth*, a little old peasant lady goes out and gathers wild things in the mountains – wild cherries, lilies of the valley, mushrooms, mistletoe – and takes her booty into the city, where she sells it in the market for vast sums. She is selling not only delicious wild produce but glimpses of some lost greenness. She is the last remaining vendor of wild things, she is a kind of ghost. Mrs Gray describes Carrara twenty years ago:

> The feeling of the mountains was never far away: retired quarrymen sold bunches of herbs they had gathered there. In summer great baskets of bilberries and wild strawberries appeared. In autumn fresh cranberries, fungi and chestnuts were brought down from the Spanish chestnut woods. In this way a dialogue between town and country was maintained . . . In those days it was still possible to feel that the Carraresi were definitely in touch with the 'earthly paradise'.

If transplanted Calabrians do grow basil in their shiny new bathtubs, perhaps they know what's what.

Mrs Gray has taken the form of the late-modern English-language cookery book to its extreme in *Honey from a Weed*, producing a kind of baroque monument of which all the moving parts work (the recipes are very sound).

(1987)

HOME

This precious stone set in the silver sea . . .

William Shakespeare

Hanif Kureishi: *The Buddha of Suburbia*

The narrator of Hanif Kureishi's ebulliant, dismayed farce introduces himself thus: 'My name is Karim Amir, and I am an Englishman born and bred, almost.' Karim, a.k.a. 'Creamy Jeans', is a child of Empire. When we first meet him, he lives with his Indian father and his English mother on the distant outskirts of London, enduring the last of school and the last of flower-power, in a state of near-terminal late-adolescent angst.

But Karim's story will prove to be most English in its heritage – that of the glorious, scabrous, picaresque, savage, sentimental tradition of low comedy that stretches from Chaucer to the dirty postcards on Brighton Pier. *The Buddha of Suburbia* is also as much an up-yours for our times as *Lucky Jim* was for the Fifties, and Kureishi himself offers another signpost in Chapter One, when Eva, Karim's father's lover, gives the boy a copy of *Candide*.

But, in some respects, Candide had it easy compared to Karim. 'I was sick of being affectionately called Shitface and Curryface.' Jamila, militant feminist, black radical, and his best friend, defines the problem: 'The thing was, we were supposed to be English, but to the English, we were always wogs and nigs and Pakis and the rest of it.'

Karim's world is soon turned upside down. His father, Haroon leaves his sweet, downtrodden wife to live with sexy, trendy Eva and practise as a guru. (He is the Buddha of the title.) Jamila, to her fury, is bullied and cajoled into an arranged marriage with the aimiable buffoon, Changez, who demands, as part of the dowry, a complete set of the works of Conan Doyle. Karim moves to the big city. Life opens up. He starts a career as an actor, his first role, to Jamila's disgust, Mowgli, in what she dubs *The Jungle Bunny Book*. Punk happens. Charlie, Eva's son, turns into a successful pop singer, although Karim is keen to assure he is a very bad one.

Karim is worshipfully in love with Charlie; by the novel's end, he has grown out of it. But *The Buddha of Suburbia* isn't so much a coming-of-age novel as a coming-to-terms novel, coming to terms with a world in which nothing, neither pleasure, nor politics, nor power, can be taken on trust. Not even violence. When a girl-friend's father turns his dog on Karim, expectations are reversed with a vengeance: 'I knew by now what the dog was up to. The dog was in love with me – quick movements against my arse told me so.'

The sexual black comedy of this episode is cruel, hilarious and desperate; Karim is training himself rigorously to see the funny side. Irony is his defence and his weapon. The ribald subject-matter is exquisitely set off by the louche prissiness of Karim's diction: 'I contemplated myself with and my wardrobe with loathing and would willingly have urinated over every garment.' When I say *The Buddha of Suburbia* is wonderfully well written, I mean it is continually tasty and interesting and full of glee. It is not like Penelope Fitzgerald.

In fact, it may be the first novel in what I trust will be a rapidly growing and influential genre – the novel designed *on purpose* to exclude itself from the Booker short-list. There's not only the richly vulgar vein of body comedy – Hanif Kureishi finds every aspect of physicality from mastectomy to anal intercourse ruefully mirthful – but he remains wonderfully Right On, politically, and lets the middle classes play little if any role in this world of squats and anti-racisim and dishevelled integrity.

He can't find a bad word to say about women, either, which is a lovely thing in this period of fashionable misogyny, but it does mean that Jamila and Eva and poor old Mum are touched with a little bit of unexpected sugar. And if some minor characters – such as Uncle Ted, the central heating engineer and part-time football hooligan – spring at once to pulsing life, others, like Jamila's mother, now a grocer, once a princess, haven't got much to do except stand round looking picturesque.

The novel ends with a wedding announcement – Haroon and Eva's – and a party. Karim ponders how things have been a mess but soon will go better. There's a sting in the tail; it is election night, in the fatal year of 1979.

A radical feminist I know paid *My Beautiful Launderette*, the movie scripted by Hanif Kureishi, her ultimate accolade: 'It almost made me like men.' His first novel almost made me nostalgic for that messy but on the whole optimistic decade, the Seventies. It is a wonderful novel. I doubt I will read a funnier, or one with more heart, this year.

(1990)

· 20 ·

Ian Jack: *Before the Oil Ran Out* and others

There is an old song by Ewan MacColl, a favourite in folk clubs thirty years ago and more, 'Dirty Old Town'. It's about Salford and enshrines all the often-parodied clichés of social realist art of the time, mucky canal and all. One day, though, the singer is going to tear that dirty old town down. Then it will be goodbye to the dark, Satanic mills for ever.

Well, the dark, Satanic mills are gone for good now. Manufacturing industry has departed this country and the great Northern cities have died even more speedily than they were born, when they doubled, tripled, tripled again their size, filth, complexity, poverty, wealth during the course of the nineteenth century. The Conservative government under Margaret Thatcher acccomplished in eight years a more radical razing of mill and foundry and pit and shipyard than any pinko troubadour ever dreamed of.

But this peremptory cleansing has left these cities bereft of everything except their inhabitants, who eke out their scant resources picking over the local tip, as described by Ian Jack in Birkenhead, in 1985. Or they can set out to scour the country for work, like post-industrial versions of the Joad family in *The Grapes of Wrath*.

Or they can turn to crime, for there *is* money around, lots of it, and if the Inland Revenue has opted out of the property redistribution business it is high time for private enterprise to take over.

If all that is solid really is melting into air, this time we are too bewildered by the speed of the vanishing to register anything but a diffuse blur. All the material evidence of the life of Ian Jack's father has gone – birthplace, workplaces – in an abrupt divorce from history, as if there was a conspiracy to ensure the old man left no trace he had ever been born.

'In this way,' says his son, 'de-industrialisation has disinherited the sons and daughters of the manufacturing classes; a benign disinheritance in many respects, because many of the places my father worked were hell-holes, but also one so sudden and complete that it bewilders me.'

Beryl Bainbridge says: 'Whenever I go back to Formby, the Lancashire village in which I grew up, I find in it nothing that reminds me of the past.' And yet, as she says somewhere else, the heart lies back there in the past, buried under the new supermarket, the multi-storey car park, the Job Centre.

Before the Oil Ran Out and *Forever England* are both collections of journalism about Britain in Year One of the Thatcherite revolution. Ian Jack used to work for *The Sunday Times*; there is a pungent coda describing his last days at Fortress Wapping.

The novelist Beryl Bainbridge's book is tied in with a television programme, an investigation of three families from the prosperous South, a symmetric three from the deprived North. She was fortunate enough to find close-knit, loving kin. One of them, a member of the long-term unemployed, opines: 'All we've really got is family.' In an era of privatisation, our greatest pleasures are private ones.

Her title suggests, in spite of everything, continuity. Ian Jack's, more ominous, suggests that our present plight, mass unemployment, homelessness, drug abuse, violence, is but the calm before the storm.

Both writers include large sections of family history, as if they feel they must offer their class credentials before seizing the nettle of present-day Britain.

And quite right, too. The national passion for Orwell surely springs from the opportunity he gave the reader to identify with an old Etonian grubbing about amongst the underclass, rather than having to face up to the fact that most of us are of working-class origins in the first place. *The Road to Wigan Pier* reminds me of what a Black American I once knew said about *Uncle Tom's*

Cabin: 'I used to weep buckets over the plight of those poor people until I realised those poor people were me.'

Ian Jack made a trip to Wigan – a Lancashire-born Scot, he did not find it so alien – and found a newsagent who remembered 'when the top of an egg were a luxury'. Recalled Orwell, too: 'I remember some folk thought he was a nark of some kind, what these days you'd call a snooper from the Social Security.'

In this solid Labour town, *The Lady* sells more copies per week than all the socialist weeklies put together. I can enlighten Ian Jack on this apparent paradox. *The Lady* carries ads from the affluent South seeking clean, reliable Northern lasses as live-in nannies.

This is a collection of descriptions of Britain moving apparently inexorably into the Third World. Sidetrips – Rhodesia before it became Zimbabwe, the Falklands before the war, Turin – only reveal the shabbiness of our pretensions. However, Ian Jack has chosen as frontispiece a family portrait. His father's. There will survive one splendid monument to the old man. It is a most moving account of a life which his son, with good reason, sees as having been exemplary. It is also a lament for the stoic, republican virtues of the old Scottish left.

It was a hard life, well lived, that of a skilled artisan, a socialist of the old school, an autodidact, a Burns lover, a good father, and, on the evidence of excerpts from the memoirs he compiled in his old age, possessed of a prose style that, alas, puts Norma Dolby's way with a pen to shame, although they would probably have recognised one another as beings cut from the same cloth.

Looking back on the earlier self who had just discovered politics and plunged into Marx, Jack London, Upton Sinclair like a dolphin into a delighted sea, Mr Jack wrote: 'We intended, and may have succeeded just a wee bit, to make the world a better place to live in. But we expected too much to happen too soon, and we did not realise how heavily the dice were loaded against us.'

Mr Jack died before the NUM strike of 1984–5 revealed just how heavily the dice were still loaded. That strike might have broken his heart. It nearly broke mine.

Norma Dolby's is an artless, month-by-month account of the slow erosion of a small mining community's faith in and respect for the police and the processes of the law, though not, finally, in justice itself: 'We want justice and are willing to fight for it.'

Mrs Dolby found her feet as a public speaker during the strike. One day, on a platform, her shyness suddenly vanished. 'All my thoughts spilled out. I really let myself go . . . If we went down, what hope had anyone else of surviving Maggie's slaughter of jobs.'

Impossible not to recall Brecht: 'When I say what things are like/Everyone's heart must be torn to shreds/That you'll go down if you don't stand up for yourself/Surely you can see that.'

But by the strike's end, her village, Arkwright Town, in Derbyshire, had almost gone down. The divide between those who stayed out until the end and those who did not ran deep. 'People dropped their eyes when they passed you and did not answer when you spoke to them.'

Mrs Dolby's husband opted for redundancy. There are rumours the pit will close. The community disintegrates, the great strike recedes into memory – but too many of us remember it for it to suffer the white-out of the past under Thatcher, even if they try very hard.

Mrs Dolby talks a great deal about the kindness of strangers – the gifts of food and money, toys, clothes, hospitality, support, from all over Britain, Europe, the world. 'Never can you measure such kindness.'

Norma, kindness had nothing to do with it. We weren't being *kind* when we shelled out for the collecting boxes. We were doing it for ourselves, because you were standing up for us, too. We were doing it for our children, and for the old men and women who wanted to make the world a better place to live in and, for a time, thought they had succeeded, even if only a wee bit.

(1987)

21

Michael Moorcock: *Mother London*

This epic portion from the kitchen of Michael Moorcock's imagination is a vast, uncorseted, sentimental, comic, elegiac salmagundy of a novel, so deeply within a certain tradition of English writing, indeed, of English popular culture, that it feels foreign, just as Diana Dors, say, scarcely seems to come from the same country as Deborah Kerr.

Mother London contains obvious input from the music hall – Josef Kiss, the central character, himself started out working the halls as a mind-reader. And Moorcock tends to create his characters with a few, swift, sure strokes, brilliant and two-dimensional, just as the characters in music-hall sketches, or, indeed, the personas of the performers themselves are created.

He also does not deny the influence of pulp fiction – a whole generation of English youth nourished its dreams on Western novels – nor of *The Magnet*, *The Gem*, nor certain kinds of teddibly, teddibly Bridish popular history. (He quotes copiously from Arthur Mee.) But across the *ad hoc* structure and the unapologetically visionary quality of it all necessarily falls the incandescent shadow of William Blake, for whom there was no distinction between the real and the imaginary and whose phantom rises again every time we see a way out of that particular trap.

It isn't really a question of 'magic realism', that much-abused term. For Moorcock's Londoners, nothing could be more magical than the real fabric of the city they love and the stories with which it echoes.

A city is a repository of the past. Therefore *Mother London* is organised as an anthology of memories – recollections from the pasts of a group of men and women who meet regularly at an NHS clinic (under threat) to collect their tablets and enjoy group therapy.

Not that any of them are deranged, exactly. But they are all sensitives, some of them perhaps too sensitive to the stories of the city and its myriad voices. The grandly eccentric old man, Josef Kiss, can hear what people think. Sometimes it drives him mad.

We can hear the voices, too. The narrative is seamed with them, voices in a multitude of tongues, speaking platitudes, mouthing sexual paranoia, prejudice, gossip, wild talk, abuse . . . the city talking to herself. She is not a loving mother. But we must take her as we find her; she is the only one we have.

During the Blitz, Josef Kiss put his talents as a mind-reader to work, seeking survivors in the burning ruins. He did not find the beautiful Mary Gasalee among the ruins, however. She walked out of the flames by herself, carrying her new-born baby in her arms.

In spite of this authentic miracle, Mary's daughter grows up to be a best-selling historical novelist, not the new Messiah. Though the novel ends with the joyously consummatory marriage of Josef and Mary, there is no suggestion this event might cue in the arrival of another saviour, even though the city that survived the fire from heaven might now be in need of divine intervention to save it from the effects of late capitalism – the property boom, the demise of history, the exile of the working class from the city they built.

For the London Moorcock celebrates is working-class London, whose history has always survived by word of mouth, in stories and anecdotes. He takes you on a grand tour of the forgotten, neglected parts of London, as far as Mitcham in the South, but always coming back to W 11, where, twenty years ago, you could see the Proverbs of Hell chalked up on the walls.

And if Josef and Mary turn out to be indestructible, as they do, perhaps there is hope in the infinite resilience of narrative itself.

Not for Moorcock the painful, infrequent excretion of dry little novels like so many rabbit pellets; his is the grand, messy flux itself, in all its heroic vulgarity, its unquenchable optimism, its enthusiasm for the inexhaustible variousness of things. Posterity will certainly give him that due place in the English literature of the late twentieth century which his more anaemic contemporaries grudge; indeed, he is so prolific it will probably look as though he has written most of it, anyway.

(1988)

22

Iain Sinclair: *Downriver*

Iain Sinclair, in the profane spirit of surrealism, has chosen to decorate the endchapters of his new work of fiction with a dozen unutterably strange picture-postcards. They show scenes such as that of six men, heavily veiled, veils held down by brimmed hats, posed with long-barrelled rifles. And two men in grass skirts, with feathers in their hair, intent on a game of billiards. They are Africans. And here are twenty-odd white men, in straw boaters, surrounding a prone crocodile. Joblard, Sinclair's friend, arranges the cards so that they tell a story. At once they become scrutable: they are images of imperialism. Joblard titles this picture story, what else, 'Heart of Darkness'.

But the twelve interconnected stories in *Downriver* don't match up with the numbered postcards, unless in such an arcane fashion it must necessarily remain mysterious to me. *Downriver* is really a sort of peripatetic biography: Iain Sinclair's adventures at the end of time, at the end of his tether, in a city of the near future with a hallucinatory resemblance to London. The decisive influence on this grisly dystopia is surely the grand master of all dystopias, William Burroughs. Jack Kerouac, asked for a quote for the jacket of *The Naked Lunch*, said it was an endless novel that would drive everybody mad. High praise. *Downriver* is like that, too.

It is mostly about the East End. This reviewer is a South Londoner, herself. When I cross the river, the sword that divides me from pleasure and money, I go North. That is, I take the Northern Line 'up West', as we say: that is, to the West End. My London consists of all the stations on the Northern Line, but don't think I scare easily: I have known the free-and-easy slap-and-tickle of Soho since toddlerhood, and shouldered aside throngs of harlots in order to buy my trousseau casseroles from Mme Cadec's long-defunct emporium, undeterred by rumoured crucifixions in nearby garages. Nothing between Morden and Camden Town holds terror for me.

But I never went to Whitechapel until I was thirty, when I needed to go to the Freedom Bookshop (it was closed). The moment I came up out of the tube at Aldgate East, everything was different from what I was accustomed to. Sharp, hard-nosed, far more urban. I felt quite the country bumpkin, slow-moving, slow-witted, come in from the pastoral world of Clapham Common, Brockwell Park, Tooting Bec. People spoke differently, an accent with clatter and spikes to it. They focused their sharp, bright eyes directly on you: none of that colonialised, transpontine, slithering regard. The streets were different – wide, handsome boulevards, juxtaposed against bleak, mean, treacherous lanes and alleys. Cobblestones. It was an older London, by far, than mine. I smelled danger. I bristled like one of Iain Sinclair's inimitable dogs. Born in Wandsworth, raised in Lambeth – Lambeth, 'the Bride, the Lamb's Wife', according to William Blake – nevertheless, I was scared shitless the first time I went to the East End.

Patrick White says somewhere that there is an intangible difference in the air of places where there has been intense suffering, that you can never get rid of the memory that pain imprints on the atmosphere. London's river runs through *Downriver* like a great, wet wound. Almost all the stories are affected in some way by the swell and surge occasioned when the pleasure boat, *Princess Alice*, sank after it collided with the *Byewell Castle*, a collier – a high-Victorian tragedy recalling the loss of the *Marchioness*, although Sinclair does nothing with the analogy, lets it lie there in the water. An estimated six hundred and forty people went down with the *Princess Alice*, including the husband and two children of Elizabeth Stride. Her family gone, she took to drink, went on the streets. She became one of the victims of Jack the Ripper – the kind of ominous coincidence that fiction needs to avoid if it is to be plausible. Life itself can afford to be more extrovert.

So can Sinclair, who has no truck with plausibility but allows or persuades his densely textured narrative to follow a logic based on the principle of allusion, engaging in a sort of continuous free collective bargaining with his own imagination. For example: there is sardonic, virtuoso description of the *Princess Alice* disaster:

> The victims chose an unlucky hour to enter the water. They were discharging the sewage from both the north and south banks into Barking Creek. Outflow. Mouths open, screaming, locked in a rictus. Rage of the reading classes. Public demand for the immediate provision of swimming-pools for the deserving poor. Let them learn breast-stroke.

Then the narrative moves like this:

> Something happens with the draw of time. With names. The *Alice*. Fleeing from the extreme interest of Lewis Carroll (weaving a labyrinth of mirrors for his English nymphet) into the tide-flow of Thames. Can you row, the sheep asked, handing her a pair of knitting-needles. Dodgsons. Dodgeson. Out on the river with another man's daughters: Lorina, Alice, Edith.

And thence to the enigmatic Canadian performance artist, Edith Cadiz, whose story we already know. By day, she worked as a nurse, nightly subsidising herself – for that income would never keep her – as a prostitute of the least exalted type. Edith Cadiz haunts the text, with her disinterested love for the mad children in her care, her unnerving stripper's act involving a dog and a set of street maps. One day, after copulating with a dog at the request of a Member of Parliament – this text is rich in dogs, some of them memorably unnerving – she disappears.

She is no less haunting a character because Sinclair makes plain she is not his own invention but the invention of another of the characters he has also invented. But many of the other characters, including Sinclair himself in a memorable walk-on ('a flannelled Lord Longford: on sulphate'), are drawn, kicking and screaming, one assumes, from real life. Some of them I recognise. One or two of them I know. That is Sinclair's autobiographical bit. Think of *Downriver* as if Alice had wept a river of tears, rather than a pool; this river, like memory, full of people, places, ideas, things, all with ambiguous reality status.

King Kole, the Aboriginal cricketer, standing at the rail of the *Paramatta*, watching a pilot-boat butt its way across Gravesend Reach, knew he had arrived at the Land of Death. Gravesend did for Pocahontas, the Indian princess, too: she died there, on her way back to Virginia. Sacrificial victims of imperialism. But less fatal presences include a writer, Fredrik Hanbury, a name transparently concealing one familiar to readers of *The London Review of Books*. There are painters, vagrants, Jack the Ripper, Sir William Gull, ritual murder, cricket, Homerton, Silvertown, 'The Isle of Doges' (VAT City plc).

Alice herself features at considerable length, in an extended meditation on Tenniel's illustration to *Through the Looking-Glass*, the one that shows Alice in the train. Alice 'allies herself with the order of birds; a feather grows from her severe black torque'. That feather might be a clue to the solution of the murders. What murders? Why, didn't you know? Spring-heeled Jack has returned. 'VAMPIRE AND BRIDE-TO-BE IN DOCKLANDS HORROR'. Edith Cadiz might have been a victim of this man.

But that is to suggest too much interconnectedness, to imply that a plot might be about to happen. *Downriver* is jam-packed with teasing little hints at possible plots, but these coy insinuations of resolution, climax, denouement are marsh-lights designed to delude the unaware reader into imagining that some regular kind of story might be in the offing. Fat chance. These stories, flowing all together, from a river without banks in which you sink or swim, like the victims of the *Princess Alice*, clutching at associations, quotations, references to other writers, if you can pick them up.

I picked up one or two. The American horror writer H. P. Lovecraft, is economically invoked with the single phrase, 'a gibbous moon'. T. S. Eliot is constantly quoted by Edith Cadiz both before and after her disappearance; she passes round a hat that once belonged to him after she does her strip. The scarlet-haired opium addict, Mary Butts, makes a brief guest appearance and Sinclair borrows a minatory quotation from her autobiography: 'I heard the first wraths of the guns at the Thames's mouth below Tilbury.'

Iain Sinclair: *Downriver*

With this mass of literary references, the sex magic, the degradations, the torture, the rich patina of black humour, this is a book that triumphantly rejects any possibility of the Booker short-list in advance. It wears its contempt for all that on its sleeve. It is, besides, a work of conspicuous and glorious ill-humour. Sinclair doesn't seem driven, like Burroughs, by an all-consuming misanthropy: he's too romantic for that. But whenever Sinclair writes about the media, he goes pink and sputters. There is a section titled 'Living in Restaurants', about trying to make a television movie about Spitalfields. 'The *consiglieri* liked the sound of it, the authentic whiff of heritage, drifting like cordite from the razed ghetto.' The media lunches, four months of heroic eating. He hates them all. He constructs stiff, epigrammatic insults, more insult than epigram. The TV producer 'has that combatant attitude so prevalent among people who spend their lives bluffing genuine enthusiasts into believing they know nothing about their own subject'.

There is an *unhandiness* about Sinclair's prose, here. It creaks. His satire is splenetic but also heavy-handed. 'The Widow was a praise-fed avatar of the robot-Maria from *Metropolis*; she looked like herself, but too much so.' No prizes for guessing who *that* is. However, *Downriver* is set just a significant little bit further forward in the future, after the privatisation of the railways. And the Widow is *still* in charge. Who could have guessed, when *Downriver* went to press, that Margaret Thatcher would have resigned by publication date? Not Sinclair. When he appears in the third person in the final story, he babbles 'some bravado sub-text about considering his book a failure if the Widow clung on to power one year after its publication'. Unless he wants to claim a preemptive strike, he'll have to concede that, like Blake, to whose prophetic books his own bears some relation, he had, as prophet, zero success rate.

At one point, the Fredrik Hanbury character opines: 'Obsession matures into spiritual paralysis.' *Downriver* is far more than the sum of its obsessions, compelling as these are. Who can ever forget that dog of dogs, the one with *no eyes*, not a dog whose eyes have been put out but one who *never had any*, grey fur there, instead. This is an image so horrifying I don't want to understand it. What is the opposite of a dog? This question begins and ends the book, this manic travelogue of a city about to burn, and I can't even begin to answer: I will have to read *Downriver* again, to find out.

Yet, in spite of, or perhaps in order to spite that central, dominating motif of the river, none of these twelve stories flow easily. There are swirls, eddies, and undercurrents but precious few stretches of clear water. When these occur, as they do, for example, two separate times in the section called 'Prima Donna' (the Cleansing of Angels)', the limpid narrative achieves genuine supernatural horrow; the bristling begins. One is the anecdote about Cec Whitenettle, driver of the hell-train bearing nuclear waste through Hackney. The other is the story of the Ripper's only personable victim, the 'Prima Donna' herself, that begins impeccably, better than Lovecraft, almost as good as Poe: 'I had not, I think, been dead beyond two or three months when I dreamed of the perfect murder.'

But Sinclair obviously isn't interested in plain sailing. His everyday prose is dense, static, each sentence weighed down with a vicious charge of imagery. Fighting the current, this reader was forced to ponder the ultimate function of fiction. This was very good for me. Is it to pass the time pleasantly, I asked myself? If so, they put some quite good things on television these days. But something is happening in this text that makes it necessary to go on reading it, something to do with time itself, even if, in order to go on, you must – to mix metaphors – crack open each sentence carefully, to inspect the meat inside.

All writers of fiction are doing something strange with time – are *working* in time. Not their own time, but the time of the reader. One of Sinclair's milder obsessions is with ritual: the project of ritual is to make time stand still, as it has apparently stood still in David Rodinsky's room in the Princelet St Synagogue since the day, twenty-odd years ago, when he disappeared. (See Tale No. Five, 'The Solemn Mystery of the Disappearing Room'.) If time could be persuaded to stand still for even one minute, then the thin skin that divides Victorian London, Pocahontas's London, Blake's accursed London, Gog and Magog's London, The City of Dreadful Night, Jack London's London (*The People of the Abyss*), *Downriver*'s London of the near future, might dissolve altogether. The partitions of time dissolve in the memory, after all. They dissolve in the unconscious.

At one point, Joblard and Sinclair watch Pocahontas being carried ashore to die, but that is altogether different, a purely literary trick with time. It is an easier one because the reader watches it being done on the page rather than experiences it in the act of reading. The thing is, you can't skip bits of *Downriver*. You have to move with currents as violent and mysterious as those of the Thames.

Its vision of London is pure hell. Madmen, derelicts, visionaries, 'wet-brains' live in the towers of abandoned mental hospitals. Academics voluptuously drown themselves in chains. Bohemians live with a dedicated ferocity. Oh! that Imar O'Hagan, with his trained snails and his 'fridge full of blocks of frozen vampire bats like an airline breakfast of compressed gloves'.

It describes a city in the grip of a psychotic crisis. One image makes this concrete – a room in Well Street ('Grade 2 listed husk'), former home of a mad, addicted girl, now a suicide. The walls are covered with shrieking graffiti, protests, denunciations, phone-numbers, pyramids, quotations, lingams, crucified sparrows, horned gods, walking fish. 'The floor was clogged with mounds of damp sawdust – as if the furniture had been eaten, and, conically, excreted. Bas-relief torcs of blood were plashed over the skirting-boards. "Dogfights," Davy explained.' This, even more than the voodoo ritual later to be enacted on the Isle of Doges (*sic*), is the true heart of darkness within the city.

On the whole, the English, except for Dr Johnson, never have liked London. Cockney Blake saw, within a crystal cabinet, a refreshed, regenerate, a garden city:

> Another England there I saw,
> Another London with its tower,
> Another Thames and other hills.

Sinclair and two companions precipitate themselves out of that nightmare voodoo ceremony by an act of will and find themselves transported to just such an earthly paradise, freshly designed for the 'Nineties by a snappy Post-Modernist', a 'morning-fresh Medieval city', a 'transported Sienna. Beneath us, along the riverside, a parade of windmills'. Windmills, the green sign of harmless energy. Benign, harmless windmills, the herbivores of the energy world. But when they look closer, they see the windmills are not windmills after all, but the sites of crucifixions.

Downriver is an unapologetically apocalyptic book that has, alas, found its moment, even if the Widow is now reduced to soundbites. Mother London, says Sinclair, is splitting into segments: a queasy glamour extinguishes the mad, bad past in Whitechapel, the rest of the places go hang . . . and yet these stories show how impossible it is to pull down an imaginary city. As Sinclair walks round London, he reinvents it, and remembered pain will always dance like heat in the air above the spot in Whitechapel where the Ripper struck down poor Lizzie Stride. The singing that turned to screaming continues to impress itself on the water where the *Princess Alice* went down. Listen, you can hear it on the slapping tide.

(1991)

London E.8
1.3.91

Dear Angela

I enjoyed your rap on *Downriver* enormously. It makes the whole business sound dangerous, difficult and insane: which is about as rich a mix as you can hope for. I would even be tempted to read the thing.

The only point I would argue is the prophetic 'failure' of Blake. (And this book.) Prophecy has nothing to do with 'accurately' casting future events, like some speedy weather-man. It has to do with *causing* future events by the power of invocation (or necessary sacrifice). Blake's razor-clawed chickens will be coming home to roost for aeons and were already doing so before he was imagined in Soho.

The prophetic element in this text is supposed to make things happen, not to second-guess banal newspaper reality. Mrs Thatcher (both more and less than the 'Widow') picked up her cards exactly one year after the typescript was handed in to Nick Austin.

It doesn't take much of a prophet to know that the family living beneath the curvature of a flying bomb are already dead as they enjoy their domestic – but posthumous – breakfast in Canning

Town. What we have to do is show what we fear most – and damn it to actually happen.

all best
Iain

AMERIKA

. . . The pure products of America go crazy . . .

William Carlos Williams

23

Robert Coover: *A Night at the Movies*

The American cinema was born, toddled, talked, provided the furniture for all the living-rooms, and the bedrooms, too, of the imagination of the entire world, gave way to television and declined from most potent of mass media into a minority art form within the space of a human lifetime. In the days when Hollywood bestraddled the world like a colossus, its vast, brief, insubstantial empire helped to Americanise us all.

A critique of the Hollywood movie is a critique of the imagination of the twentieth century in the West. Could this be what Robert Coover, most undeceived and quintessentially American of writers, is up to in this new collection of stories, characterised as they are by his particular quality of heroic irony? Certainly they are located almost entirely within the territory of the American film except for a side-trip into a British one, 'Milford Junction 1939: a Brief Encounter', which gets onto the bill for *A Night at the Movies* under the description of travelogue.

Strangers used to gather together at the cinema and sit together in the dark, like Ancient Greeks participating in the mysteries, dreaming the same dream in unison. But Coover is no respecter of mysteries. The book kicks off in the cinema, with a story called 'The Phantom of the Movie Palace'. But nowadays the cinema is a rat-haunted, urine-scented wreck, inhabited only by a lonely projectionist screening reels at random for his solitary pleasure.

'The Phantom of the Movie Palace' describes the method of much of what is to follow, as the projectionist puts together his flickering collages:

He overlays frenzy with freeze frames, the flight of rockets with the staking of the vampire's heart, Death's face with thrusting buttocks, cheesecake with chaingangs, and all just to prove to himself over and over again that nothing and everything is true. Slapstick *is* romance, heroism a dance number. Kisses kill.

At last the projectionist finds himself flattened into two dimensions, up there on the screen, 'surrendering himself finally . . . to that great stream of image activity that characterizes the mortal condition'.

Coover exacts a similar surrender from the reader. There is some exceptionally strenuous image activity ahead in these stories that precisely reactivate the magnificent gesticulations of giant forms, the bewildering transformations, the orgiastic violence that hurts nobody because it is not real – all the devices of dream, or film, or fiction. Coover is also diabolically, obscenely, incomparably funny.

The collection includes, besides the travelogue already mentioned, a weekly serial, some shorts, a cartoon, a musical interlude, and not one but three main features – a Western, a comedy, a romance. Every aspect of the mortal condition, besides every type of Hollywood genre, is comprehensively covered. Some of the movies invoked are imaginary; some, like the musical, *Top Hat*, reinvent the familiar in hallucinatory terms: 'he had some pretty fancy moves, but all that nimble-footedness looked to me like something he mighta learned tippytoeing through the cowshit.'

'Shoot Out at Gentry's Junction' starts off deceptively straightforwardly: 'The Mex would arrive in Gentry's Junction at 12:10. Or had arrived. Couldn't be sure . . . Sherriff Henry Harmon grunted irritably and eased his long pointed boots to the floor.'

So far, so good: already the stereotypes are briskly in play and, as so often in Westerns, the set-up is strictly Freudian. If Hank Harmon, clearly the Henry Fonda role, 'a tough honest man with clear speech and powerful hands', stands for the Superego, then the Mex is, as ever, the Id incarnate. 'Here he is in the schoolhouse demonstrating for the little childrens the exemplary marvels of his private member.'

The presence of the Mexican bandit, his grotesque Hispanic

accent, that amazing private member, the appalling stench of his fart – 'The goddam Mex had let one that smelled like a tomb' – his presence transforms the genre. With the Mex at the centre, all becomes a bloody carnival of sex and death.

It soon becomes obvious the terrible Mexican must triumph at the shoot-out. 'Adios to Gentry's Junction! . . . The storekeeper, the banker, the preacher, they swing with soft felicity from scaffolds and the whisky he is running like blood.'

The two other main features exhibit no less manic invention. 'Charlie in the House of Rue ' – yes; it *is* that Charlie – takes slapstick via its own remorseless logic of paranoia and anxiety to a place of the deepest anguish and disquiet, as darkness, 'like the onset of blindness,' irises in on the clown. 'What kind of place is this? Who took the light away? And why is everybody laughing?'

If Coover turns a Western into a savage fiesta and a Chaplin two-reeler into an analysis of the compulsion to repeat, he is cruellest of all to the love story that is, of all film romances, most precious to buffs, for he turns *Casablanca* into a blue movie in which Rick and Ilsa get it on again in no uncertain manner: 'he's not enjoyed multiple orgasms like this since he hauled his broken-down black-listed ass out of Paris a year and a half ago . . . '

This is desecration on the grand scale, a full frontal attack on – or, rather, a full frontal revision of – one of the sacred texts of American cinema. But Rick and Ilsa also founder amongst gathering shadows and uncertainty. The other characters wait downstairs in the bar for the lovers to get up and dress and the action to continue but is that possible, now? Hasn't everything been changed? The story, nostalgically titled 'You Must Remember This', ends the book; the ending is an unanswered, unanswerable plea: 'And then . . . ? Ilsa . . . ? And *then* . . . ?'

It is a wild night, this marathon night's viewing, in the semi-derelict picture palace of twentieth-century illusion, from which gangsters can whisk you away in an unmarked car during the 'Intermission', send you spinning through a dozen different hazards – sharks, seraglios, dud parachutes, etc. – and drop you back in your seat in time for the shorts.

But, wait. Something has happened while you have been away. Now the audience is 'all sitting stiffly in their seats with wierd flattened-out faces, their dilated eyes locked onto the screen like they're hypnotized or dead or something'. The most virtuoso single exercise in the book, the strangest, the most exemplary in its demonstration of the transforming resources of narrative, 'After Lazarus,' concludes with a coffin being lowered towards the camera. 'Sudden blackness.'

At this moment, impossible not to recall, as if they were prophecy, the final words of *Weekend*, Jean-Luc Godard's great film of the Sixties, 'Fin du cinema. Fin du monde'.

(1987)

· 24 ·

Hollywood

In its heyday, the period 1917–60 dealt with in *The Classical Hollywood Cinema*, Hollywood was a gold-rush boom town, a place of pilgrimage, when the young and the beautiful, the cynical and the depraved, the talented, the lucky, and the doomed thronged to seek their fortunes. That was how it was supposed to be, at any rate, and, oddly enough, that was really the way the capital city of illusion was, as if Hollywood itself were its own greatest production.

Easy to forget, nowadays, how unprecedented the movie industry was in its mobilisation of vast amounts of capital, both financial and human, in the production of pleasure. Easy to forget the religious fervour that possessed the audiences, those communities of strangers crowded together in the dark. (How appropriate that, according to *Hollywood Anecdotes*, one of the abandoned Art Deco picture palaces in New York has been consecrated as a Pentecostal tabernacle.)

Hollywood was, still is, always will be, synonymous with the movies. It was the place where the United States perpetrated itself as a universal dream and put the dream into mass production. 'We take Hollywood seriously, treating it as a distinct mode of movie practice with its own cinematic style and industrial conditions of existence,' state the authors of *The Classical Hollywood Cinema*, and proceed, comprehensively to do so.

But there was an extra dimension of scandal and glamour that was also an essential part of the product. John Ford said that you couldn't geographically define Hollywood. Almost as soon as the studios went up, the town was recreated via the twentieth-century arts of publicity as the home of an ever-increasing pantheon of deities; major, minor, and all sizes in between. Star worship wasn't a perversion but a genuine manifestation of the religious instinct. (Some of that sense of the sacred rubbed off the movies on to the US itself, too, which is why we all venerate the Stars and Stripes.)

Janet Leigh thought the MGM lot in the Fifties was like fairy-land. Other actresses did not. ' "Darling," drawled Tallulah Bankhead to Irving Thalberg, "how does one get laid in this dreadful place?" '

But did she really say it, or did somebody put the words in her mouth? 'Hollywood thrives on apocryphal aphorisms,' say the authors of *Hollywood Anecdotes*. At least one of their stories – the one about the cameraman who apologises for not getting as good shots as he did ten years before – has a variable heroine, either Greer Garson or Marlene Deitrich or Norma Shearer. The authors categorically deny that another story, told by Elizabeth Taylor about herself, ever happened at all. A favourite story of Hitchcock's has no basis in fact, either.

This is genuinely folkloric material. 'Telling a story is the basic formal concern,' according to *The Classical Hollywood Cinema*. That is what the Hollywood cinema is there for. Telling stories about the people engaged in telling stories is a basic informal concern, and no matter if these are twice-told tales – they gain richness and significance with repetition.

Much of the contents of *Hollywood Anecdotes* will be familiar to buffs, and loved because it is familiar. There is the MGM lion ('Ars Gratia Artis') who in old age, had to be fitted with dentures, and also the lions (25 lions at 25 dollars a head) who pissed on the assembled Christian martyrs in Cecil B. de Mille's *The Sign Of The Cross*. Though, alas, the toothless lion of whom Victor Mature (*Androcles and the Lion*) said 'I don't want to be gummed to death', is missing.

Sam Goldwyn's famous deformations of English are lavishly quoted: 'You've got to take the bull by the teeth,' etc. Boller and Davis are fond of funny accents; they wouldn't dream of omitting Michael 'Bring on the empty horses' Curtiz.

They cite genuine curiosities, like the brothel, Mae's, staffed by film-star lookalikes ('Claudette Colbert' spoke excellent French). Ben Hecht's celebrated dictum gets another airing: 'Starlet is a name for any woman under 30 not actively employed in a brothel.' Otherwise, Boller and Davis are decently reticent about the abundant sexual folklore of Hollywood, which the prurient are advised to seek in Kenneth Anger's two volumes of *Hollywood Babylon*.

All in all, the tone of *Hollywood Anecdotes* is oddly similar to those little Sunday school compilations of the sayings of saints and worthies. Any incident, no matter how trivial, is worth recounting if it concerns a star or near-star. Christopher Plummer, it is said, hated *The Sound of Music* so much he nicknamed it *The Sound of Mucus*. Abbot and Costello once threw a suitcase of condoms at their director in the middle of a scene. Well, well, goodness gracious.

Close-Ups – designed to look like a mock-up of a Thirties movie annual – is the very stuff of legendary history, a collection of star ephemera spanning seventy-odd years complete with iconic representations. Odd little snippety articles go with the photographers, some of them historic documents such as Alvah Bessie's obituary of Marilyn Monroe and Budd Schulberg's weird threnody for Judy Garland, other bits of makeweight scribble even if the by-line makes you blink – Sergio Leone on Henry Fonda, for example.

Danny Peary, the editor, describes *Close-Ups* as a scrap-book. Leafing through it is an unnerving experience; like flicking through the channels late at night on television, catching snatch after snatch of old movies diminished by their transmission through the indifferent air. When we talk about Hollywood nowadays, we talk about nostalgia, but Brecht described his own experience in Golden Age Hollywood: 'Every morning to earn my bread,/I go to the market where lies are bought/Hopefully/I take up my place among the sellers.'

The hell of it was, they made wonderful movies, then, when nothing in Hollywood was real except hard work, mass production, the conveyor belt, the tyrants, and madmen running the studios.

The Classical Hollywood Cinema quotes François Truffaut: 'We said that the American cinema pleases us and its film-makers are slaves. What if they were freed? And from the moment that they were freed, they made shitty films.'

(1988)

· 25 ·

Edmund White: *The Beautiful Room is Empty*

This account of an American sentimental education starts off according to the conventions of such things: 'I met Maria during my next-to-last year in prep school.' In the US, prep school prepares you for college; the narrator is on the threshold of adulthood but, although an intense friendship with Maria, painter, socialist, Lesbian, nascent feminist, will be central to his life, she is far from being the romantic heroine who will administer his lessons of the heart.

Yet, in a sense, she saves his life, or, at least, his sense of self by introducing him into the hard-working, easy-going Bohemia of the Fifties, where our existentially dishevelled hero can feel, if still not quite at home, at least less abandoned in the world.

Love as such will come much later, almost at the novel's end. As for passion – well, perhaps the preconditions for passion won't arise until after the novel is over, because you need high self-esteem to engage in a passionate attachment, you need to believe yourself worthy of one, and the narrator of this lucid book spends the greater part of it coping, with considerable fortitude, with the conviction he is depraved, or mad, or worthless.

After he has finally found, and lost, his first great love, he tries to exorcise the pain by writing about it: 'Yet how could I like myself, or ask the reader to take seriously a love between two men?' The novel itself is an answer to that question.

The Beautiful Room is Empty is a sequel to Edmund White's *A Boy's Own Story*, and takes the anonymous hero of the earlier book from late adolescence, to the further shores of youth, his late twenties. It also takes him from the stern repression of the

139

mid-West to New York City; from the 'frumpy cuteness' of Fifties Middle America to the ravishing diversity of the late Sixties; from the solid, merciless, deranged, white middle class to the rootless urban intelligentsia with its mix of race and class and desire.

But, essentially, the narrator's sentimental education concerns neither men nor women but the nature of his own desires. It begins in a painful contradiction: 'As half-consciously I inched towards my desires for men, I clung to my official goal of stifling these desires.' Driven by a curiosity he believes to be as perverse as its promptings are irresistible, his encounters are bleak with irony, characterised by a deliberate absence of pleasure, as if to enjoy them would make them even more wicked. The narrator's secret life, indeed, most of his sexual life, consists of meeting anonymous flesh in the public toilets he obsessively cruises, the 'long sentence' served on his knees from which Edmund White extracts an astonished poetry.

In a coffee shop, on a night out with a reckless gaggle of queens – 'Grab your tiaras, girls' – he notes straight couples stare with open disgust. 'I was no longer a visitor to the zoo, but one of the animals.' Meanwhile, the narrator's father grudgingly coughs up for the analysis that is supposed to 'cure' his son. But the ministrations of Dr O'Reilly, speed freak and alcoholic, teetering on the verge of his own breakdown, collapse, only induce more anxiety: 'If I started from the premise I was sick (and what could be sicker than my compulsive cruising?) then I had to question everything I thought and did. My opinions didn't count, since my judgement was obviously skewed.'

Damaged ghosts, victims of America, drift past. Annie Schroeder, real-life Warhol superstar *avant le jour*, yearns to be a top New York model. A bulimic, she blocks up the drains when she regurgitates the whole ham and entire turkey from which she has made a midnight snack during a Christmas visit home with the narrator; her gesture of disgust and rejection is so comprehensive, if involuntary, that it is a wonder the narrator never thought of bulimia himself.

Into this world of guilt, lust, and occasional fierce excitement erupts Lou, the 'handsome, ugly man,' scarred, alchoholic, heroin-addicted, irresistible, who loves Ezra Pound, and 'everything deformed by the will towards beauty', and who loves, too, the 'beautiful poetry of gay life'. The narrator clearly hadn't thought of it like that before.

Lou's own huge potential for tragedy has been arrested by his equal potential for the dramatic glamour of the life of homosexual crime celebrated by Burroughs and Genet, the lure of, the necessity for transgression. In the terms of the period, you might say that Lou *enjoys* being a pervert.

It speaks volumes for the narrator's good sense and emotional stability, in spite of all, that he eschews the 'demon lover' aspect of his new friend and cultivates, instead, a loving friendship. His scandalised mother, for whom the enigmatic Lou is the last straw, suggests an implant of female sex hormones will solve her son's problems: ' . . . oestrogens neutralise your sex drive altogether; they neuter you and soon you're free to lead a normal life.'

And yet she loves her son. She truly believes she has his welfare at heart.

Lou suggests the narrator leave Chicago for New York with him, the archetypal journey for the American writer, the mid-West to the Big Apple. Here, normalcy is a more flexible condition; the Sixties are just beginning; the streets are full of what Lou calls 'Cha-cha queens, hairburners and glandular cases', and the narrator begins, for the first time, to see homosexuality not as deviancy but as a way of being.

And the beautiful stranger arrives at last. The blond Sean. Perhaps love is not so inaccessible, after all. Yet Sean soon cracks up, breaks down, because loving another man is too much evidence that he is homosexual – a recurrent theme of the book, the wish to gratify desire whilst evading stigma, whilst avoiding self-identification whilst evading membership of a stigmatised group. That's putting it in bare, sociological terms. It was a system of repression that killed. Sean goes to live with a cowboy; nobody, he writes, would ever guess this cowboy was gay . . .

The narrator despairs. 'If as a child I'd known my whole long life was going to be so painful, I'd never have consented to go on leading it.'

But the novel is not over. It is quietly moving towards a remarkable and joyous conclusion that takes place, unfashionably enough, on the barricades, probably the first barricades in the history of street warfare manned by people who saw the funny side of a revolution.

On the day of the death of Judy Garland, the narrator and Lou find themselves in a gay bar, one summer's night; the police raid. There is a riot. The bar was the Stonewall; at this point, the novel enters real history. 'Lily Law shouldn't have messed with us the night Judy died,' says Lou. Somebody shouts out: 'Gay is good.' Gay Liberation is about to be born. The Stonewall riot was, the narrator says, 'The turning point of our lives'. The rioters were not protesting their right to depravity, neuroses, or psychic derangement, but a simple right to be human.

This exemplary novel is written in prose as shining and transparent as glass; it lets you see life through it. It describes how the survivor of a psychological terror campaign retains his humanity.

If I were a teacher, I would recommend this book to every student who asked me why it was necessary to fight the amendment to the Local Government Bill presumably designed to prevent me doing just that. Nobody who has seen the inside of the closet would wish to condemn anyone to return to it.

(1988)

· 26 ·

Paul Theroux: *My Secret History*

The title of Paul Theroux's new novel recalls that of the Victorian autobiographical masterpiece of erotomania, Walter: *My Secret Life*, with which Theroux's book has something in common. Theroux himself makes a more inscrutable reference to Arthur Waley's *The Secret History of the Mongols*, which Theroux's peripatetic hero, Andre Parent, reads on his way to commit adultery, surely a rather precious choice.

My Secret History is divided into six sections that take Parent from adolescence in 1956 to middle age in 1984 in a series of self-contained leaps. In the first person, it begins briskly and attractively: 'I was born in rich America. . .' The voice is fluent, conversational, confiding; the novel would pass the time pleasantly on one of those marathon train rides of which Theroux, in his guise of travel writer, has made such a speciality.

But, under this moderately beguiling surface, there is something stronger and stranger. The real subject of *My Secret History* is libidinal gratification expressed as a basic, irrepressible hunger. At one point, Parent says to an African acquaintance: 'America's a very hungry country.' Which would be tasteless – Africa is starving to death, after all – were it not a metaphor. Parent's history suggests that to be 'born poor in rich America' is to be born with a metaphysical lust that nothing, not success, wealth, or the love of women, can satisfy. There is an acknowledged madness in Parent. He wants to fuck the world.

Parent speedily outlines for us the nature of his two lives – one, that 'of the dreamer, or the sneak', hidden, the other led in public. (Later, he puts it more succinctly: 'One was sex, the other work.')

And that is enough of that. Theroux does not allow his hero to indulge in introspection, nor to speculate either upon his own motives or those of other characters. As a result, the novel is so free from psychologising that Parent becomes almost a perfect existential hero who does what he does, and, indeed, *who* he does, because he does it.

Part One. Young Parent is the horny sprig of a dour Catholic family in a small New England town. He forms an attachment to a drunken yet charismatic Irish priest not a hair's breadth away from cliché. The priest dies; Andre gets laid. A typical 'male awakening' scenario, not insensitively done.

Four years pass. Now Andre is at college. He is determined to become a writer, as if writing were a form of phallic mastery. He is still horny as hell; happily, he is maturing into one of those young men, familiar in fiction, whose very presence impels women to remove their clothing but when a girlfriend suffers a vile abortion he is briefly filled with guilt and determines to leave the US.

Another four years pass. Andre is now in Black Africa, teaching school, and screwing local bar girls omnivariously, taking crabs and VD in his stride, kicking the girls out in the morning before they bore him with their chatter. Four years later, he's a dead mark for the first girl he meets who screws *and* talks about T. S. Eliot. Jenny. 'It was wonderful to be with this woman. We talked about books we liked. We took turns quoting poetry we had memorised.' Wow. It must be Love. Jenny is not Black African but blonde English; Parent proves conventional enough in his marriage choice.

Again, a lapse of four years. The couple have settled in London where Andre, returning from amassing material for a travel book, discovers Jenny has been unfaithful in his absence. His bizarre revenge is to discharge at her lover a water-pistol filled with urine. Jenny is angry but soon begs forgiveness, an episode which needs more finesse than Theroux gives it to make plausible. This section ends with a touch of pure Hollywood, a phone call from an agent to say the travel book is about to do extremely well.

Skip a decade. Andre is rich and famous, with not only a lavish house, Jenny and their child in London but also a lavish house and mistress on Cape Cod to mark his triumphant return to Massachusetts. The mistress, Eden, with her dyed black hair, gourmet cooking, and girlish lisp when randy ('If I'm bad you'll have to put me to bed') is clearly a refugee from an early Feiffer cartoon but Parent likes her style and takes her on a trip to India.

A few weeks later, neurotically anxious to duplicate his life in every way, he takes Jenny on the same trip in what, to the reader, looks a transparent bid to be found out. He is found out; Jenny says Parent must choose and the novel ends as Parent announces he knows 'exactly what to do' but teasingly fails to tell us.

I'd suggest a vasectomy. As it stands, Parent's career usefully demonstrates the interconnectedness of sexism and racism; I hope this was Theroux's point.

(1989)

· 27 ·

Gilbert Hernandez: *Duck Feet*

Gilbert Hernandez' comic strips in the series, *Heartbreak Soup*, of which this collection, *Duck Feet*, is the second portion available in Britain, are about gossip. Especially, about yesterday's gossip, about the memories our parents share with us so we almost come to think that they are our memories too. The intimate folklore of family. Gilbert Hernandez' family, of course, is not my family, or your family, but this kind of folklore has a cross-cultural similarity, most of all in cultures where people often find themselves short of a bob.

Families, particularly extended families – and the families in *Heartbreak Soup* are often stretched to the limit – flourish best in small towns. This involves Gilbert Hernandez in a celebration of small-town life. In the very small town of Palomar (population 356), the narratives of its inhabitants' lives weave in and out of each other with the same claustrophobic compulsiveness of the lives in the marvellous novels of Louise Erdrich (*Love Medicine*, *The Beet Queen*), set in remote townships in the American mid-West.

The novel composed of interwoven small-town lives has a long tradition in the United States. Sherwood Anderson's *Winesburg, Ohio* (1919) is a classic. But Palomar is not in the United States; it is somewhere south of the border. And although the strip sometimes goes out of its way to pay homage to a painter, the Mexican artist, Frida Kahlo, there is nothing in the least 'literary' about *Heartbreak Soup*. Nevertheless, Hernandez shares the same project as Erdrich and Anderson: the recreation of a place and time that explains why and what we are, here and now.

146

Erdrich and Anderson were raised in communities much like the ones they write about. Gilbert Hernandez does not even speak the Spanish which is the mother tongue of his characters. That gives his project an even greater urgency.

He says that the stories came, mostly, from his mother, told with her apron on while she was making the dinner or ironing. Stories about Mexico, when she was a girl, and her first years in the States. Gilbert and his brother, Jaime, creator of the comic strip, *Love and Rockets*, live in Oxnard, sixty miles outside Hollywood. In California, the signs in bus stations are in both English and Spanish: bilingual education is a burning public topic: the state is re-Hispanicising itself while you watch and yet its image and aspirations remain securely Anglo.

But the Spanish arrived in California first. Hence the place names: San Diego, La Jolla, Sacramento, and so on. Indeed, they got to the entire bottom bit of the USA first: Arizona, New Mexico, Texas, Florida. After a century or so in the back seat, the Spanish are staging a come-back, recolonising the lost territory of the Mexican Empire to such effect that there are towns like Palomar deep in the heart of Texas – towns just as fly-blown and dirt-poor, teeming with barefoot kids, in which English, if spoken at all, is a reluctantly acquired second language. This invasion has been caused by economic desperation, not a desire for cultural expansion; what will happen when the barefoot kids, children of recent immigrants, grow up and demand a share of the All-American apple pie is anybody's guess.

Oxnard, however, is suburban, multi-cultural, Los Angeles in miniature, with 'nothing to do at night', say the brothers. Neither Gilbert nor Jaime speaks more than the odd phrase of Spanish. Their position is complex. And Palomar is, for them, the Old Country. The foreign place where one's parents grew up. 'Home' at second hand, of which the knowledge is our inheritance, not our birthright. It is a place known only to the children of immigrants and therefore one with a special resonance in the American imagination, and, increasingly, the British.

The daily life of Palomar is a cruel parody of the chaste suburbia pictured in that family newspaper strip of my childhood, *Blondie*. It is a world of brawling kids and feckless, licentious, drunken men, dominated in every sense of the word by endlessly fecund earth mothers, furiously sexy women who might have come undulating straight out of the crudest kind of male fantasy if they didn't pack such big punches. Such big punches that a man can boast of them, even regret their absence; a grieving widower laments, 'She needed no dishes to render me into submission, her flying dropkick was enough.'

Sexiest and most furious of all is Luba of the big breasts and uncertain temper. The strip charts her progress from humble beginnings, crammed with her kids in the van where she plied her original trade of bath-house keeper, to cinema proprietor and a nice house, with porch and fence in a decent part of town. Not that any of this changes Luba; 'None of my daughters know who their fathers were . . . and I'm keeping it that way. They're too young to have to know what kind of men their mother was stupid enough to get involved with.'

These are matrifocal families, in the main. Sisters, or female relatives – Luba lives with her cousin, Ofelia – share a selection of children. A foundling, like the irrepressible Carmen, will be fitted in somewhere. Paternity, as Luba notes, is hypothetical. And the men are often away, anyway, working or looking for work; employment opportunities are few in Palomar. Money is a problem.

After the routing of an incompetent male sheriff, law and order rest in the capable hands of one Chelo, former bath-house keeper, former midwife. Indeed, she brought most of Palomar's inhabitants into the world. Now, in the name of the law, she occasionally dispatches one of them from it. But, although Chelo has the power of life and death, and Luba is eternal mother, the mythic dominance of women in the community does not, it should be noted, prevent the men of Palomar from treating them like shit from time to time.

Story lines are as absorbing and inconsequential as the ones a neighbour tells over a back fence, or a stranger in a bar. You feel somebody, one of the characters in the strip, or Gilbert Hernandez himself, is taking you into their confidence about Palomar, telling you its secrets. While you are reading the strip, Palomar becomes 'our town', even if you've never been in a town like that.

When is all this supposed to be taking place? Hard to say. Note that television has not yet come to Palomar. In the early days of the strip, nobody remarked on it. Nowadays, however, visitors congratulate the inhabitants on the absence of TV, and the inhabitants congratulate themselves. Indeed, their lives are already so much like soap operas, why should they feel the need to watch them?

But the absence of television, like the relative absence of cars, like the characteristic hour-glass shape of the women and the 'Silvana Mangano in *Bitter Rice*' type shorts they like to wear, like the flat-top haircuts of the men, are evidence that the town is stuck in the Fifties even when its calendars tell you that the Eighties are here. The roughest edges of poverty are absent too, edges as rough then as they are now. I don't think this has been done on purpose, as a cosmetic exercise; it has happened because Palomar is already suffused with the glow of second-generation nostalgia.

One of the inhabitants of the town who *is* bang up to date is the prim, rather bourgeois wise woman, who charges ten dollars a throw and prescribes aspirin more readily than eye of newt. A more folkloric witch visits occasionally, toting a fetish bag; she, however, is given to bouts of prediction as follows: 'American moviemaker Steven Spielberg wins an Oscar for his adaptation of *The Catcher in the Rye* in 1998. Art then is legally declared dead.'

This is one of those moments when you might almost suspect that Gilbert is making mild fun of those among his admirers who, confusing the teller with the tale, assume the creator of these simple, vital peasant types must be a simple, vital peasant himself.

Enter the ghost of Gabriel Garcia Marquez. Well, not ghost, exactly; he isn't dead, yet. Shall we say, the vexed question of the influence on the Hernandez series of the Colombian author of *One Hundred Years of Solitude*, with its unique, remote, fantastic township of Macondo. *Heartbreak Soup* has been consistently compared with *One Hundred Years of Solitude* since the strips began to appear in the early Eighties. Evidently Gilbert Hernandez didn't get around to reading the novel, although urged to do so, until a short while ago, but it soon made a personal guest appearance in the strip. Carmen and Heraclio, one of the few more-or-less happily married – indeed, one of the few more-or-less married – couples in Palomar come to blows over it. Carmen hates to see him reading. She throws *One Hundred Years of Solitude* away: 'This is the last time you're going to ignore me for this junk!'

There are things about *Heartbreak Soup* that make me think

Gilbert Hernandez must respond sympathetically to the politics of *One Hundred Years of Solitude*; but, of course, he didn't have to know about Macondo to invent Palomar. They are both places that existed once, in a continent caught between post-colonialism and neo-imperialism; but to think of *Heartbreak Soup* as a sort of Classic Comics version of Garcia Marquez is to do Gilbert Hernandez a great disservice. What *Heartbreak Soup* is most like is life.

Both Hernandez brothers cite Federico Fellini's movies as a real influence, and it is easy to see why. Think of Fellini's own home town, with its top-heavy women, horny youths, venomous feuds, as he recreated it for his autobiographical film, *Amarcord*, a word that in the dialect of Fellini's part of Italy, means 'memory'.

Heartbreak Soup is put together with such imagination and verve that it is easy to talk about it as if it were a novel; and it isn't, of course. But it *is* fiction, a category that includes novels, movies, soap opera, sit com, tragedy, comedy, and comic strips. Gilbert Hernandez is using the comic strip to tell us important stories about love, and death, and poverty, and grinning and bearing it, and the past we all carry with us wherever we go.

(1987)

· 28 ·

Louise Erdrich: *The Beet Queen*

Perhaps most writers in the US simply do not know how strange its daily life is. Certainly Louise Erdrich's writing, violent, passionate, surprising, arrives in the midst of a torpid time for American letters. She deals with small towns, the prairies, people trashed by circumstance, sexual obsession – all the matter of the classic American novel, in fact. But most people haven't been tackling these immense verities for ages. *The Beet Queen*, her second novel, imparts its freshness of vision like an electric shock.

Like Toni Morrison and other Black women writers, Louise Erdrich approaches the American novel from a doubly marginalised position – that of women; and also that of an ethnic minority, in Erdrich's case, American Indian. Perhaps even trebly marginalised; she was raised in the remoter parts of the farm belt, hick country. She is part of the wedge being driven deep into WASP fiction from new contenders for their share of the Great Tradition.

And WASP fiction is in a bad way. The vogue during the Reagan years has been for the sentimental petit bourgeois naturalism of which Raymond Carver is the most influential, and the most glum, exponent. The sensibility is grey, the mood one of discontented acquiescence.

You'd never guess, from reading Carver, that, as William Carlos Williams once stated, 'The pure products of America go crazy'. That craziness shows up on TV news bulletins, rarely in the typical WASP well-crafted short story.

These craftspersons never even hint at the furious contemporary folklore of America enshrined in those magazines at supermarket check-outs brimming with the raw material of the marvellous

– stories about UFOs, levitation, unnatural births ('73-year-old mother's 16-month pregnancy'), weird deaths (the girl who succumbed to hypothermia after eating too much ice-cream).

Back in the Sixties, this kind of thing provided nourishment for important writers – for Pynchon, Barth, Coover. Nowadays, most US writers are content to ignore the exuberance and variety of the imaginative life manifesting itself in all its convulsive beauty outside the creative writing departments that seem to constrain more and more of them. There are a few exceptions. Louise Erdrich is one.

The imaginative lives of Louise Erdrich's vast gallery of characters are rich to the point of excess, although financially they run the gamut from dirt poor to just coping and tend to have eschewed the benefits of higher education.

The Beet Queen is closely related to the earlier *Love Medicine*, neither a sequel nor a prequel but an overlap – some of the same characters appear, some of the same landscapes. There is very much the sense of one continuous story, or, rather, a continuous braided sequence of interlinked narratives, and no real reason why, now she has begun, she should ever stop.

Like Garcia Marquez in *One Hundred Years of Solitude*, Louise Erdrich has appropriated the family saga as a suitable form in which to describe the processes of history at work amongst and within ordinary people. She has also chosen, as he did, a small town at the back of beyond.

The time span of *The Beet Queen* extends from the 1930s to the 1970s; the town of Argus in North Dakota survives the Depression in good shape to move into a prosperity we know with hindsight will not last. Around the town stretch the formidable distances of the Great Plains. There is a sense of isolation and abandonment, in which the travelling salesman is genuinely a figure of romance.

The Beet Queen, like *Love Medicine*, is composed of many sections of narrative in the voices of a number of narrators, because Louise Erdrich's method with the family saga is to explode it. The very structure of her novels is unstable and not like other novels, as if she were experimenting with effects derived from the oral tradition. The impression is as of a river of memory bursting its banks and overflowing upon the page in an irresistible flood.

Yet there is a functional aspect to all this remembering. Ms Erdrich is out to reconstruct that most mysterious of sites, the recent past, the time of the lives of our parents before we were born; out of these family romances we make our identities.

The principal participants in *Love Medicine* are Chippewa who live on the reservation. Those of *The Beet Queen* are white and do not. The Lamartine and Kashpaw families live the tumultuous lives of extravagant poverty – in which love and violence are the only pleasures that cost nothing.

The mood of the first novel is epic. Mary Adare, her brother, her cousin, her friends, usually have just a little more cash and are therefore, on the whole, more repressed. The mood of *The Beet Queen* is one of lyrical desperation and black comedy.

There is a miracle in *The Beet Queen*. A face, taken by some to be the face of Christ, appears in a shattered sheet of ice in a convent school playground. The miracle is as inconsequential as the apparition of the face of the Virgin Mary in an oil slick on a pond in Oklahoma, which happened – no, *really* happened – last year. The mother of Mary Adare and her brother Karl, whom we meet in Chapter One, riding boxcars as in a Woody Guthrie song, has flown away in a small plane, while they watched her, flown away and never come back.

And indeed, Mary and her friends and relations are variously cracked, and crazed, and barking mad; but never, for all the elements of the fantastic, less than true to life. If Louise Erdrich's fiction has the compulsiveness of remembering, then it has the dream-like exaggeration, the metaphorical quality of memory.

But at times this veers perilously close to a kind of Dakota Gothic. When Mary dreams of an imaginary lover: 'His eyes were the same burnt-butter brown as his hair, and his horns branched like a young buck's.' Her cousin Sita's restaurant ('Chez Sita, home of the flambeed shrimp') looks, thinks Mary, like the ship of the dead.

And there is a bizarre vignette of a spider weaving its web in a baby's hair that would be at home in a Buñuel film, beautiful, but somehow uncomfortable, here. But Ms Erdrich is a writer who takes risks on every page, so it would hardly be fair if she did not, once or twice, risk a little too much.

It is impossible to make a synopsis of *The Beet Queen*. Too much happens; the flow and counter-flow of the narratives defy summary. But the many narratives centre, more or less, on the life-long friendship, which becomes almost a form of marriage, between Mardy Adare and a girl called Celestine James. The vagaries of this friendship encompass the birth of a child to Celestine, fathered by Mary's errant brother. This child, squat, savage, fearless Dot, grows up to become the Beet Queen of the title, chosen to reign over Argus for a day when its prosperity peaks due to the cultivation of the sugar beet. How drab, how everyday, how James M. Cain; How magical.

This parsimonious sketch gives little indication of the infinite richness of the novel. Ms Erdrich is a writer who can give you a whole chunk of social history complete in one exquisitely precise piece of observation: 'They were heavy people, Germans, Poles or Scandinavians, rough-handed and full of opinions, delicate biters because their teeth hurt or plates did not fit well.'

And she throws that away in the course of a description of a butcher's shop. She is so thoroughly in tune with the surreal poetry of America that when you read her you can hear America singing, the discordant choruses of its multitude of voices, its rough music, its requiems for disappointed dreams.

(1987)

Grace Paley: *The Little Disturbances of Man* and *Enormous Changes at the Last Minute*

What can put you off Grace Paley's stories is their charm. 'An Interest in Life' in the collection called *The Little Disturbances of Man* begins: 'My husband gave me a broom one Christmas. This wasn't right. No one can tell me it was meant kindly.' It is so scrupulously disarming an intro that it is bound to put people who like Joan Didion very much on their guard. And it is alarmingly easy to fall into the language of the Martini ad when writing about Grace Paley – wry, dry, tender, ironic, etc.

The snag is, her work *has* all these qualities: it is an added irony that, since the *fin* has come a little early this *siècle* and anomie is all the rage, wry, dry tenderness is a suspect commodity. Not that Paley appears to give one jot for psychosocial hem-lengths. She is, as we used to say, 'for life', and clearly cannot imagine why anybody should be against it. Not that the wonderful world of Grace Paley is all sunshine: the heroine of 'An Interest in Life' is kept from despair only by a Micawberesque sustaining illusion that the broom-giver, now defected, will return. (It's obvious that, if he does, she'll really be in trouble.)

But the charm is a problem, though, both infuriatingly irresistible and, since couched in the *faux-naif* style, verging dangerously on the point of cloy. The title story of the collection called *Enormous Changes at the Last Minute* almost goes over the top. A middle-aged social worker, Alexandra, is surprised into bed with a feckless hippy. 'That's my bag. I'm a motherfucker,' he crows complacently. He impregnates her. Her aged father is justifiably enraged. 'After that, Alexandra hoped every day for her father's death, so that she could have a child without ruining his life at the very end of it when ruin is absolutely retroactive.'

But Paley contrives to transcend this Shirley Maclainesque scenario completely. Alexandra reorganises her apartment as a refuge for pregnant teenagers, setting an interesting precedent in social work. Her father falls, bangs his head, clears his brain, begins again 'with fewer scruples'. The hippy composes a celebratory anthem about parent–child relationships that is a hit from coast to coast and is 'responsible for a statistical increase in visitors to old-age homes by the apprehensive middle-aged and the astonished young'.

That single adjective, 'astonished', is sufficient to illuminate retrospectively this everyday story of marginal folk. We see that it is not a quaint tale of last-minute motherhood so much as an account of that reconciliation with old age and kinship which is, in itself, a reconciliation with time. Extracted from the text, the characters are patently emblematic: an old man, his daughter, a young man, a chorus of girls, a boy child. There is even an off-stage cameo guest appearance by Alexandra's ex-husband, the Communist Granofsky. ('Probably boring the Cubans to death this very minute,' opines her father.)

As in the *News of the World*, the whole of human life is here, and, indeed, many of Paley's plots would not disgrace that journal. Other stories feature a man shot by a jealous cop, his neighbour's husband; a White runaway raped, beaten, dead, in a Black neighbourhood – Paley extends tenderness and respect even to the rapists. There are shot-gun marriages and catatonic boys. But do not think that, Ophelia-like, Paley can turn hell itself to favour and to prettiness. In *Enormous Changes at the Last Minute*, two stories – 'Gloomy Tune' and 'Samuel' – are done as straight as case-histories. 'Gloomy Tune' is an analysis of social deprivation. The problem children 'never stole. They had a teeny knife. They pushed people on slides and knocked them all over the playground. They wouldn't murder anyone, I think'. They are doomed. 'Samuel' is probably one of the great works of fiction in our century, although it is but four pages long. He is a bold child killed at dangerous play on the subway. His mother is young and soon pregnant again. 'Then for a few months she was hopeful. The child born to her was a boy. They brought him to be seen and nursed. She smiled. But immediately she saw that this baby wasn't Samuel.'

I love to think how Joan Didion would hate Grace Paley. If a continent divides Paley's seedy, violent multi-ethnic New York from Didion's neurasthenic vision of LA as a city of the plain, their sensibilities are those of different planets. But, then, the poor always have an unfair moral edge on the rich, and most Paley characters are on Welfare.

Those who manage to keep their heads above water tend to come from good socialist stock. Even in retirement with the Children of Judea, one old man plots to organise the help. Ex-husbands constantly send committed postcards from developing countries. Ex-husbands are far more frequent on these pages than husbands, though, as in 'The Used-Boy Raisers' and 'The Pale Pink Roast', often turning up again like the refrain of an old song – mysterious, irrelevant, yet never quite consigned to oblivion.

Paley does not efface herself from the text. A homogeneous, immediately recognisable personality pervades everything she writes. Nevertheless, she is a ventriloquist *par excellence*, and speaks the American that has been moulded by Russian, Polish, and Yiddish as eloquently as she can personate the speech of Harlem. She can change sex, too: as a first person, she credibly becomes a man, young or old. Shape-shifting is no problem – thin, fat. 'I was popular in certain circles, says Aunt Rose. I wasn't no thinner then, only more stationary in the flesh.' This is 'Goodbye and Good Luck', in *The Little Disturbances of Man*, the only one of all these stories that has a strong flavour of another writer. In this case, Isaac Bashevis Singer, with whom Paley shares a tradition and an idiom.

All the same, all the narrative roles Paley undertakes are those of the same kind of marginal people, with essentially the same exhausted, oblique tolerance as those child-besieged women, usually called Faith (she has a sister, Hope), who seem most directly to express the real personality of the writer. One of them describes her own marginality: 'I was forced by inclement management into a yellow-dog contract with Bohemia, such as it survives.' And perhaps the continuous creation of this fictive personality, whom we are always conscious of as the moving force behind the narratives, is the real achievement of these two marvellous collections. As if, somehow, this omnipresent meta-narrator is, finally, more important than the events described. I think this meta-personality is, in fact, something like conscience.

The charm turns out to be a stalking-horse, a method of persuasion, the self-conscious defensive/protective mechanism characteristic of all exploited groups, a composite of Jewish charm, Black charm, Irish charm, Hispanic charm, female charm. It is part of the apparatus of the tragic sense of life.

Technically, Grace Paley's work makes the novel as a form seem virtually redundant. Each one of her stories has more abundant inner life than most other people's novels; they are as overcrowded as the apartments they all live in, and an enormous amount can happen in five or six pages. Her prose presents a series of miracles of poetic compression. There are some analogies for her verbal method – e. e. cummings, perhaps, also a smiler with a knife, but she rarely plumbs his depths of cuteness. She has the laconic street eloquence of some of the Beats. This is not *English* English; scarcely a Wasp graces these pages. Yet the cumulative effect of these stories is that of the morality of the woman of flexible steel behind them; most of all, because of her essential gravity, she reminds me, strangely enough, of George Eliot. But, within its deliberately circumscribed compass, Grace Paley's work echoes with the promise of that sense, not of optimism, but of *inexhaustibility*, which is the unique quality of the greatest American art.

(1980)

LA PETITE DIFFERENCE

Vive la petite différence!

Old French saying

· 30 ·

Charlotte Brontë: *Jane Eyre*

In 1847, a young woman of genius, vexed at publishers' rejections of *The Professor*, the first novel she had completed, on the grounds that it 'lacked colour' and was too short, sat down to give the reading public exactly what she had been told they wanted – something 'wild, wonderful and thrilling', in three volumes. Rarely, if ever, has such a strategy proved so successful. The young woman's name was Charlotte Brontë and the novel she produced, *Jane Eyre*, is still, after a century and a half, 'wild, wonderful and thrilling'. It remains the most durable of melodramas, angry, sexy, a little crazy, a perennial bestseller – one of the oddest novels ever written, a delirious romance replete with elements of pure fairytale, given its extraordinary edge by the emotional intelligence of the writer and the exceptional sophistication of her heart.

Charlotte Brontë lived during one of the greatest periods of social change in English history. In all her novels, she is attempting to describe a way of living that had never existed before and had come into being with the unprecedented social and economic upheavals of England in the early industrial revolution. Jane Eyre herself is the prototype Charlotte Brontë heroine – a woman on her own for whose behaviour there are no guidelines. This woman is not only capable of earning her own living but also must and needs to do so; for her, therefore, love is a means of existential definition, an exploration of the potentials of her self, rather than the means of induction into the contingent existence of the married woman, as it had been for the previous heroines of the bourgeois novel.

I don't think for one moment that Charlotte Brontë knew she was doing this, precisely. When she wrote *Jane Eyre*, she thought she was writing a love story; but in order for Charlotte Brontë, with her precise configuration of class background and personal history, to write a love story, she had, first of all, to perform an analysis of the operation of erotic attraction upon a young woman who is not rich nor beautiful but, all the same, due to her background and education, free to choose what she does with her life.

The clarity and strength of Charlotte Brontë's perception of her heroine's struggle for love is extraordinary. Yet, of all the great novels in the world, *Jane Eyre* veers the closest towards trash. Elizabeth Rigby, writing in the *Quarterly Review*, 1848, makes the exact point that the novel combines 'such genuine power with such horrid taste'. She went on, a touch petulantly: 'the popularity of *Jane Eyre* is a proof how deeply the love of the illegitimate romance is implanted in our nature.' In order to do something new, in order to describe a way of being that had no existing language to describe it, Charlotte Brontë reverted, to a large extent, to pre-bourgeois forms. *Jane Eyre* is the classic formulation of the romance narrative, with its mysteries of parentage, lost relatives miraculously recovered, stolen letters, betrayal, deceit – and it fuses elements of two ancient fairytales, *Bluebeard*, specifically referred to in the text when Thornfield Hall is compared to Bluebeard's castle, and *Beauty and the Beast*, plus a titillating hint of *Cinderella*. The archaic sub-literary forms of romance and fairytale are so close to dreaming they lend themselves readily to psychoanalytic interpretation. Episodes such as that in which Rochester's mad wife rips apart the veil he has bought Jane to wear at his second, bigamous wedding have the delirium of dream language. As a result, *Jane Eyre* is a peculiarly unsettling blend of penetrating psychological realism, of violent and intuitive feminism, of a surprisingly firm sociological grasp, and of the utterly non-realistic apparatus of psycho-sexual fantasy – irresistible passion, madness, violent death, dream, telepathic communication.

The latter element is so pronounced that it gives the novel a good deal in common, not with *Emma* or *Middlemarch*, but with certain enormously influential, sub-literary texts in which nineteenth-century England discussed in images those aspects of unprecedented experience for which words could not, yet, be found: Mary Shelley's *Frankenstein*, Bram Stoker's *Dracula*. 'There are times when reality becomes too complex for Oral Communication,' says the computer in Jean-Luc Godard's 1967 movie, *Alphaville*, 'but Legend gives it a form by which it pervades the whole world.' *Jane Eyre* has this quality of legend and, like *Frankenstein* and *Dracula*, has proved infinitely translatable into other media: stage, screen, radio. As a child, I first encountered *Jane Eyre* in a comic-strip version. The text easily secretes other versions of itself. Jean Rhys' *Wide Sargasso Sea*, restores the first Mrs Rochester, Jane's predecessor, to the centre of the narrative. One of the great bestsellers of the mid-twentieth century, Daphne du Maurier's *Rebecca*, shamelessly reduplicated the plot of *Jane Eyre*, and went on to have the same kind of vigorous trans-media after-life.

Nevertheless, if Jane Eyre arrives, like Bluebeard's wife or Beauty, at an old, dark house, whose ugly/beautiful master nourishes a fatal secret, she arrives there not as a result of marriage or magic, but as the result of an advertisement she herself had placed in a newspaper. She has come to earn her own living and the fairytale heroine, as she travels to the abode of secrets and the place of initiation, is fully aware of her own social mobility, which is specifically the product of history. 'Let the worst come to the worst,' she ponders, 'I can advertise again.'

Jane is only pretending to be a heroine of romance or fairytale. She may act out the Gothic role of 'woman in peril' for a while at Thornfield Hall, when she is menaced by her lover's first wife, but, when things become intolerable, she leaves. She might be trapped by her desires, but she is never trapped by her circumstances. She is, in terms of social and literary history, not a romance figure at all but a precursor of the rootless urban intelligentsia who, seventy years later, will take the fictional form of the Brangwen sisters in D. H. Lawrence's *Women in Love*. Like the Brangwen sisters, and like Lucy Snowe in *Villette*, Jane Eyre must earn her living by teaching. There is no other 'respectable' option, except writing fiction, and, since Jane is a character in a piece of fiction, she would give the game away if she resorted to that. When Jane sets out on her journey to her new place of employment, she says things that no woman in fiction has ever said before:

It is a very strange sensation to inexperienced youth to

feel itself quite alone in the world; cut adrift from every connection, uncertain whether the port to which it is bound can be reached, and prevented by many impediments from returning to that it has quitted. The charm of adventure sweetens the sensation, the glow of pride warms it: but then the throb of fear disturbs it.

Independence is not a piece of cake. But, for Jane, it is essential. It isn't surprising to find her saying

Nobody knows how many rebellions besides political rebellions ferment in the masses of life which people the earth. Women are supposed to be very calm generally; but women feel just as men feel; they need exercise for their faculties, and a field for their efforts as much as their brothers do.

The history of Charlotte Brontë and her family has itself been the subject of much fiction and speculation, as if it, too, were the stuff of legend. Certainly, the six Brontë children seem to have tried hard to be ordinary, but could not help making a hash of it. The Reverend Patrick Brontë, their father, may have passed his life as the 'perpetual curate' of Haworth Parsonage, near Keighley, in Yorkshire, but he early exhibited that discontent with the everyday that marked out the clan when he celebrated his arrival in England from his native Ireland by changing his spelling from Brunty. (The umlaut is a master stroke.) Of all of them, he repressed the discontent the best, which may be why he lived the longest, outliving his last surviving child, Charlotte, by six years, to die at the age of eighty-four in 1861; Charlotte died in 1855, at thirty-nine years old.

From childhood, the Brontë children knew there were no such things as happy endings. Cancer claimed Mrs Maria Brontë in 1821, when Charlotte was five. The two eldest daughters, Maria and Elizabeth, died at the school Charlotte Brontë barely fictionalised in *Jane Eyre* as Lowood. (Charlotte claimed Maria as the prototype of Jane's unnaturally self-abnegating friend, Helen Burns.)

Charlotte, Emily, Branwell, the only boy, and Anne lived to grow up. The family home at Haworth was close to both the majestic landscape of the Yorkshire moors but also to the newly built, sombre milltowns surrounding Leeds; their life was not as isolated as might be supposed. They read voraciously and extremely widely. Their father does not appear to have censored their reading at all.

From an early age, they amused themselves by writing stories and poems. After a failed attempt to set up a school following the period Charlotte and Emily spent in Brussels in 1842, studying French, Charlotte persuaded her sisters to publish an anthology of their poetry under the sexually indeterminate names, Currer, Ellis, and Acton Bell. Charlotte wrote that they 'did not like to declare ourselves women because . . . we had a vague impression that authoresses are liable to be looked on with prejudice'. That's an elegant piece of irony, especially since there have been persistent attempts to attribute not only *Wuthering Heights*, Emily Brontë's great novel, to the authorship of Branwell Brontë, but also virtually the entire *oeuvre* of all the other sisters too. Branwell, in fact, possessed little literary talent but, alone of them, exhibited signs of a genuine talent for physical excess that might have passed unnoticed at the time of *Tom Jones* but dissipated itself in drink and scandal at Haworth Parsonage.

Jane Eyre was published under the name of Currer Bell in 1847 and was an immediate and smashing success. It was followed, successfully, by *Shirley* in 1849 but Charlotte Brontë can have taken little pleasure in her growing fame; Branwell, Emily, and Anne all died of tuberculosis between September 1848 and May 1849. The unusually closely knit and self-sufficient family was gone. Charlotte and her father lived on together. In 1853, she published *Villette*, one of the most Balzakian of English novels, a neurotic romance that uses fantastic and grotesque effects sparingly to heighten an emotionally exacerbated realism in a most striking way. In 1854, Charlotte Brontë finally ceased to rebuff the advances of her father's curates, who had been proposing to her in relays all her adult life, and married the most persistent, the Rev. Arthur Nicholls, in 1854. Less than a year later, she was dead, possibly from tuberculosis, possibly from complications of pregnancy.

Few lives have been more unrelievedly tragic. It is salutory to discover that her novels, for all their stormy emotionalism, their troubling atmosphere of psycho-drama, their sense of a life lived on the edge of the nerves, are also full of fun, and of a wonderfully sensuous response to landscape, music, painting, and to the small, domestic pleasures of a warm fire, hot tea, the smell of fresh-baked bread.

There is also a spirit of defiance always at large. It is an oddly alarmed defiance; Charlotte Brontë's frail yet indomitable heroines burn with injustice, then collapse with nervous exhaustion after they have passionately made their point. All the same, Matthew Arnold put his finger on it when he expostulated that her mind 'contains nothing but hunger, and rebellion, and rage'. As orphaned children, as Englishwomen abroad, as wandering beggars, as governesses, as lovers, Charlotte Brontë's heroines do not know their place. They suffer from a cosmic insecurity that starts in the nursery. Their childhoods are full of pain.

The first relation with the family, the elementary institution of authority, is often distorted or displaced. After the infant Jane suffers a kind of fit, or seizure, while being punished by her Aunt Reed, the local apothecary is sent for: 'I felt an inexpressible relief, a soothing conviction of protection and security, when I knew there was a stranger in the room.'

Aunt Reed's husband, who might have protected her, is dead. Jane's own father is long dead. When she is befriended by the Rivers family, they are freshly in mourning for their father. *Jane Eyre* is a novel full of dead fathers. As if to pre-empt the possibility of his own demise, Mr Rochester himself staunchly denies paternity – he refuses to accept little Adèle Varens, daughter of a former mistress, as his own child, causing Jane to cry out protectively: 'Adèle is not answerable for either her mother's faults or yours: I have a regard for her, and now that I know that she is, in a sense, parentless – forsaken by her mother and disowned by you, sir – I shall cling closer to her than before.'

The question of whether Rochester actually *is* Adèle's father is left interestingly moot. But something curious happens at the end of the novel. After Rochester has been blinded and maimed, we are left with the image of himself and Jane, a grizzled, ageing, blind man, lead by the hand by a young girl (Jane is young enough to be his daughter). Suddenly, astonishingly, they look like Oedipus and Antigone, having ascended to the very highest level of mythic resonance. (Charlotte hastily restores the sight in one of his eyes before the first child of the union is born, and that is an interesting thing for her to do, too.) Jane has transformed Rochester into a father. Her mediation lets him live.

Jane Eyre begins, magnificently, with a clarion call for the rights of children. Jane, at ten years old, squares up to her Aunt Reed, who has signally failed to care for the orphaned child left in her charge.

> 'I will never call you aunt again as long as I live. I will never come to see you when I am grown up; and if any one asks me how I liked you, and how you treated me, I will say the very thought of you makes me sick, and that you treated me with miserable cruelty.'

No child in fiction ever stood up for itself like that before. Burning with injustice, the infant Jane, true child of the romantic period, demands love as a right: 'You think I have no feelings, and that I can do without one bit of love or kindness: but I cannot live so.'

Indeed, she specifies love as a precondition of existence. And not love in a vacuum, love as a selfless, unreciprocated devotion, either. There isn't a trace of selfless devotion anywhere in *Jane Eyre*, unless it is the selfless devotion of the missionary, St John Rivers, to himself. After all, it is very easy to love, and may be done in private without inconveniencing the object of one's affections in the least; that is the way that plain, clever parson's daughters are supposed to do it, anyway. But Jane *wants to be loved*, as if, without reciprocity, love can't exist. This is why, towards the end of the novel, she will reject St John Rivers' proposal of marriage although he has half-mesmerised her into subservience to him. She rejects him because he doesn't love her. It is as simple as that.

It is also exhilarating, almost endearing, to note that, in spite of the sentimental pietism which Charlotte Brontë falls back on almost as a form of self-defence against her genuinely transgressive impulses, she can also – see the entire treatment of Blanche Ingrams, Jane's alleged rival for Mr Rochester's affections – be something of a bitch.

Although the sober, *The Professor*, published posthumously in 1857, was the first novel that Charlotte Brontë completed, it is *Jane Eyre* that exhibits all the profligate imagination we associate with youth. However much it may have been written with a bitter ambition for fame foremost in the author's mind, the novel remains firmly rooted in the furious dreams of a passionate young woman whose life never quite matched up to her own capacity for experience. It is the author's unfulfilled desire that makes *Jane Eyre* so haunting.

The writing that the Brontë children had engaged in since childhood was of a very particular kind. They spent their adolescence constructing together a comprehensive alternative to the post-romantic world of steam engine and mill chimney they were doomed to inhabit. Charlotte and Branwell chronicled a territory they named Angria; Anne and Emily constructed the history of the island of Gondal. This alternative universe, 'with its emperors and its seas, with its minerals and its birds and its fish', just like the encyclopedic other-world in Borges' marvellous story, 'Tlon, Uqbar, Orbis Tertius', was so intensely imagined that sometimes its landscapes and inhabitants pushed aside the real ones that surrounded their creators:

> Never shall I, Charlotte Brontë, forget . . . how distinctly I, sitting in the school-room at Roe-head, saw the Duke of Zamorna . . . his black horse turned loose grazing among the heather, the moonlight so mild and exquisitely tranquil, sleeping upon that vast and vacant road . . . I was quite gone. I had really utterly forgot where I was and all the gloom and cheerlessness of my situation. I felt myself breathing quick and short as I beheld the Duke lifting up his sable crest which undulated as the plume of a hearse waves to the wind . . . [1]

At nineteen, Charlotte Brontë had lost her heart to a creature of her own invention, the irresistibly seductive, sexually generous Duke of Zamorna, a Byronic *homme fatal* untouched by irony. It is easy to say that real life never could have lived up to this, that Charlotte Brontë's wonderfully discontented art comes out of a kind of Bovaryism, a bookish virgin's yearning for a kind of significance that experience rarely, if ever, provides. Jane Eyre, before her discontent is made glorious summer by the charismatic Rochester, who himself bears some resemblance to the Duke of Zamorna, often allows herself to 'open my inward ear to a tale that was never ended – a tale my imagination created, and narrated continuously; quickened with all of incident, life, fire, feeling, that I desired, and had not in my actual existence'.

But Charlotte Brontë *did* possess a sophistication, a temperament, that could, perhaps, be equalled by her immediate family, but by precious few other Englishmen and women of the period. Thackeray, whom she admired, patronised her. 'The poor little woman of genius! The fiery little eager brave tremulous homely-faced creature!' he said, as if passion was, by rights, the perquisite only of those blessed with conventional good looks. But Europe was full of artists exhibiting the same temperament as Charlotte Brontë – Berlioz, Delacroix, De Musset. Charlotte Brontë herself admired George Sand. Yet she went to Brussels to study French, not Paris, and her Protestantism, which can amount to fanaticism, springs into operation as soon as she arrives in a Catholic country, as if to protect herself from *giving herself away*. Charlotte Brontë's fiction inhabits the space between passion and repression. She knows she must not have the thing she wants; she also knows it will be restored to her in her dreams.

What would have happened if Charlotte Brontë really had met Byron? Although I doubt a spark would have flared between those two; Claire Clairmont and Lady Caroline Lamb had taught Byron to steer clear of women of passion. But Shelley, now . . .

Byron and Shelley were dead and gone by the time Charlotte Brontë was growing up in those dour, Northern school-rooms. Yet those James Deans of the romantic period burned their images of beauty, genius, and freedom on the minds of more than a generation. If the Byronic hero contributed in no small measure to the character of Edward Fairfax de Rochester, the man whom Jane habitually, in masochistic ecstasy, calls 'my master', he also contributed towards the ambitions of the young woman who invented Rochester.

But there is more to it than that. Mr Rochester's name irresistibly recalls that of the great libertine poet of the Restoration, the Earl of Rochester – the 'de' is as elegant a touch as the umlaut in Brontë – and he is evidently libido personified. Not only is his a history of sexual licence but he is also consistently identified with fire and warmth just as Jane's other suitor, St John Rivers, is associated with coldness and marble.

If Rochester is libido personified, then libido is genderless. He is not only the object of Jane's desire but also the *objectification* of Jane's desire. *Jane Eyre* is the story of this young woman's desire and how she learns to name it. Name it, and tame it. Charlotte Brontë cuts him down to size – literally so. Rochester loses a hand and an eye as well as his first wife, that swollen, raging, purple-skinned part of himself, before Charlotte Brontë finally consents to mate him to Jane. But, in taming him, Charlotte is also taming Jane, domesticating her passions, banishing the Duke of Zamorna from the family hearth forever.

If Rochester is the id, however, then St John Rivers is the super-ego. The second of Jane's suitors, this chaste and austere clergyman, attracts less attention than Mr Rochester and his unconventional ménage (which comprises not only a deranged wife but also a putative daughter). But he represents the opposite pole to Rochester; Rochester is love and St John Rivers marriage. He is the super-ego. And he is monstrous.

When Jane finds refuge with Rivers' sisters at Moor House after she has fled Thornfield Hall, St John himself arrives as the perfect antidote to the squalor and mess of passion. Indeed, he is the antidote to the squalor and mess of life itself. There is an element of sadism in Rochester's emotional teasing of Jane, in the bizarre episode where he dresses up as a gypsy woman and quizzes her about her secrets, for example. But St John Rivers is a different kind of sadist, one who regards his lust for domination as a God-given right.

Rochester is a libertine but, worse than that, a cad, as well. He exhibits his caddishness not only because of his actual treatment of the first Mrs Rochester, but – as Jane is quick to note – because of the way he talks about her. It should be said that Jane is wise not to trust Rochester. She exhibits an exemplary perceptiveness, and, indeed, an exemplary female solidarity in her refusal to trust him. When Rochester finally confesses the truth about the existence of his hated but legal and living wife, Jane says, reasonably and also honourably, that the poor woman 'cannot help being mad':

'If you were mad, do you think I should hate you?'
'I do indeed, sir.'

One cannot imagine Emma Bovary, in a similar situation,

saying that. Some things about life you can't learn from books. Jane Eyre may burn with the longing for love, but that does not prevent her from making a bleak, clear-eyed appraisal of the realities of the situation. Rochester invites her to live with him in the South of France, not as his wife but as a companion; she turns down that offer with alacrity. She speculates that, when he is tired of her, he will dismiss her and, after that, talk about her in the contemptuous way he has told her about his other women. 'I now hate the recollection of the time I passed with Celine, Giacinta and Clara.' Yet he must have told each one of them he loved her, once upon a time, and Charlotte Brontë cannot think of a good reason why a libertine and sensualist like Rochester, who has fixed upon tiny, plain, uncanny-looking Jane because of her difference, should not, one day, some day, want a difference from that difference.

The fire burns his wife and burns his home and disfigures him and, after that, he ceases to be a cad and becomes . . . something else. A husband. A father. He loses the shaggy grandeur with which unfulfilled desire has dowered him. There is a dying fall, a sadness, to the last chapter, the one that begins so famously: 'Reader, I married him.' Marriage is not the point of their relationship, after all.

However St John Rivers is even worse than a cad; he is a prig. Turning his back on his own sensual response to the beautiful heiress, Rosamond Oliver, he concentrates all his energies on subjugating Jane, indeed, on killing her spirit. He succeeds in inspiring her with his enthusiasm for the mission field, although he seems the very type of missionary who, one hopes, will end in the pot. He virtually forces her to learn Hindustani. ('Rivers taught you Hindostanee?' says Rochester, when he and Jane are reunited, echoing the incredulity of the reader.) His intention is to bully this young woman into marriage. He says to her one of the nastiest things a fictional man ever said to a fictional woman: 'God and nature intended you for a missionary's wife.' Jane would gladly accompany him to India as a companion; she foresees none of the same problems that would have arisen had she accompanied Rochester to Marseilles. But St John Rivers will admit of no such impropriety. He will marry her, without – and Charlotte Brontë is perfectly explicit about it – any kind of sexual feeling for Jane on his part, almost as if to mortify his flesh.

Yet Jane knows he would feel it necessary, once they were married, to perform his duty as a husband. She is fully aware of what this would entail and the prospect freezes her blood. She describes her idea of what their married life would be in a passage of chrystalline perceptiveness:

> . . . yet, if forced to be his wife, I can imagine the possibility of conceiving an inevitable, strange, torturing kind of love for him; because he is so talented; and there is often a certain heroic grandeur in his look, manner and conversation. In that case my lot would be unspeakably wretched. He would not want me to love him; and if I showed the feeling, he would make me sensible that it was a superfluity, unrequired by him, unbecoming in me.

The clarity and strength of Charlotte Brontë's observation and sensitivity is astonishing. She uses melodrama and excess to say what otherwise could not be said. Yet *Jane Eyre* remains an intensely personal novel, with a quality of private reverie about it, of a young girl's erotic reverie, that disguises itself as romantic dreaming to evade discovery and self-censorship. There is a tender embarrassment about re-reading *Jane Eyre* in middle age; one wants the world to be kind, not to Jane, but to the girl who invented Jane, and, in doing so, set out so vividly her hopes and fears and longings on the page. We know the world was not particularly kind to her, that fame came mixed with grief and death. And her achievement is singular; in *Jane Eyre* she endowed a modern heroine, a young woman not dissimilar from Teresa Hawkins in Christina Stead's *For Love Alone*, not dissimilar from the early heroines of Doris Lessing, with the power and force, the extra-dimensional quality, of a legendary being. If she had not died so young, the course of English fiction would have been utterly different. Anything would have been possible.

(1990)

David Kunzle: *Fashion and Fetishisms*

David Kunzle starts off thinking about corsets from an angle which, I'm ashamed to say, had never occurred to me. It may be described most simply, thus: that women, as a whole, are *not* silly and, when they do things that, at first glance, may seem to be silly, like wearing extremely tight-fitting corsets, or tottering along in stiletto-heeled shoes, there is, at base, an impeccable, if unconscious, logic to it; that these voluntary self-mutilations are a paradoxical expression of sexual defiance and gender self-esteem.

Kunzle doesn't put it quite like that, but this is one message that may be drawn from his book, and it shocks me to think that, for so long, I went along with the standard feminist line on sexually specific clothing – that it showed women were the mere dupes of male fancy. How has it come about that feminists have picked up on the masculine notion that those women who aren't self-confessed feminists don't know what they're doing, half the time?

However, Kunzle's book is not an apologia for the corset but an argument, conducted with awe-inspiring sobriety, about the role of certain practices involving the distortion of the female (and sometimes the male) form that become exaggerated at certain moments in history. His historical range extends from the wasp-waisted athletes of ancient Crete (both male and female, and they all wore padded codpieces, too), to Mrs Ethel Granger, of Peterborough, who has latterly entered the *Guinness Book of Records* as the possessor of the World's Smallest Waist (13 inches).

Nevertheless, the nineteenth century was the reign of Queen Corset, when everybody wore corsets, only some people wore them with more dedication than others. And this is the period in which Kunzle is able to elaborate most convincingly on his general predicate that tight-lacing was practised 'by women, always the disenfranchised *vis-à-vis* men, aspiring to social power by manipulating a sexuality which the patriarchy found threatening'.

He is interested primarily in excessive corseting, when, as he says in his Preface, '"Fashion" (the culturally dominant mode of dress) and "fetishism" (the individual or group redirection of the sexual instinct on to an aspect of dress) collide and merge in the unique phenomenon of tight-lacing'. A practice that has never, precisely, been fashionable, since exhibitionism is always beyond fashion, though corsets were a European universal until this century.

He also provides a running historical commentary on the related sub-class of excessively high heels, which make a woman look either a quivering sex object always deliciously about to fall flat on her face, an erotic spectacle in itself with all the connotations of the 'fallen woman', or else the epitome of sexual aggression, ready to trample some prone man underfoot.

These forms of 'body sculpture' – of modifying, sometimes dramatically so, the natural human shape – obviously fly in the face of nature and therefore cock an all-too-visible snook at that god in whose form we were created. The Christian pulpit, always quick to pick up hints of burgeoning female sexuality, has fulminated consistently against 'unnatural' dress, from the horned headdresses of the middle ages to toreador pants, and directed considerable ire against the close-fitting corset, although Kunzle illustrates an iron corset of the sixteenth century that looks like a penitential garment and perhaps was.

Suffering for God and being ugly in a hairshirt was all right, apparently; suffering for the devil with a wasp waist and frilly petticoats was not. The corset it is that makes a woman's body an erotic hour glass, all tits and bum, yet armoured with whale bone and impossible to get at without permission.

Repression gives birth to austere, solitary pleasures and, in the nineteenth century, extravagantly sexual forms of women's fashions – the crinoline, the bustle, both emphasising a tiny, if not tiny-tiny, waist – blossomed in an atmosphere of general sexual repression, in which a particular veil was drawn over the reality of female desire. Kunzle quotes a shocked physician who discovered a young girl masturbating with the aid of her corset. However, there is rather more to sexual satisfaction than simple orgasm.

He provides extensive descriptions from practising twentieth-century tight-lacing fetishists as to the physiological satisfactions of the practice, the voluptuous palpitations, the 'disembodied', almost mystical feeling, the sense of mastery and achievement. These tally with letters to nineteenth-century women's magazines elaborating on the painful pleasure of a 15-inch waist, the sensation of being erotically in control, as in horse-back riding, the correspondence between self-control, self-discipline, and the magical ability to control the world. He suggests a relation between tight-lacing and the current female plague of anorexia nervosa, in which the irritating female flesh is curbed by dietary methods, often by young women who feel there is more to life than the conventional female role but may not know precisely what that something more might be.

He cites a Victorian phrenologist, thus: 'Compression produces inflamation, retains the blood in the bowels and neighbouring organs and thereby inflames all the organs of the abdomen, which thereby excites amative desires . . . ' So *that* is the source of corset phobia! Especially since, once the corset has thoroughly awakened the sleeping demon in a woman's belly, the compressive organ itself will deal efficiently with the consequences. It was widely believed that tight-lacing procured abortion.

At this point, Kunzle's theory that tight-lacing was a means 'to protest the ever-breeding, child-centred mother' becomes hard to resist. And the foeticidal Victorian coquette, anxious to profit from her only capital, her body, by means of an upwardly socially mobile marriage or high-class prostitution, to do something, anything, to assert herself, becomes a sister under the skin.

Certainly, on the evidence Kunzle produces, fanatical nineteenth-century hatred of tight-lacing did not come from the female emancipation movement – which, after all, had far more important things to think of than what women did with their waistlines – but from those who saw women's primary function in terms of domestic labour and childbearing, both of which are activities contra-indicated by tight-lacing.

Renoir, celebrant of the 'natural' woman, spreading, naked, dumb, available for rape at any moment, hated and feared corsets.

He told his six-year-old son that women who wore them must inevitably suffer from dropped wombs. In his memoirs, Pierre says ' . . . this idea of the womb tumbling down gave me nightmares.' You bet. Hogarth, however, adored 'stays', out of a metaphysical passion for a perfect, sinuous, rococo, artificial 'line of beauty' that is better than the natural, since it is a human creation. Baudelaire always preferred art over nature, and particularly enjoyed seeing men in corsets.

One of Kunzle's most curious and interesting byways is his discussion of the military corset, the tight waists of Russian and Prussian heroes. In an appendix, he includes an interview (made in 1967) with an English baronet, a Member of Parliament for fifty years, who habitually wore a corset and found he always delivered a House of Commons speech better when supported.

Though often witty, Kunzle is never facetious, although facetiousness has often been the way of making these fetishistic items socially acceptable, and also of reducing their implicit menace, somehow transferring the responsibility for their effect from women back to men again. Advertising copy from the wasp-waist revival of the 1950s demonstrates this admirably: 'Steel hand in the velvet glove' (but not your own hand); 'How can you look so naughty and feel so nice?'

Most histories of costume are lightweight gossipy journalism. *Fashion and Fetishisms* is, however, exactly how it describes itself: a piece of social history, instinct with intellectual curiosity and spiritual generosity towards the human race and its various contradictory ways of asserting its humanity.

From the photograph on the back-flap, it looks – though I could be wrong, and if so, I am sorry – as if David Kunzle may have donned, if not a waspy, at least a virile and inconspicuous corset of the 'military' type for the benefit of the camera.

(1982)

· 32 ·

Christina Stead

To open a book, any book, by Christina Stead and read a few pages is to be at once aware that one is in the presence of greatness. Yet this revelation is apt to precipitate a sense of confusion, of strangeness, of anxiety, not only because Stead has a rare capacity to flay the reader's sensibilities, but also because we have grown accustomed to the idea that we live in pygmy times. To discover that a writer of so sure and unmistakable a stature is still amongst us, and, more, produced some of her most remarkable work as recently as the Sixties and Seventies, is a chastening thing, especially since those two relatively recent novels – *Cotters' England* (1966) and *Miss Herbert (the Suburban Wife)* (1976) – contain extremely important analyses of postwar Britain, address the subject of sexual politics at a profound level, and have been largely ignored in comparison with far lesser novels such as Doris Lessing's *The Golden Notebook*. To read Stead, now, is to be reminded of how little, recently, we have come to expect from fiction. Stead is of that category of fiction writer who restores to us the entire world, in its infinite complexity and inexorable bitterness, and never asks if the reader wishes to be so furiously enlightened and instructed, but takes it for granted that this is the function of fiction. She is a kind of witness and a kind of judge, merciless, cruel, and unforgiving.

Stead has just reached the age of 80 and, according to Australian newspapers, is still writing. Born in Australia, she has lived in Britain, Europe, and the US and has written novels set in cities in various countries as if she were native to them all. This phenomenon of ubiquity helps to explain her relative obscurity:

177

she appears to acknowledge no homeland and has therefore been acknowledged by none until her return to her native country after almost a half-century of absence. Lawrence, in exile, remained British to the core; Joyce took Dublin in his back pocket wherever he went. Stead becomes absorbed into the rhythms of life wherever she finds herself. Furthermore, although she has always written from a profound consciousness of what it is to be a woman, she writes, as they say, 'like a man': that is, she betrays none of the collusive charm which is supposedly a mark of the feminine genius. As a result, because she writes *as* a woman, not *like* a woman, Randall Jarrell could say of *The Man Who Loved Children* (1940): 'a male reader worries: "Ought I to be a man?"'

Jarrell thought that *The Man Who Loved Children* was by far Stead's best novel and believed its commercial and critical failure blighted her subsequent development. (Why did he say that? Was it revenge for having his machismo deflated?) However, at least three of her other novels – I'd say *For Love Alone* (1945), *A Little Tea, A Little Chat* (1948) and *Cotters' England* (1945) – equal that novel, and in some ways surpass it, while *Letty Fox: Her Luck* (1946) is, unusually for Stead, a fully achieved comic novel of a most original kind.

However, it wasn't surprising that *The Man Who Loved Children* should acquire the romantic reputation of a unique masterpiece, especially when it was the only novel of hers in print. The single-minded intensity of its evocation of domestic terror gives it a greater artistic cohesion than Stead's subsequent work, which tends toward the random picaresque. And Stead permits herself a genuinely tragic resolution. The ravaged harridan, Henny, the focus of the novel, dies in a grand, fated gesture, an act of self-immolation that, so outrageous has been her previous suffering, is almost a conventional catharsis. One feels that all Henny's previous life has been a preparpation for her sudden, violent departure from it and, although the novel appals, it also, artistically, satisfies, in a way familiar in art. Later, Stead would not let her readers off the hook of life so easily. She won't allow us the dubious consolations of pity and terror again.

Since Stead went home, she has become more and more known as an Australian writer. This geographical placement is, of course, only right and proper and geographically correct, and contains within it the enticing notion of a specific kind of post-colonial sensibility which might serve as a context for her illusionless power. But only one of her novels has a wholly Australian setting, and that the earliest, *Seven Poor Men of Sydney* (1934). Even here, she has already established her characteristic milieu as that of the rootless urban intelligensia, a milieu as international as it is peculiar to our century. Teresa Hawkins in *For Love Alone* is the only major Australian character in Stead's later fiction, and Teresa is the most striking of these birds of passage, who sometimes become mercenaries of an ideology, sometimes end up as flotsam and jetsam.

Stead is also one of the great articulators of family life. There is no contradiction here. Stead's families – the Pollitts in *The Man Who Loved Children*, the Foxes in *Letty Fox: Her Luck*, the Hawkinses in *For Love Alone*, the Cotters of *Cotters' England* – are social units that have outlived the original functions of protection and mutual aid and grown to be seedbeds of pathology. These are families in a terminal state of malfunction, families you must flee from in order to preserve your sanity, families it is criminal folly to perpetuate – and, on the whole, Stead's women eschew motherhood like the plague. (Stead's loathing of the rank futility of home and hearth is equalled, in literature, only by that expressed by the Marquis de Sade.) These are degenerated, cannibal families, in which the very sacrament of the family, the communal meal when all are gathered together, is a Barmecide feast at which some family member, wife or child, is on the emotional menu. One characteristic and gruesomely memorable family dinner, with its exaggerated hysteria and elements of high, diabolic farce, is that in *Cotters' England*, at which raw chicken and dementia are served. Once away from the nest, Stead's birds of passage tend to eat in the neutral environments of restaurants – as do the runaway lovers in *The Beauties and Furies*.

These rancid, cancerous homes may provide a useful apprenticeship in the nature of tyranny (several times in *The Man Who Loved Children* Stead stresses that children have 'no rights' within the family): that is all. The only escape is a plunge into an exponential whirl of furnished rooms, cheap hotels, constant travelling, chance liaisons, the blessed indifference of strangers. Stead's families, in fact, produce those rootless, sceptical displaced persons she also describes, who have no country but a state of mind, and yet who might, due to their very displacement and disaffection, be able to make new beginnings.

In *For Love Alone*, we actually see Teresa Hawkins performing this trajectory, from the mutilating claustrophobia of her father's house – 'home' in Stead is almost always the patriarchal cage – into that homelessness which is the prerequisite of freedom. In *The Beauties and Furies* this process founders. Elvira leaves her husband in London for a lover in Paris, but Elvira is a dreamily narcissistic, emotionally contingent being, who scarcely knows what freedom is and who will, inevitably, return home. (There is a remarkable consistency in Stead. Elvira, the romantic, self-obsessed Englishwoman, of this, one of her earliest novels, has much in common with the Eleanor Herbert of her latest.) But Stead does not direct us to condemn Elvira – nor to pity her. Stead's greatest moral quality as a novelist is her lack of pity. As Blake said,

> Pity would be no more,
> If we did not make somebody poor,

and, for Stead, pity is otiose, a self-indulgent luxury that obscures the real nature of our relations with our kind. To disclose that real nature has always been her business. Essentially, she is engaged in the exposition of certain perceptions as to the nature of human society. She does this through the interplay of individuals both with one another and with the institutions that we created but which now seem to dominate us. Marriage; the family; money.

She has, obviously, from the very beginning – her first publication was a collection of short stories modelled on the *Decameron* – been a writer of almost megalomaniac ambition. The literary project of Louie, the unnatural daughter of *The Man Who Loved Children*, was to compose for an adored teacher 'the Aiden cycle . . . a poem of every conceivable form and also every conceivable metre in the English language', all in Miss Aiden's praise. This seems the sort of project that would attract Stead herself. Hers may even be the kind of ambition that is nourished by neglect, of which she has received sufficient. (Had people believed Cassandra, she would have known something had gone badly wrong.) To read some of Stead's more possessed and driven novels – *Cotters' England* and *A Little Tea, A Little Chat*, in particular – is to be reminded of what Blake said about his Bible of Hell: 'which the world shall have whether they will or no.' If, as seems the case, we are now ready to accept Stead as one of the great writers of our time, this does not mean the times are going well.

It is possible to be a great novelist – that is, to render a veracious account of your times – and a bad writer – that is, an incompetent practitioner of applied linguistics. Like Theodore Dreiser. Conversely, good writers – for example, Borges – often prefer to construct alternative metaphysical universes based on the Word. If you read only the novels Stead wrote after *The Man Who Loved Children*, it would seem that she belonged to the Dreiser tendency. She patently does not subscribe to any metaphysics of the Word. The work of her maturity is a constant, agitated reflection upon our experience in *this* world. For her, language is not an end-in-itself in the current, post-modernist or 'mannerist' mode, but a mere tool, and a tool she increasingly uses to hew her material more and more roughly. Nor does she see the act of storytelling as a self-reflexive act. Therefore, as a composer of narrative, she can be amazingly slipshod. She will allow careless lapses in continuity. People can change names, parentage, age, occupation from page to page, as though she corrected nothing. They can also slip through holes in the narrative and disappear. Miss Aiden is honoured, arrives for a typically vile family supper with the Pollitts, and is then written out of the script like a soap-opera character with a contract elsewhere. All this would be unforgivable if, in Stead, narrative mattered, much. It does not. Her narrative is almost *tachiste*: she composes it like a blind man throwing paint against a wall. Her narratives shape themselves, as our lives seem to do.

Interestingly enough, she started her career as a very mannered writer indeed. *The Salzburg Tales* of 1934 is a collection of glittering, grotesque short fictions, parables and allegories not dissimilar to the *Seven Gothic Tales* that Isak Dinesen published in the same year. *The Salzburg Tales* are contrived with a lush, jewelled exquisiteness of technique that recurs in *The Beauties and Furies*, which first appeared in 1936. At one point in that novel, Coromandel, the antique-dealer's daughter, recites just such a little Gothic tale, 'The Story of Hamadryad'. Oliver's adventures in the Club of the Somnambulists at the end of the novel and the dreams of several of the characters have a similar overblown, highly decorated, romantic extravagance. It is rather unusual for Stead's characters to dream with quite such abandon – 'She saw a rod with two headless snakes emerging from a dusky ivory egg . . . ' – and it is tempting to hypothesise some influence from the surrealists, especially since this novel takes place in a Paris that is decidedly Paul Eluard's *capitale de la douleur*. And, at this stage, Stead is assimilating influences from every conceivable source. She is a self-consciously brilliant young writer. *The Beauties and Furies* is evidence of a love-affair with language which produces felicities such as: 'Not a blade of grass moved and not a bird flew down the perspective of the great water, but, under thickety trees, officers and children skated with coloured cloaks and gloves over a pond. Beyond, dazzling and enchanted, lay the leafless forest.' Very finely crafted, too, though this love-affair can induce logorrhoea, and the same novel contains much purple: 'Imprisoned by her marauding hair, she lay, and turned dark, silent eyes upon me.' And so, on. Fine writing must have come easily to her; roughness, ungainliness, ferocity were qualities for which she had to strive.

In *House of All Nations* (1938), which comes after *The Beauties and Furies*, the puppy-fat is already beginning to fall away from the bare bones of Stead's mature style, and of her mature purpose, for this is a novel straightforwardly about the root of all evil: that is, banking. However, the complications of its plotting recall the Jacobean drama at its most involuted, so that it is quite difficult to tell exactly what is going on. In fact, the elaborately fugal plotting of *House of All Nations* is beginning to dissolve of its own accord, just because too much is going on, into the arbitrary flux of event that characterises Stead's later novels. And she is beginning to write, not like a craftsman, but like an honest worker.

At the time of *The Man Who Loved Children*, she relinquished all the capacity of the language of her narrative to bewitch and seduce. But Sam Pollitt, the father almighty or Nobodaddy of that novel, uses a babbling, improvised, pseudo-language, a sort of Pollitt creole, full of cant words – 'cawf' for coffee, 'munch-time', 'orfus' – with which to bemuse, delight, and snare his brood. This is the soft, slippery, charming language of seduction itself. Louie invents an utterly opaque but grammatically impeccable language of her own and confronts him with a one-act play in it, acted by her siblings. 'Mat, rom garrots im.' (In translation: 'Mother, father is strangling me.') Sam is very angry. Louie's ugly language is vengeance. Stead does not go as far as Louie. Her later style is merely craggy, unaccommodating, a simple, functional, often unbeautiful means to an end, which can still astonish by its directness: 'With old Mrs Cotter after the funeral, time had been, time was and time might be again, but it was all one time: she knew no difference between the living and the dead.' So, without pathos or elaboration, she depicts senility in *Cotters' England*.

Since she is technically an expressionist writer, in whose books madmen scream in deserted landscapes, a blue light turns a woman into the image of a vampire and a lesbian party takes on the insanely heightened melodrama of a drawing by George Grosz, the *effect* is the thing, not the language that achieves it. But there is more to it than that. The way she finally writes is almost as if she were showing you by demonstration that style itself is a lie in action, that language is an elaborate confidence trick designed to lull us into acceptance of the intolerable, just as Sam Pollitt uses it on his family, that words are systems of deceit. And that truth is not a quality inherent in any kind of discourse, but a way of looking at things: that truth is not an aspect of reality but a test of reality. So, more and more, Stead concentrates on dialogue, on language in use as camouflage or subterfuge – dialogue, or rather serial monologue, for Stead's characters rarely listen to one another sufficiently to enable them to conduct dialogues together, although they frequently enjoy rows of a polyphonic nature, in which it is not possible for anybody to hear anybody else. If the storytellers in *The Salzburg Tales* reveal their personalities through the gnomic and discrete fables they tell, Stead's later characters thunder out great arias and recitatives of self-deceit, self-justification, attempted manipulation, and it is up to the reader to compare what they say with what they do and draw his or her conclusions as to what is really going on. The monologue is Stead's forte, dramatic monologues comparable to those of Robert Browning.

In *Letty Fox: Her Luck* (1946) she extends this form of the dramatic monologue to the length of an entire novel. It is an elaborate imitation autobiography almost in the manner of Defoe, a completely successful impersonation of an American woman, in which we are invited to extract bare facts from Letty's account of her own life – the life of a 'generous fool' who has no luck with men because of the careless magnificence with which she throws herself away on them – and construct from the bare facts the *real* life of Letty Fox. Letty, it turns out, is joylessly promiscuous, hysterically demanding, a self-righteous bitch, and a heartless betrayer. But Letty does not know any of these things about herself and when, as from time to time happens, her friends tax her with them, she hotly denies them. The disjuncture between what she is and what she thinks she is is wonderfully comic. It is, curiously, not comic at Letty's expense. Letty finally does no harm to anyone but herself, and Stead graciously allots her the best one-liner in her entire *oeuvre*: 'Radicalism is the opium of the middle-classes.' Letty is as full of bad faith as Nellie Cotter but is saved by her unpretentiousness and by what Stead calls somewhere the 'inherent outlawry' in women. Letty is not named after the predatory and raffish fox for nothing and if her only ambition is to marry, which defines her limited aspirations, it takes two to tie the knot. Letty longs for children and is only truly happy when pregnant, but any social worker would recommend a termination when, at the novel's end, we leave her pregnant, in a cheap hotel, with a penniless playboy husband – all she has finally managed to ensnare. The final joke is that this greedy vixen of an amateur prostitute will, as a wife, be the perfect poacher turned gamekeeper: all her life she has been a matriarch manquée – hence her ill-success as a free woman – and now the matriarch has found herself and can begin. The amoral predator will become the solid citizen. Why rob banks when you can run them, to paraphrase one of the maxims in Brecht's *Threepenny Opera*, and Letty is too dishonest to live for long outside the law.

Others in Stead's gallery of monsters of existential bad faith – Sam Pollitt, Nellie Cotter, Robert Grant in *A Little Tea, A Little Chat* – are not treated so genially. They are killers. They precipitate suicide and madness in those who come close to them. Letty uses bad faith to bolster her faltering self-respect: these pernicious beings base their entire self-respect on bad faith. The mouths of these grotesque, nodding carnival heads are moving all the time as they rage, bluster, cajole, manipulate, provoke, enlightening us as to what bad faith does.

Stead's fictional method obviously presupposes a confidence in the importance of fiction as the exposition of the real structures on which our lives are based. It follows that she has gained a reputation as a writer of naturalism, so much so that, in her Introduction to the Virago edition of *The Beauties and Furies*, Hilary Bailey seems disconcerted that 'this great writer of naturalism' should have produced a novel so resistant to a naturalist reading. (Any novel in which a prostitute advertises her wares by reciting the poetry of Baudelaire is scarcely in the tradition of George Gissing.) Stead is certainly not a writer of naturalism nor of social realism, and if her novels are read as novels about our lives, rather than about the circumstances that shape our lives, they are bound to disappoint, because the naturalist or high-bourgeois mode works within the convention that there exists such a thing as 'private life'. In these private lives, actions are informed by certain innate inner freedoms and, however stringent the pressures upon the individual, there is always a little margin of autonomy which could be called 'the self'. For Stead, however, 'private life' is itself a socially determined fiction, the 'self' is a mere foetus of autonomy which may or may not prove viable, and 'inner freedom', far from being an innate quality, is a precariously held intellectual position that may be achieved only at the cost of enormous struggle, often against the very grain of what we take to be human feeling.

Teresa Hawkins achieves selfhood only through a fanatical, half-crazed ordeal of self-imposed poverty and an act of willed alienation which takes her across half the world, from Australia to England. But this ordeal does not prepare Teresa for any reconciliation with the world: it only toughens her up for what is going to happen next. Louie, in *The Man Who Loved Children*, plots her parents' murder and succeeds in abetting her step-mother's death to a point beyond complicity. Then she runs away, leaving a houseful of small children to the tender mercies of Sam Pollitt. That is what Louie must do, in order to enter the fragile state of freedom-in-potential which is all Stead will offer in the way of hope. (She sometimes reminds me of what Kafka said to Max Brod: 'There *is* hope – but not for us.') But many, in fact most, of Stead's characters remain trapped in the circumstances which have produced them. These include Sam Pollitt, Letty Fox, Nellie Cooke and her brother, Robert Grant and his blonde, fatal mistress – and the eponymous 'Miss Herbert, the

Suburban Wife'. (*Miss Herbert* is one of the oddest novels and, after much thought, I take it to be a reversion to certain allegorical elements present in her earliest writing and always latent in it: to be nothing more nor less than a representation of the home life of Britannia from the Twenties until almost the present day.) The lovers in *The Beauties and Furies* are incapable of responding to the challenge of their romantic attachment: they drift, vacillate, betray one another and all in a kind of lapse of consciousness – like the sleepwalkers their friend Marpurgo says they all are. 'I prefer to be a somnambulist. I walk on the edge of precipices safely. Awake, I tremble.' Earlier, Elvira has said: 'I am a dead soul; life is too heavy for me to lift.' Happily for them, they never wake; happily for her, she never gets sufficient grip on life to give it a good shove.

The hard edges and sharp spikes of Stead's work are rarely, if ever, softened by the notion that things might be, generally, other than they are. It is tempting to conclude that she does not think much of the human race, but it is rather that she is appalled by the human condition. It is illuminating that Teresa, in *For Love Alone*, says to herself, near the end of the novel: 'I only have to do what is supposed to be wrong and I have a happiness that is barely credible.' Teresa has freely chosen to be unfaithful to her beloved lover, to follow her own desire. To become free, she has exercised her will; to remain free, she follows her desires. Stead rarely states her subversive intent as explicitly as this, nor often suggests that the mind-forged manacles of the human condition are to be so easily confounded. But when Teresa meditates, 'It was easy to see how upsetting it would be if women began to love freely', she is raising the question of female desire, of women's sexuality as action and as choice, of the assertion of sexuality as a right, and this question, to which she returns again and again in various ways, is at the core of Stead's work. The latter part of *For Love Alone*, the section in London where Teresa learns to love freedom, is rendered as a mass of dense argument within Teresa herself, unlike the discussion of women and marriage that occupies most of the earlier, Australian section of the book, where it is dramatised through the experiences of women in Teresa's circle. As a result, the triumph of desire simply does not strike the reader as vividly as the early grisly *tableaux vivants* of repression, such as Malfi's wedding. Perhaps Stead found this subject of the triumph of desire almost too important to be rendered as pure fiction; it is the exultant end of Teresa's ordeal.

For Love Alone is an account of a woman's fight for the right to love in freedom, which the anarchist Emma Goldman claimed as 'the most vital right'. (All Teresa's meditations on free union recall Goldman.) This is a fight we see one woman, Teresa herself, win: Teresa, who has the name of a saint, and also – Hawkins – kinship with a bird of prey noted for its clear vision. Stead then published *Letty Fox: Her Luck*, a crazy comedy about a girl who fights, and fights dirty, to get a ring on her finger. It is as if Stead were saying: 'There is Teresa, yes: but there is also Letty.' ('Letty Marmalade', as she signs herself, 'Always-in-a-Jam'.) It is as if the successive novels were parts of one long argument.

Stead's work always has this movement, always contains a movement forward, and then a withdrawal to a different position. *A Little Tea, A Little Chat*, her New York novel of 1948, presents us with another kind of woman: the thoroughly venal Barbara Kent, who is depicted almost exclusively from the outside. She is a mystery, with a complicated but largely concealed past, and she does not say much. She is like a secret agent from the outlawry of women, on a mission to destroy – but that is not her conscious intention. She and the shark-like war-profiteer, Robert Grant, form a union of true minds. They are both entrepreneurs, although Barbara Kent's only capital is her erotic allure. However, she is able to, as they say, screw him. Grant, for himself, screws everything that moves. The novel makes a seamless equation between sexual exploitation and economic exploitation. It thoroughly trashes all the social and economic relations of the USA. It etches in acid an impressive picture of New York as the city of the damned. It is also, as is all Stead, rich in humour of the blackest kind. It occurs to me that Stead has a good deal in common with Luis Buñuel, if it is possible to imagine a Buñuel within a lapsed Protestant tradition. A Calvinist Buñuel, whose belief in grace has survived belief in God.

However, this definitive account of a New York fit to be destroyed by fire from heaven is followed, in 1952, by *The People with the Dogs*, a description of a charming clan of New York intelligentsia who are modestly and unself-consciously virtuous and, although bonded by blood, are each other's best friends. Why is Stead playing happy families, all of a sudden? What, one wonders, is she trying to prove? Perhaps, that amongst the infinite contradictions of the USA, where anything is possible, even Utopia might be possible. In the USA, Utopias have certainly been attempted. The generously loving Oneida Massine, not matriarch – that would be too much – but principal aunt of this extended family, is named after one of the Utopian experimental communities of nineteenth-century America. And, like perfect communards, the Massines exist in harmony and tolerance with one another in a New York which has transformed itself from the City of Dreadful Night into the shabby, seedy, comfortable kind of place where birds of passage, Stead's habitual displaced *dramatis personae*, can all roost happily together – a city of strangers, which is to say a city with infinite possibilities. Tiring of the city, the Massines can enjoy pastoral retreats in an idyllic country house left them by a wise father who has had the decency to die long before the action begins. Stead seems to be saying that, given a small private income, beautiful people can lead beautiful lives, although the very circumstances which nourish their human kindness are those which succour the morally deformed profiteers and whores of *A Little Tea, A Little Chat*.

But there is something odd about *The People with the Dogs*, as if the dynamo of her energy, ill-supplied with the fuel of distaste, were flagging. She permits the Massines to be charming and even writes about them in a charming way, as if she herself has been moved by the beautiful promise of the Statue of Liberty, which always touches the heart no matter how often it is betrayed. There is nothing fraudulent about this novel, although, perhaps revealingly, it is exceedingly carelessly written. It would be interesting to know whether an unpublished novel, *I'm Dying Laughing*, set during the period of the HUAC investigations, was written before or after *The People with the Dogs*. According to a recent Australian newspaper article, this novel remained unpublished because of subsequent tragedies in the lives of the people involved. Certainly *The People with the Dogs* may be softening up the reader for a blow which, in the end, was never delivered.

An internal logic of dialectical sequels connects all Stead's work in a single massive argument on the themes of sexual relations, economic relations, and politics. There has been scarcely any large-scale critical appraisal in the UK, to my knowledge, though at the moment more of her fiction is in print, here, than at any single time before. If I were to choose an introductory motto for the collected works of Christina Stead, it would be, again, from Blake, from *The Marriage of Heaven and Hell*. It would be: 'Without contraries is no progression. Attraction and repulsion, Reason and Energy, Love and Hate, are necessary to Human existence.' One might take this as a point to begin the exploration of this most undervalued of our contemporaries.

(1982)

Christina Stead completed the original manuscript of *I'm Dying Laughing* in 1966 and was urged to revise it, to clarify its background of politics in the US in the Forties. For the next ten years, she worried away at the novel until at last she bequeathed a mass of confused material to her literary trustee, R. G. Geering, with instructions to publish it after her death.

The Stead connoisseur will note that Mr Geering's editorial hand is evident in an internal consistency far from characteristic of the novelist in her later years. *I'm Dying Laughing* is a mess, but a tidy mess. Characters do not change their names and appearances from page to page; events do not occur in an entirely arbitrary manner. All the same, it has that chaotic sense of flux that makes reading Stead somehow unlike reading fiction, that makes reading her seem like plunging into the mess of life itself, learning things, crashing against the desperate strategies of survival.

Thematically, it belongs with the group of political novels she completed much earlier, in the Forties – *Letty Fox, Her Luck, A Little Tea, A Little Chat, The People with the Dogs*, novels about the life and times of the American Left. *I'm Dying Laughing* concludes this sequence; it is a kind of obituary.

I'm Dying Laughing begins at a time that now seems scarcely credible, those far-off days when the Left was in fashion in the US. In those days, careerists joined the Party and the Party itself was a career. In 1935, Emily Wilkes and Stephen Howard meet, fall in love, and marry, to the strains of the Internationale.

They are superficially an odd couple. She, a big, gaudy, loquacious mid-Westerner with huge appetites and mighty laughter. He is the scion of an upper-crust East Coast family. He has abandoned his patrimony for the Party. The Howards' greatest bond is the struggle. They love passionately, with a quality of *amour fou* that already suggests a tragic outcome.

Emily is a writer, and Stead makes us believe this comic, greedy, self-deceiving, self-dramatising woman might possess some kind of genius, although her husband spends a good deal of time attempting to convince her she has only the profitable fluency of a hack. This does not make the portrait of their marriage any less gripping; it is one of the happiest if most tempestuous marriages in literature, and destructive precisely to the degree of their mutual passion.

Stephen, however, is more an all-purpose Marxist intellectual. Emily ritually defers to Stephen's superiority in dialectics but it is she who rakes in the money. The Roosevelt years are ripe for her home-spun tales of small-town life.

By the end of the war, they are in Hollywood, hobnobbing with a Communist élite of script-writers and living high on the hog's back. They are already very partial to a place on the hog's back.

In his Preface, R. G. Geering observes that *I'm Dying Laughing* is 'not a political novel in the manner of Koestler's *Darkness at Noon* or Orwell's *Nineteen Eighty-Four*'. Quite so. It is certainly not a novel about the bankruptcy of an ideology. Stead takes the validity of the ideology for granted. The world of her fiction is analysed as consistently from the left as Evelyn Waugh's world is described from the right. She gives her own characteristically bleak and sardonic account of the novel's protagonists: 'At the same time they wanted to be on the side of the angels, good Communists, good people, and also to be very rich. Well, of course . . . they came to a bad end.'

But the side of the angels has its drawbacks. The first full-scale set piece in the novel is a trial – an informal one, conducted after a good dinner in a spirit of the most sanctimonious self-righteousness, by a cabal of Hollywood Communists. The Howards, it seems, have been judged deviationist. Especially roaring, ranting Emily, who is 'making deviationist speeches every time she opens her mouth. It's a very serious thing'.

Their crimes are individualism. Bohemianism. They won't accept Party discipline. They are unreconstructed Marxist-Leninists and the 'good party Communists' don't see why such disordered creatures should be permitted to take care of Stephen's daughter by his first wife. Indeed, they are prepared to go to court to help contest his custody of the girl.

It is an extraordinary scene, a 'trial without jury, entirely in the spirit of the mid-century and their society'. The Howards are subjected to what is virtually a moral crucifixion – 'It was thought necessary by us all to get you here and be frank and clear,' they are told.

At this point, the Hollywood Communists have a great deal of power and do not even realise when they are abusing it. With hindsight, one knows all those gathered in the room will shortly face real trials of their own; it is one of Stead's singular achievements to make us understand fully some of the powerful bitternesses that came to flower in the days of HUAC.

But the Howards remain proudly unreconstructed. 'Still on the train that started from the Finland Station,' as Stephen says, he is determined to stay on it until the end. They compile a litany of the sins of the Soviet Union, the 1923 Party purge, the expulsion of Trotsky, the labour camps. 'And to think we're losing our shirts and our faces, standing up for such a nation, such betrayers of all that's dear to the romantic hearts of the parlour pinks,' says Emily. Then she damns herself: 'Heigh-ho! History doesn't bear scrutiny.'

The Howards flee, not the Party but their country. Like the representatives of the Lost Generation immediately preceding them, they go to Paris. They set up a vast entourage of children, nannies, maids, cooks, governesses, and proceed to live the life of Riley although, in the aftermath of the Second World War, the necessities of life are scarce and luxuries virtually unobtainable. But the Howards live happily, lavishly, off the Black Market, financed by Emily's earnings. Slowly, the contradictions of their situation destroy them.

They meet former collaborators and former resistants and people whose experience under Fascism has driven them to despair. The Howards are at sea. Increasingly corrupted by money and the privileges it can buy in a poor country, they guitily discover they enjoy the company of the collaborators, their style, their fine food, rather better than the European comrades, with their dour air, their poverty, their patronage of typical little workers' bistros where the food wreaks havoc with Stephen's ulcer and on Emily's increasingly refined palate.

Emily gives herself over to gluttony; soon they are like Mr and Mrs Jack Spratt. Stephen querulous, dyspeptic, is increasingly given to shady practices with the money that has been settled on his daughter and the nephew whom they have adopted, for Emily's earning power is on the wane.

But still they spend, spend, spend, as news comes of the witch hunts at home. The leaders of the red élite that so berated them, those 'pious, stiff-necked people', as Emily calls them, are now in prison; they pleaded the First Amendment, they refused to name names. Communism has fallen out of fashion with a vengeance in the US.

The European comrades, the governesses, and shabby businessmen who turn out to be great heroes of the Resistance, are not interested in living well, to which the Howards by now are fatally addicted although Emily's writing, like Communism, has gone out of fashion and their debts are piling up. Has the time come at last to get off that 'slow train from Finland'?

Emily, half-mad with worry and balked ambition, gives in first, hoping that if she recants she will be forgiven and once more be rich and famous. Once she has done so, Stephen, heart and spirit broken, follows suit. Stead does not make a big issue of the scenes where the Howards name names, as if she cannot bear to linger on it.

Emily might have been able, out of her chronic Bohemianism, to patch herself together and go on, Stephen has nothing left to live for. That 'bad end' their author has prepared for them is nigh.

(1987)

Phyllis Rose: *Jazz Cleopatra*

'She just wiggled her fanny and all the French fell in love with her,' said Maria Jolas to Josephine Baker's biographer, Phyllis Rose. Maria Jolas, evidently still bewildered after all these years by the insouciant ease with which the washerwoman's daughter from St Louis, Missouri, conquered Paris in 1925.

But by all accounts that wiggle was an unprecedented event even in the uninhibited world of Parisian spectacle. Her posterior agitated as if it had a life of its own. Phyllis Rose theorises about it: 'With Baker's triumph, the erotic gaze of a nation moved downward: she had uncovered a new region for desire.' Surely Ms Rose is being a little unfair; the French reputation for sexual sophistication may be exaggerated but the *habitués* of Montmartre cabaret *must* have seen a bare bum before.

And, of course, it wasn't as simple as that. Baker herself put her finger on the source of her attraction: 'The white imagination sure is something when it comes to blacks,' she said. When Baker sailed the Atlantic in 1925 with a group of African-American artists, including Sidney Bechet, to take a little taste of show-stopping Harlem nightlife to Europe, she left behind nascent Broadway stardom as a comic dancer, an elastic-limbed, rubber-faced clown, grimacing, grinning, crossing her eyes, to find her-self freshly incarnated as a sex-goddess without, it would seem, changing her act very much at all.

She even, although glammed up to the nines, continued cross-ing her eyes at odd moments: she must have felt it necessary to make her own ironic comment on herself to her audiences, so rapt and breathless was the Parisian reaction to the *Revue Négre*.

'Their lips must have the taste of pickled watermelon, coconut, poisonous flowers, jungles and turquoise waters,' enthused one scribe.

Yes, of course there is an implicit racism behind that purple prose, but it is a better thing to be adored for one's difference than shunned for it and Phyllis Rose describes eloquently the extraordinary sense of liberation these black artists felt when they arrived in Europe. Life acquired a grand simplicity; any bar would serve them, and waiters said: 'sir', and 'madame'. They could check into any hotel they wanted. To use a public convenience did not provoke a race riot. Later on, in the US in the Fifties, Baker would battle valiantly in the Civil Rights Movement; in Paris in the Twenties, she allowed herself to enjoy being a girl. She was Cinderella, the papers said; all she need do now was try on the slipper and marry the prince.

As toothy, exuberant, not-precisely-pretty Josephine Baker grew into her new role of jungle queen, savage seductress and round Baudelairean Black Venus, she left off making faces. At night, she hit the town in Poiret frocks. She never married a prince but Georges Simenon always said he would have married her had he not been married already; then, staggering thought, she would have been, in a sense, Madame Maigret. She had plenty of other offers, too; Phyllis Rose does not drop many names, although she gives a teasing vignette of the architect Le Corbusier, whom Baker met on an ocean liner. 'He and Josephine became great pals and he went to the ship's costume ball dressed as Josephine Baker, with darkened skin and a waistband of feathers.'

She acquired a pet, a leopard named Chiquita, 'a male despite his name', who sported a diamond collar. (She had a Bardot-like passion for animals.) Chiquita went everywhere with her, her exquisite objective correlative; the French wanted her to be herself a jewelled panther and good humouredly she gave them what they wanted. Baring her breasts, she danced in the Folies Bergéres wearing a girdle of bananas and sealed her fame. From henceforth, this garment, which is, I think, unknown in any form of dress in any part of the world, which is purely the invention of a mildly prurient exoticism, would be associated with her.

In 1928, she danced in Berlin. Louise Brooks, there to film *Pandora's Box* for Pabst, and something of an expert in the methodology of exploited sexuality, saw her. When Josephine Baker appeared, naked except for a girdle of bananas, it was precisely as Lulu's stage entrance was described by Wedekind: "They rage there as in a menagerie when the meat appears at the cage".' Phyllis Rose doesn't record Brooks's observation, suggesting as it does that there was, perhaps, rather more raw eroticism about Baker's early performances than Rose lets on.

La Baker came back to the Casino de Paris and sang: 'J'ai deux amours. Mon pays et Paris.' That became *her* song. In return for her youth, her sex, her exoticism, the French gave her love, cash, and respect. She briefly returned to Broadway in 1935 and arrived at a party for Gershwin in full drop-'em-dead French glamour-queen glad rags: 'Who dat?' said Bea Lillie. In France once again, now and then she'd change the words of her song: 'Mon pays, c'est Paris.' After a war in which she proved her loyalty to her adopted country, smuggling secret information in invisible ink on her sheet music, would you believe, the French gave her the Légion d'Honneur.

She died in her seventieth year, in 1975, in the white heat and ostrich plumes of her umpteenth come-back, an institution, a heroine, mourned by the dozen children – her multi-ethnic 'Rainbow Tribe' – she adopted in her forties, something glorious if faintly touched by the ludicrous, at last, a geriatric sex-queen cherished in old age by the French loyalty to the familiar as she had been fêted when young by the French passion for the new.

(1990)

· 34 ·
Murasaki Shikibu: *The Tale of Genji*

The Tale of Genji is a masterpiece of narrative fiction and was written a thousand years ago by a woman whose real name we do not know (she's always been known by the name of her own main heroine, Murasaki). Its most immediately affecting quality is that of an exquisite and anguishing nostalgia. Not a whisper of the morning of the world, here; all regret at the fall of the leaf and remembrance of things past.

It is also endlessly long, constructed with great skill and composed in a Japanese so archaically elusive that many modern Japanese will use Seidensticker's definitive English translation as a handy crib. Murasaki Shikibu had the capacity for dealing with emotional complexity of a Stendhal and a sensibility rather more subtle than that of Proust.

Kyoto, the Imperial capital of Japan of the Heian period, which is her setting, was a dazzling place, where fine handwriting, a nice judgement in silks and the ability to toss off an evocative 60-syllable tanka at the drop of a cherry blossom were activities that achieved the status of profound moral imperatives for the upper classes.

The major work of English literature extant at roughly the same period is butch, barbaric, blood-boltered *Beowulf*, a fact that makes the Japanese giggle like anything. Though Murasaki does not by any means capture all the world in her silken net; cultured as all hell her courtiers may be but they are the élite of an élite and when her hero, Genji, in exile, catches a glimpse of the life of the common fisherman, he finds it difficult to believe other people are altogether human. Murasaki's imperial court is a claustrophobic place.

And it is a curious fact that a novel so variously beautiful, so shot through with rainbow-hued poetry, so sophisticated, so instinct with that heart-wrenching sense of the impermanence of the world the Japanese call 'mono-no-aware' (the sadness inherent in things) should procure in this reviewer at least the sense of having gorged herself on a huge box of violet-centred chocolates.

At least Arthur Waley's Bloomsburyish and truncated version (which Seidensticker's monumental achievement is bound to supersede) gave the inescapable lady-novelist quality of *The Tale of Genji* its due. Seidensticker's chaste, occasionally transatlantic, idiom errs only on the side of a lack of self-indulgence.

The polygamous and promiscuous Heian court – 'court life is only interesting when all sorts of ladies are in elegant competition,' opines Genji – produced a bumper crop of lady writers; in the endless boredom of rarely visited harems, in the well-screened apartments of retired empresses, there were dozens of bright, clever, highly educated, twitching, neurotic women, scribbling away – poems, novels, diaries, commonplace books, anything to pass the time.

Life revolved around the suns, the shining ones, the emperor, and chief ministers. The character of Genji himself, the sentimental rake who never forgets a one-night stand and always commemorates it in a wee personalised poemlet on the loveliest notepaper, the first great romantic fictional hero in the world, is indeed supremely fictional. It is not a characterisation but an idealisation, a model for polygamous husbands.

But the life of the Imperial sprig, Genji, is not the whole meat of the novel. It is essentially a family saga, the family the enormous clan of the Imperial family, with the extraordinary network of relationships that multiple wives, child marriage, and institutionalised illegitimacy makes possible. It flows on and on, with no apparent reason for stopping, then halts abruptly in midstream – possibly because Murasaki died, or became a nun.

After Genji dies, about three quarters of the way through, Murasaki concentrates her attention on the tormented love-affairs of the frivolous Niou, and of Kiaru, with his repressed sexuality and general oddness. There is a definite change of emphasis, now, a sharpening of focus, an increase in psychological realism. It is as though the lives of Genji and his lovely consort, Murasaki, had been an account of a golden age, now past; the world is running downhill, no more descriptions of snow-viewing or incense-making competitions. The glamour of all those beautiful people is definitely tarnished.

Beautiful people Niou and Kiaru certainly are, but as deeply unpleasant as most beautiful people. As one ex-concubine remarks of the father of her child: 'The Prince at Uji was a fine, sensitive gentleman but he treated me as if I were less than human,' and the unfortunate product of this liaison is hounded to the point of suicide by the conflicting attentions of our predatory heroes.

One suspects that, by page 1,000, it is beginning to occur to our narrator herself that the Heian Court, from the point of view of one of those ladies in elegant competition, is really a meat-market with a particularly pretty decor. That ineffable Buddhist gloom, which makes Calvinism look positively sprightly, begins to suffuse the text.

Nevertheless, the decor is absolutely ravishing. Murasaki depicts an exquisite, pictorial life. The first chapters unfold themselves like a succession of painted screens, in which the beauties of nature and the seasons and the weather have the function of pure decoration. There are the rituals of bird and butterfly dances; the shuttered, sequestered women with their black-painted teeth and six-foot swatches of hair, in robes of white silk lined with red, yellow lined with russet, arrange and rearrange those irridescent sleeves that are all custom allows of them to be seen beneath their curtains, sleeves often wet with tears due to the demands of their highly cultivated hearts.

Flowers, everywhere; women named for flowers. Gardens. Ruined houses where neglected ladies sit like Mariana in the moated grange ('he cometh not,' she said). And, dominating everything, an absolute tyranny of good taste, a Stalinist regime of refinement. Choose a singlet of the wrong shade of red and your life is as good as over.

Yet the ominous thunder of the river in which poor Ukifune tries to drown herself reverberates through the last chapters like the very voice of stern Buddhist morality itself. It's all the dream of a dream, you see. All of it. It is curious that this wonderful and ancient novel that Seidensticker's translation makes so

voluptuously deliciously readable should have so little hope in
it.

(1977)

· 35 ·

Eric Rhode: *On Birth and Madness*

This book begins like a novel: 'A woman attends a funeral. The coffin is lowered into the grave. A man approaches her and says: "He was not your father."' But the reader's expectation of continuous narrative is excited only to be disrupted; Eric Rhode prefers to work in discrete sections of speculation, each independently, often curiously titled – 'Father into Foetus', 'Eyes Pregnant with a Mother's Babies'. This method of organisation is reminiscent of the collections of brief, aphoristic essays by Theodor Adorno, although Eric Rhode's intellectual method is rather less rigorous than Adorno's. Rhode's speculation centres on work as a psychiatrist in a puerperal breakdown unit – that is, a place where women are sent who have gone mad in connection with the process of childbirth. However, his scope extends far beyond the specificity of his book's title.

It is a favourite saying among women of my type that if men could have babies, then abortion would be as readily available as light ale. Nevertheless, it is in just this physical difference that the whole opposition of the sexes lies. If men could have babies, they would cease to be men as such. They would become the 'other'. They would become magical objects of strangeness, veneration, obloquy, awe, disregard, and oppression, recipients of all the effects of the syndrome of holy terror. I wonder if it has occurred to Eric Rhode that, but for a chance division of cells while he was an undirected foetus, he, too, might have had babies. Certainly he seems to imply that parturition is not a function of the psychiatric profession itself: 'Psychiatrists talk about a mental unhinging round about the seventh month: is this true? We need

more evidence, especially from the pregnant delegates themselves.' So there aren't any women psychiatrists around who can
supply the necessary?

Don't think I don't realise that Rhode doesn't mean this. It is
only the sloppy way he has phrased it. Yet the question need
not have remained rhetorical. Even if he does not know any
psychiatrists who have been pregnant, if that is possible, then his
list of acknowledgements includes known mothers who could
have told him. Semantic sloppiness usually goes hand in hand
with mental sloppiness. For example, is it just some psychiatrists
or all psychiatrists who claim that women become 'unhinged' –
whatever that means – in late pregnancy? If it is the opinion of
the entire profession, as he implies, how was it arrived at – by a
postal ballot or by a show of hands? Rhodes is not fond of
footnotes, on the whole. Nor, I suspect, of empiricism. On the
other hand, he has far more female intuition than I do.

It occurs to me, thinking about this wayward, infuriating book
with its shining flashes of metaphysics, its linguistic imprecision,
its mass of references (Blake, Kierkegaard, Shakespeare, Giorgione, Walter Benjamin, and more, and more) how deeply
psychoanalysis is concerned with culture. Not only broadly, with
culture as opposed to nature, but also with culture in its narrowest
sense – that is, high-bourgeois culture. Easel painting, symphonic
music, literature. As if Freud had condemned the entire profession
to the taste of a cultivated Viennese at the turn of the century.

Rhode is prepared to advance pure cultural product as the sacred
book of the Freudian calling. By page three, he is already talking
about 'a Greek play often read as psychoanalytic holy writ, Sophocles's *Oedipus the King.*' But he does not think of *Oedipus the King*
as a cultural product, with the specific conditions of the time and
place of its composition mediating its universality. Nor does he
treat the play as if Sophocles had dreamed it. Rather, he seems
to think of the Oedipus family as though they were real people
with real problems, an approach similar to that of the literary
criticism of A. C. Bradley. He talks about the Hamlets the same
way; they might even be patients, although he does not pause to
entertain the Bradleian-style gloss I've always put on the play
myself: that it only makes sense if Hamlet is really the son of
Claudius and not of 'Hamlet's Father' at all.

One could argue that *Oedipus the King* is really, deep down, about the overthrow of Mother Right, that the play contains, transforms, subverts, patricises the ideology of those antique, matrilinear communities around the Mediterranean celebrated somewhat circumspectly in *The Golden Bough*, and increasingly cherished by women of my type as we reach a certain age, in which kingship was attained by marriage with the queen and terminated in ritual combat with the inevitable defeat by a more nubile successor when the hapless consort's hairline started to recede or his ardour flag. This is the version Robert Graves gives in his *Greek Myths*, and though Graves's anthropology is just as shaky as J. G. Frazer's, I love the poetic truth at the kernel of it. Certainly the question 'Who is your father?' only becomes pressing when property is inherited through the male line.

Children, since they are polymorphously perverse by nature and, furthermore, do not usually possess property, can be much nicer, wiser, and kinder than culture. In an early essay, Melanie Klein tells about a small boy who, informed how babies are made, is told that he can do it himself when he grows up. '"But then I would like to do it to Mama." "That can't be, Mama can't be your wife [*sic*] for she is the wife of your papa, and then papa would have no wife." "But we could both do it to her!"' The heart, or hearts, of many-breasted Cybele would warm to that. (I wonder if Melanie Klein believed women became unhinged in the seventh month of pregnancy.)

I understand perfectly well that Sophocles' play is about aspects of human relations that transcend the immediate circumstances of its composition. Oedipal conflict pre-dates Sophocles. On the other hand, the play isn't the pure product of Sophocles' unconscious either – art is not the dream of culture. But Sophocles and Rhode are both very much concerned with crude biologism *vis-à-vis* the Oedipal situation. Indeed, Rhode is so interested in paternity that he introduces a woman concerned about her own paternity in the first paragraph of a book that is supposed to be about maternity.

'He was not your father.' In the terms of the real world in which we live and where we try to cherish our dear ones, Oedipus *does* escape his fate. He does not murder the man who saved him from death, nurtured him, gave him a bicycle, had his teeth straightened, paid for driving lessons, etc. Nor does he impregnate the woman who wiped his bum, taught him to sneeze, and catered to all the indignities of childhood that effectively de-eroticise the relationship between mothers and sprogs. Oedipus's genuine filial feelings are not outraged. His biological parents are perfect strangers. To emphasise the biological aspect of parenthood is to deny culture in a way that makes us less human. That dreadful question – how do we know whose child we are? – has dogged patriarcy since its inception, yet it is a profoundly absurd question. Put it another way: an American friend discovered her son had financed his grand tour of Europe by selling shots of his sperm to an AID agency. 'My grandchildren!' she cried and then fell silent, suddenly aware of the absurdity, to even think of them like that.

There never has been a way to know. Not truly know. Until just now, in the late twentieth century, when genetics can help us. And that is somewhat late in the day for the human race, which has been forced to rely for so long on its mother's word when women are so notoriously duplicitous. But the question has been so pressing it has even resolved itself in metaphysics, in the invention of an omnipotent but happily non-material father to whom everyone can lay claim as a last resort.

'Father' is always metaphysics: a social artefact, a learned mode. Rhode is prepared to concede this, using his favourite device of the rhetorical question. 'Who is my father, my mother, my brother, my sister? In a sense, the answer is simple – in regard to our mother, at least.' (In regard to all the others, it may be unbearably complex.) 'There is documentation; and the documentation is unlikely to have been faked.'

Unlikely, but not improbable. Raising the unwanted child of a sister, or a daughter, as one's own is not uncommon among working-class families, often causing a good deal of existential anxiety. On the other hand, although a mother can fake the documentation of her condition, she cannot fake the physical event of birth.

The fact of maternity has become a good deal more problematic in the late twentieth century than it has been hitherto, however. For example: am I the mother of the fertilised egg I carry when it does not originate in my own ovary? I'd say: yes, of course. But where does the child who eventually comes out of this egg stand in relation to such a mother in terms of incest taboo? What degree of kinship would the Sphinx ascribe? If Jocasta had donated a fertilised egg to Merope, what then?

These are academic, even scholastic points. But they underpin a good deal of the discussion about mechanical intervention in the processes of maternity, where the culture of high-tech surgery manifests itself at its most 'unnatural' by taking on, and succeeding at, a job that Mother Nature shirked. And if this train of thought is followed to the end, we must conclude that 'mother' is also primarily a conceptual category. Just like 'father'.

Yes, but. If these basic, physically determined relationships are not 'natural', then what is? And why do women, having given birth – the most natural thing in the world, as they constantly tell you at the antenatal clinic – so frequently go mad, as if the violent collision of culture and nature which is the event of childbirth shatters us?

Rhode does not really attempt to deal with this question. Instead, he manages to invest biological motherhood with an almost occult quality. Discussing Oedipus: 'That he fails to see the old man he meets at the crossroads (and murders) as his father is not improbable; that he fails to sense that the bereft queen (whom he marries) might be his mother strains credulity.'

Why? Some young men find older women quite attractive, and though Jocasta might be a touch long in the tooth, she is still capable of giving Oedipus four healthy children, so she can't be that old. Freud says the feeling of *déjà vu* is always inspired by the memory of the body of the mother – *déjà vue*. Perhaps Rhode feels that Oedipus, whilst having intercourse with Jocasta, was bound to have recognised his intra-uterine address. Or is he trying to warn young men off older women because if you screw them you will go blind? Because there is always the chance she might be his mother?

Surely it should be the other way around, anyway. Augustus John used to pat the heads of all the children whom he met when he walked down the King's Road because he wasn't sure who was or wasn't his and didn't like to leave anybody out. Similarly, we should all treat all old men with respect, just in case. Seed is a random thing. There isn't the same margin for error with mothers, for whom it is a case of one egg, one birth, as a rule.

Meanwhile, Rhode is constructing an edifice of radiant surmise around that extraordinary clash of culture and nature, childbirth.

He is in love with the gnomic. He is so pleased with that sentence about our eyes being pregnant with our mother's babies that he repeats it twice, subtly varying it. He is rich in ideas that are marvellous, in the sense of the word that the surrealists used – magical, breathtaking, spurting from a sumptuous vein of his own unconscious. 'Adam's semen, the *semina aeternitatis*, contains all mankind,' he says. He has been discussing seventeenth-century philosophers; it has induced a seventeenth-century turn of phrase – or indeed, of mind. And the entire book is self-consciously in the form of a series of meditations of a doctor-philosopher, a sort of *Religio Medici* for our times. He condenses images into a dense, suggestive mass; he adores infinity.

And then one stumbles over a piece of nonsense. 'What does a father see when he looks at the beauty of his wife?' he demands rhetorically. But fathers do not necessarily have wives, nor, if they do, are these wives necessarily beautiful. I think I can see how this sentence has come about; Rhode is so concerned with the rhetoric of it he has not engaged in a little practical criticism. I suspect it ought to read: 'What does a father see when he looks at the beauty of his child's mother?'

The sentence remains a grid of patriarchal definitions: the mother is presented solely in terms of the gaze and vanity of the father, to whose credit it redounds to boast a 'beautiful' mate, and of her biological relation to both subjects. But at least it is no longer nonsense and the little bit of gratuitous romanticism about beauty suggests Rhode is really a nice man, even if carried away by his own rhetoric when he contemplates the fact of our arrival on this earth in its blood, its banality, its glory.

In fact, its romanticism is one of the most gripping things about the book, which could, perhaps, be subtitled 'A Psychiatrist in Search of the Soul'. Rhode is fairly sure he can locate that slippery concept even in the womb. 'Reluctantly I have come to the view that our heritage at infancy is some articulated yet unconscious Platonic idea, a necessary substrate to our capacity for having experiences.' H'm.

But then we come to the mad women themselves, in their bereft abandonment. He quotes from Etienne-Dominique Esquirol, who wrote down stark descriptions of women in breakdown in the 1830s. 'A woman feeding her child was startled by a clap of thunder. Her milk dried up. She lost her reason.' This makes

Rhode think of a painting by Giorgione, *The Tempest*. It makes me think of Munch, *The Scream*. When he arrives at the voices of the women in the puerperal breakdown unit themselves, it is scarcely tolerable. This is suffering beyond metaphor:

> She just screamed and screamed when I tried to feed her. I thought, it's my own child and she doesn't want me. In the end, I didn't want to get up in the morning. I felt so guilty. I didn't feel capable of looking after her. My neighbour fed her and I sat there and cried.

'When I'm washing her clothes and squeezing them out, I think I'm wringing her neck.' A woman describes a recurring dream: 'I remember closing my eyes – and I could see a knife sticking into a baby. I could see someone swinging the baby in our hall at home, swinging the baby round and round in the hall.'

Language crumbles under the weight of this pain. Mystification of this pain is a lie. This is what it is to be a mother and be mad.

(1988)

Envoi: Bloomsday

Now I will make my own legend and stick to it.
> Letter from James Joyce to Lady Gregory, 1904

Cities have sexes: London is a man, Paris a woman, and New York a well-adjusted transsexual, but – what is Dublin? Has it made up its mind? Yet if the Thames, as is well known, is Old Father, then Dublin's river is as famous a woman, is Anna Liffey, with her broad curves gracious as those of a *fin de siècle* bum. On 16 June, the name of the bridge at Chapelizod was officially changed to the Anna Livia Bridge, thus putting the unequivocal sex of Mother Liffey squarely on the map at last, even if in tribute to Dublin's most protean if least-grateful son, who irreverently changed 'Liffey' to 'Livia' after a Triestine housewife.

' . . . riverrun past Eve and Adam's, from swerve of shore to bend of bay . . . ' Invitation to the swell and ebb of sleeping and waking, to the world inside the book, which is the world, which is the river, which is the book. And so on. But *Finnegans Wake* is postgraduate stuff, still; as it turns out, *Ulysses* is for *everybody*.

Dubliners wished one another: 'A Happy Bloomsday.' Florists cashed in on a pardonable pun: 'Buy a bloom for Bloomsday,' and many, Anthony Burgess for one, sported Blazes Boylan buttonholes. Some said it should have been a national holiday. The entire inner city was *en fête* and, no, it did not rain. Thus Dublin ingeniously secularised and took back unto itself the first authentic post-modernist literary festival, a day devoted to the celebration of the fictional texts of James Joyce, in which the author took a back seat to his inventions.

For though 1982 is his centenary year, Joyce was not born nor did he die on 16 June, but chose to moor *Ulysses* to this point in time and place because, on that day, in 1904, Nora Barnacle

consented to walk out with him. You could say that, on that day,
Joyce's real life began for his greatest novels make of the role of
Husband the peak and summit of masculine aspiration. Joyce was
one of nature's husbands, incomplete until he found his wife, and
none the less so because he did not marry her for a decade or
two after; a husband, still, in his unconsummated dreams of
cuckoldry.

On Bloomsday, though, it was not Bloom's imaginary and
antlered head that graced the postage stamps, but the Brancusi
drawing of Joyce's own, the gaunt, bespectacled, subtly odd,
familiar face of the legend. But I prefer that infinitely moving
photograph of young Joyce, every inch a Jim, taken when he was
22 in that very blessed 1904 itself, hands in his pockets, almost a
*Boy's Own Paper*ly heroic stance. Such an undeniably handsome
face you see why Nora fell, and his eyes not yet dimmed nor
hidden away behind glasses. 'Asked what he was thinking when
C. P. Curran photographed him, Joyce replied: "I was wondering
would he lend me five shillings".'[1]

Note Joyce's syntax, here. His English, as he well knew, had
been moulded by another tongue, by one not even his mother
tongue since her monoglot English, too, had been moulded by
the language long lost within it. (The name of Dublin, Baile Atha
Cliath, in Irish so dignified and remotely foreign, turns, when
Anglicised, into the almost comically accessible Ballyattaclee: the
English knew how to make the languages of the ethnic minorities
of the British Isles ridiculous.)

This questing young man is already determined on earth-shat-
tering fame: 'Now I will make my legend and stick to it.' He
stares at us with almost a Jack London look of purpose. He is, I
think, already pondering a magisterial project: that of buggering
the English language, the ultimate revenge of the colonialised.

'Aren't there words enough for you in English?' the Bliznakoff
sisters asked Joyce. 'Yes . . . ,' he replied. 'But they aren't the
right ones.'

However many there were, there would never be the right
ones, since Joyce spoke a language that had been translated into
English and must always have suffered a teasing feeling that most
of the meaning had been lost in the process. Somewhere, perhaps
in the European languages, lurked that unimaginably rich
original.

What is more, we carry our history on our tongues and the history of the British Empire came to exercise a curious kind of brake upon our expression in the English language, as it became less and less the instrument of feeling and more and more that of propaganda. Something even odder has happened since Joyce's day, in these last years, when English, in the great world, has become synonymous with the language spoken in America, which, though it uses the same words, is an entirely other communications system. Indeed, American threatens to leave us entirely stranded, now, on a linguistic beach of history with English turning into a quaint dialect, another Old World survival, like Castillian Spanish, stiff outmoded, unapposite.

And what shall we do then? Why, we shall be thrust back on Joyce, who never took English seriously and so he could continue, as we will do.

However, the world-wide provenance of English, its ubiquitous if fading *functionability*, the reason why there *were* enough words in it, even if they had to be kicked around a bit and shown their place, is inseparable from the history of the British Empire, when English needed to be in a lot of different places at the same time. Happy for Shakespeare he did not speak Serbo-Croat and his Queen embarked on a policy of expansion. If you speak a language nobody understands, you can babble away as much as you like and nobody will hear you. Even had he wished to use it, the grand but archaic language of Ireland would not have suited a man who wished to straddle the world.

In *Ulysses*, only an Englishman is fluent in Irish. 'I'm ashamed I don't speak the language myself,' mutters a crone addressed in her native speech.

On the other hand, the Celtic revivalists were theoretically correct. The only way to get us off their backs was to ensure we could not understand what they were saying. But unfortunately, we *needed* to hear them and, by the turn of the century, Ireland was already committed to that tongue of the wicked stepmother – fortunately for us. And this is the tongue that Joyce systematically deformed, excavated, imploded, you might say; he made sufficient space within that appropriated language to accommodate the next phase of history.

He sheared away the phoney rhetoric that had been accreting over the centuries. In *Ulysses*, he transformed English into something intimate, domestic, demotic, a language fit not for heroes but for husbands, then did it over again, stripped it of its linguistic elements, in fact, and put it together in a polyglot babble that, perhaps, begins to approximate something like a symphonic Euro-language, in which English is no more than a dominant theme. He disestablished English.

Although American academia was especially prominent among the massed scholarship arriving in Dublin for Bloomsday Week and the VIII International James Joyce Symposium in order to get their heads down over a susurrating mass of learned papers, this question of the disestablishment of English is, of course, not an American problem. The American language had something exponential built into it from the start, although the chances are that American will harden its arteries somewhat if the United States dons the mantle of world leadership with too much enthusiasm. All the same, there is nothing culturally troubling about Joyce for Americans. There is for me. Troubling and consoling.

I do believe that, had Joyce opted for a career as a singer, as Nora wished, I, for one, as a writer in post-imperialist Britain, would not even have had the possibility of a language, for Joyce it was who showed how one could tell the story of whatever it is that is going to happen next. Not that he would have cared. Whatever it was he thought he was up to, it certainly wasn't making it easier for the British to explain their past and their future to themselves. He wasn't doing it for *our* sakes, he made *that* clear.

Nevertheless, he carved out a once-and-future language, restoring both the simplicity it had lost and imparting a complexity. The language of the heart and the imagination and the daily round and the dream had been systematically deformed by a couple of centuries of use as the rhetorical top-dressing of crude power. Joyce Irished, he Europeanised, he decolonialised English: he tailored it to fit this century, he drove a giant wedge between English Literature and literature in the English language and, in doing so, he made me (forgive this personal note) free. Free not to do as he did, but free to treat the Word not as if it were holy but in the knowledge that it is always profane. He is in himself the antithesis of the Great Tradition. You could also say, he detached fiction from one particular ideological base, and his work has still not yet begun to bear its true fruit. The centenarian still seems avant-garde.

'The value of the book is its new style,' he said of *Ulysses* to a friend in Paris.

And another thing . . . Poet of the upper-working and lower-middle classes as he was – that is, of the artistically most despised and rejected, poet of those exiled from poetry – he never succumbed to the delusion that people who do not say complicated things do not have complicated thoughts. Hence, the stream-of-consciousness technique, to bring that inner life into the open. It's simple. Just as, when you hear Joyce read aloud in the rhythms of Irish, it, too, all falls into place.

That is what Radio Telefis Eirann did, for Bloomsday. RTE broadcast *Ulysses*, read aloud, from early morning on 16 June till the next day. All over the city, transistors fed it to the air. RTE propose to sell cassettes of this mammoth and inspired occasion for the sum of £1,000 each, which would have gladdened Joyce's heart of a balked entrepreneur. (He set up the first cinema in Dublin, the Volta, in 1909, with Triestine money. It failed. RTE's project, with a market of American universities, will probably succeed.)

'History is a trap from which I am trying to escape,' said Stephen Daedalus. The Bloomsday of 1982 takes place in the capital city of the Republic of Ireland. It is a country which Bloom Joyce, the wandering Irishman, would find amazing. A state reception was held for him in Dublin Castle, and this reception turned out to be the very kind of riotous party Joyce adored. American Express offered the city the Bloomsday present of Joyce's head in bronze; the President himself, Dr Patrick Hillery, unveiled it. (Nobody thought to gratify Joyce's gleeful and malicious ghost by slipping say, an item of ladies' underwear under the veil and, indeed, it would have marred the dignity of the occasion.) Bloomsday was celebrated with such stylish and imaginative joyousness it seemed a pity the old boy missed it.

But the old city is pulling itself down. Freed at last from that 'hemiplegia of the will' which Joyce diagnosed as his country's most significant malady in a letter to his brother in 1903, Dublin, all bustle, thrust, traffic-jams, and businessmen concluding suave deals, is no longer the city I remember from even twenty years ago, which, then, pickled in the sour brine of poverty, was sufficiently like the city of the book to make you blink.

Nobody knows what tomorrow will bring.

The squares, the terraces, the grand parades, going, going, deserted, weed-grown, the city of the Raj, waiting for the demolition men, gone. The city seethes with gossip, rumour, and speculation about the activities of property speculators. Up go the mirror-clad slabs of office-blocks; Ireland has at last followed Joyce into Europe.

Everything has changed. If 16 June was Bloomsday, 26 June was Gay Pride Day. In the personal column of the magazine, *In Dublin*, the 'Legion of Mary' finds itself at hazard of alphabetical listing, nudging against 'Lesbian Line'. Decorating each street corner, exquisitely spiked and studded Irish punks have, overnight, discovered Style. The city, the country, whose inhabitants once seemed to leap with one bound from babyhood to middle age now seethes with the youngest population in Europe who have a look in their eyes that suggests they will not be easily satisfied. One doubts both the old sow's appetite for *this* farrow and her ability to digest it.

But nobody lives at 7, Eccles Street, anymore. The house where the imaginary Blooms never lived is now a tumbledown shell. Its door graces the Bailey Bar, in Duke Street. Before this abandoned house, however, at three in the afternoon of Bloomsday, a facsimile of Molly Bloom disposed herself upon a makeshift bed while Blazes Boylan made his way towards her and her husband pottered pooterishly round the town. Because this is what Dublin did for Bloomsday: it peopled the streets of the city with the beings of the book: the Word made Flesh, in fact.

For one hour, just one hour, up they all popped, in costume, large as life, and even 'William Humble, Earl of Dudley, and Lady Dudley, accompanied by Lieutenant-Colonel Hesseltine' riding out from the viceregal lodge in a cavalcade of carriages and antique horseless carriages. And exquisite children in pinafores and sunbonnets and ladies in tight bloomers on tricycles and blind men and one-legged sailors and look it up in your Bodley Head edition, the 'Wandering Rocks' episode in *Ulysses* (pages 280, 328), this slice of teeming 1904 Dublin life rendered as street theatre, like a marvellous hallucination. Nothing could have been more perfect, as the city adopted Bloomsday and revisited its own vanishing past with a tourist's eager curiosity and the devotion of a trustee.

These are, perhaps, the last few years when Joyce's fictional blueprints of Dublin will correspond at all to the real outlines of the city. Dublin appears, the final tribute, to be 'fixing' the city of the book as perfect fiction by tidying away the real thing so that Joyce's Dublin can gloriously survive as its own monument, the book which is the city, the metaphysical city of the word, while whatever it is that happens next gets on with it.

Jorge Luis Borges at the Bloomsday banquet, proposing the toast to Joyce and Ireland ('since for me they are inseparable'), opined that, one day, 'as with all great books', *Ulysses* and *Finnegans Wake* would become books for children. One day, one fine day, one universal Bloomsday, when, perhaps, the metaphysics depart from the book and it becomes life, again.

(1982)

Notes

Introduction

1. From the essay, 'Readers respond to Rousseau', in Robert Darnton, *The Great Cat Massacre* (London: Allen Lane, 1984).

1. *Milorad Pavic:* Dictionary of the Khazars

A review of Milorad Pavic, *Dictionary of the Khazars: A Lexicon Novel in 100,000 Words*, trans. Christina Privicevic-Zoric (London: Hamish Hamilton), *London Review of Books*, 1989.

2. *Milorad Pavic:* Landscape Painted with Tea

A review of Milorad Pavic, *Landscape Painted with Tea*, trans. Christina Privicevic-Zoric (London: Hamish Hamilton), *The Independent on Sunday*, 1991.

3. Irish Folk Tales, Arab Folktales

A review of *Irish Folk Tales*, ed. Henry Glassie (Harmondsworth: Penguin Books) and *Arab Folktales*, trans. and ed. Inea Bushnaq (Harmondsworth: Penguin Books), *Guardian*, 1987.

4. *Danilo Kis:* The Encyclopedia of the Dead

A review of Danilo Kis, *The Encyclopedia of the Dead* (New York: Farrar, Straus & Giroux), *New York Times Book Review*, 1989.

Notes

5. *John Berger:* Pig Earth

A review of John Berger, *Pig Earth* (London: Writers and Readers Publishing Co-operative), *New Society*, 1979.

6. *John Berger:* Once in Europa

A review of John Berger, *Once in Europa* (New York: Pantheon Books), *Washington Post*, 1989.

7. The German Legends of the Brothers Grimm

A review of *The German Legends of the Brothers Grimm*, trans. and ed. Donald Ward (London: Millington Books), *Guardian*, 1981.

8. *Georges Bataille:* Story of the Eye

A review of Georges Bataille, *Story of the Eye* (London: Marion Boyars), *New Society*, 1979.

9. *William Burroughs:* The Western Lands

A review of William Burroughs, *The Western Lands* (London: Picador), *Guardian*, 1988.

10. *William Burroughs:* Ah Pook is Here

A review of William Burroughs, *Ah Pook is Here* (London: John Calder), *Guardian*, 1979.

11. *J. G. Ballard:* Empire of the Sun

A review of J. G. Ballard, *Empire of the Sun* (London: Victor Gollancz), *Time Out*, 1984.

12. *Walter de la Mare:* Memoirs of a Midget

Written as the Introduction to Walter de la Mare, *Memoirs of a Midget* (Oxford University Press, 1982).

13. *The Alchemy of the Word*

First published in *Harpers & Queen*, 1978.

14. *An Omelette and a Glass of Wine* and other Dishes

A review of Ann Barr and Paul Levy, *The Official Foodie Handbook* (London: Ebury Press), Elizabeth David, *An Omelette and a Glass of Wine* (London: Hale), and Alice Waters, *Chez Panisse Menu Cookbook*, Foreword by Jane Grigson (London: Chatto & Windus), *London Review of Books*, 1984, with subsequent correspondence, *London Review of Books*, 1985.

15. *Redcliffe Salaman:* The History and Social Influence of the Potato

A review of Redcliffe Salaman, *The History and Social Influence of the Potato*, ed. J. G. Hawkes (Cambridge University Press), *London Review of Books*, 1986.

16. *Food in Vogue*

A review of *Food in Vogue: Six Decades of Cooking and Entertaining*, ed. Barbara Tims (London: Harrap), *New Society*, 1977.

17. *Elizabeth David:* English Bread and Yeast Cookery

A review of Elizabeth David, *English Bread and Yeast Cookery* (London: Penguin Books), *New Society*, 1987.

18. *Patience Gray:* Honey from a Weed

A review of Patience Gray, *Honey from a Weed: Fasting and Feasting in Tuscany, Catalonia, the Cyclades and Apulia* (London: Prospect Books), *London Review of Books*, 1987.

19. *Hanif Kureishi:* The Buddha of Surburbia

A review of Hanif Kureishi, *The Buddha of Suburbia* (London: Faber & Faber), *Guardian*, 1990.

Notes

20. *Ian Jack:* Before the Oil Ran Out *and others*

A review of Ian Jack, *Before the Oil Ran Out: Britain 1977–86* (London: Secker & Warburg), Beryl Bainbridge, *Forever England: North and South* (London: Duckworth/BBC Books), and *Norma Dolby's Diary: An Account of the Great Miners' Strike* (London: Verso), *Guardian*, 1987.

21. *Michael Moorcock:* Mother London

A review of Michael Moorcock, *Mother London* (London: Secker & Warburg), *Guardian*, 1988.

22. *Iain Sinclair:* Downriver

A review of Iain Sinclair, *Downriver* (London: Paladin), *London Review of Books*, 1991, and letter from the author.

23. *Robert Coover:* A Night at the Movies

A review of Robert Coover, *A Night at the Movies, or, You Must Rember This* (London: Heinemann), *Guardian*, 1987.

24. *Hollywood*

A review of David Bordwell, Janet Staiger, and Kristin Thompson, *The Classical Hollywood Cinema: Film Styles to 1960* (London: Routledge), Paul F. Boller jr and Ronald L. Davis, *Hollywood Anecdotes* (Basingstoke: Macmillan), and *Close-Ups: The Movie Star Book*, ed. Danny Peary (New York: Fireside), *Guardian*, 1988.

25. *Edmund White:* The Beautiful Room is Empty

A review of Edmund White, *The Beautiful Room is Empty* (London: Picador), *Guardian*, 1988.

26. *Paul Theroux:* My Secret History

A review of Paul Theroux, *My Secret History* (London: Hamish Hamilton), *Guardian*, 1989.

27. *Gilbert Hernandez:* Duck Feet

Written as the Introduction to Gilbert Hernandez, *Duck Feet* (London: Titan Books, 1988).

28. *Louise Erdrich:* The Beet Queen

A review of Louise Erdrich, *The Beet Queen* (London: Hamish Hamilton), *Guardian*, 1987.

29. *Grace Paley:* The Little Disturbances of Man *and* Enormous Changes at the Last Minute

A review of Grace Paley, *The Little Disturbances of Man* (London: Virago) and *Enormous Changes at the Last Minute* (London: Virago), *London Review of Books*, 1980.

30. *Charlotte Brontë:* Jane Eyre

Written as the Introduction to Charlotte Brontë, *Jane Eyre* (London: Virago, 1990).
1. *The Poems of Charlotte Brontë and Patrick Branwell Brontë*, ed. T. J. Wise and J. A. Symington (Oxford: Blackwell, 1934).

31. *David Kunzle:* Fashion and Fetishisms

A review of David Kunzle, *Fashion and Fetishisms* (George Prior Associated Publishers), *New Society*, 1982.

32. *Christina Stead*

A review of Christina Stead, *The Beauties and Furies*, Introduction by Hilary Bailey (London: Virago), *London Review of Books*, 1982 and *I'm Dying Laughing* (London: Virago), *Guardian*, 1987.

33. *Phyllis Rose:* Jazz Cleopatra

A review of Phyllis Rose, *Jazz Cleopatra: Josephine Baker in her Time* (London: Chatto & Windus), *The Tatler*, 1990.

Notes

34. *Murasaki Shikibu:* The Tale of Genji

A review of Murasaki Shikibu, *The Tale of Genji* (London: Secker & Warburg), *Guardian*, 1977.

35. *Eric Rhode:* On Birth and Madness

A review of Eric Rhode, *On Birth and Madness* (London: Duckworth), *London Review of Books*, 1988.

Envoi: Bloomsday

First published in *New Society*, 1982.
1. *James Joyce*, Richard Ellman (New York: Oxford University Press, 1959).

219

Index

A la carte (magazine) 77
Acker, Kathy 45–6
Adorno, Theodor 200
Amis, Kingsley 18, 46: *Lucky Jim* 109
Amis, Martin 47
Anderson, Sherwood 147: *Winesburg Ohio* 146
Anger, Kenneth: *Hollywood Babylon* 137
Anglo-American Cyclopaedia 12
Appollinaire, Guillaume 71: *Les Mamelles de Tiresias* 71
Apuleius 1, 9
Arabian Nights Entertainment, The 9, 12
Aragon, Louis 68, 70, 73
Ardizzone, Edward 93
Arnold, Matthew 166
Arp, Jean 71
Artaud, Antonin 70
Atlee, Clement 4
Austen, Jane 57–8: *Emma* 162

Bailey, Hilary 185
Bainbridge, Beryl: *Forever England* 113
Baker, Josephine 193–5
Ballard, J. G. 4, 46–7: *The Atrocity Exhibition* 44; *The Concrete Island, Crash!* 46; *Empire of the Sun* 44–50; *High Rise* 46; 'The Drained Swimming Pool', 'The Open-Air Cinema', 'The Fallen Airman' 47; 'Why I want to fuck Ronald Reagan' 44, 66; *The Unlimited Dream Company* 47
Balzac, Honoré de; *Lost Illusions* 62
Barr, Ann and Levy, Paul; *The Official Foodie Handbook* 77–9
Barth 45, 152
Barthelme 45
Barthes, Roland 38, 39
Bashevis Singer, Isaac 157
Bankhead, Tallulah 136
Bataille, Georges: *Story of the Eye* 37–8
Baudelaire, Charles 68, 176, 185
Beaton, Cecil 93
Bechet, Sidney 193
Bedford, Sybille 80
Beerbohm, Max 60, 68
Bellmer, Hans 45
Benjamin, Walter 7, 201
Berger, John 4, 104: *Once in Europa* 30–2; *Into their Labours* (trilogy) 32; *Pig Earth* 27–9, 105
Berkeley, Bishop George 73
Berlioz, Hector 169
Blake, William 54, 73, 116, 120, 123, 124, 126, 180, 181, 201: *The Marriage of Heaven and Hell* 189
Borges, Jorge Luis 12, 54, 168, 181, 213
Boswell, James 1
Boxer, Arabella 92
Bradley, A. C. 201
Brandel, Fernand: *Capitalism and Material Life* 88
Brecht, Bertold 115, 137: *The Threepenny Opera* 184

Index

Breton, André 67, 68, 70, 71, 72, 73:
 First Manifesto of Surrealism 73;
 Second Manifesto of Surrealism 71;
 Najda 72
Brontë, Anne 164, 165, 168
Brontë, Branwell 164, 165, 168
Brontë, Charlotte 161, 164, 165, 166,
 168: *Jane Eyre* 161–172; *The
 Professor* 161, 167; *Shirley* 165;
 Vilette 163, 165
Brontë, Emily 164, 165: *Wuthering
 Heights* 165
Brooks, Louise 194–5: *Pandora's Box*
 194
Browne, Sir Thomas 57, 103
Browning, Robert 183
Buñuel, Luis 68, 153, 187: *L'Age d'or*
 38, 68; *Un Chien Andalou* 68
Burgess, Anthony 46, 95, 207
Burns, Robert 114
Burroughs, William 4, 73, 123, 141:
 Ah Pook is Here 42–3; *Cities of the
 Red Night* 39; *The Place of Dead
 Roads* 39; *The Western Lands* 39–41;
 The Phantom of Liberty 71; *The
 Naked Lunch* 119
Bushnaq, Inea: *Arab Folktales* 21, 22–3
Butterworth, Arthur 55
Byron, George Gordon, Lord 169

Calvino, Italo 10–11: *The Castle of
 Crossed Destinies* 17
Carrier, Robert 92
Carrington, Leonora 73
Carroll, Lewis 73: *Through the Looking
 Glass* 122
Carter, Jimmy 44
Carver, Raymond 151
Casablanca 133
Cecil, Lord David 52
Cesares, Bioy 12
Chaucer, Geoffrey 99
Clairmont, Claire 169
Classical Hollywood Cinema, The 135,
 136, 137
Cobbett, William 101
Colbert, Claudette 137
Coleridge, Samuel Taylor 56
Conan Doyle, Sir Arthur 109
Connolly, Cyril 39
Coover, Robert 11, 16, 45, 152: *A
 Night at the Movies* 131–4

Crevel, René 70
Cromwell, Oliver 22

Dada (magazine) 71
Dadas, the 67, 71
Dalai Lama, the 70
Dali, Salvador 68, 72: *L'Age d'or* 38;
 Un Chien Andalou 68
Dali, Gala 72
Darnton, Robert 20
Daubmannus, Joannes 11–12
David, Elizabeth 77, 89, 101: *English
 Bread and Yeast Cookery* 94–9; *An
 Omelette and a Glass of Wine* 77–84
Day Lewis, C. 52
de Chirico, Giorgio 71: *Hebdomeros* 71
Delacroix, Eugène 169
de la Mare, Walter: *On the Edge* 54–5;
 Come Hither 52, 56; *Memoirs of a
 Midget* 51–66; *Peacock Pie* 52; *The
 Return* 53; *Tea with Walter de la
 Mare* 53; *Three Royal Monkeys* 53,
 65; *Rupert Brooke and the Intellectual
 Imagination* 53
de Mille, Cecil B.: *The Sign of the
 Cross* 136
de Musset, Alfred 169
Desnos, Robert 70–1, 72
Desnos, Youki 73
Didion, Joan 155, 157
Dietrich, Marlene 136
Dinesen, Isak: *Seven Gothic Tales* 181
Dors, Diana 116
Dostoievsky, Fyodor 71
Douglas, Norman 80, 101
Dover Wilson, J. 52
Dreiser, Theodore 181
Driver, Christopher: *The British at
 Table 1940–1980* 82–3
Du Maurier, Daphne: *Rebecca* 163

Eco, Umberto: *The Name of the Rose*
 12
Eliot, George 158: *Middlemarch* 162
Eliot, T. S. 70, 122, 144: *The
 Wasteland* 39
Eluard, Paul 68, 70, 72, 182
Encyclopedia Britannica 12
Erdrich, Louise 146, 147: *The Beet
 Queen* 146, 151–54; *Love Medicine*
 146, 152, 153
Ernst, Max 45, 70–1

Index

Esquirol, Etienne-Dominique 205

Farrell, J. G.: *The Singapore Grip* 48
Fellini, Frederico 150: *Amarcord* 150
Fiedler, Leslie: *Freaks, Myths and
    Images of the Secret Self* 60
Fielding, Henry: *Tom Jones* 165
Firbank, Ronald 99
Fisher, M. F. K. 107: *The Art of Eating*
    104
Fitzgerald, Penelope 110
Fonda, Henry 137
Food in Vogue 90–3
Ford, John 135
Freud, Sigmund 15, 68, 201, 204: *The
    Interpretation of Dreams* 70

Garland, Judy 137, 142
Garson, Greer 136
Geering, R. D. 189, 190
Genet, Jean 141
Giorgione 201: *The Tempest* 206
Gissing, George 185
Glassie, Henry: *Irish Folk Tales* 21
Godard, Jean-Luc: *Weekend* 134;
    Alphaville 163
Goldfayn, George 72
Goldman, Emma 187
Goldwyn, Sam 136
Gould, Tony 5
Graves, Robert: *The Greek Myths* 202
Gray, Patience: *Honey from a Weed*
    100–105; *Plats du Jour, or Foreign
    Food* 100
Gray, Thomas 20
Greene, Graham 9
Gregory, Isabella, Lady 21, 207
Grimm, Brothers: *German Legends*
    33–6
Guide to World Literature 13
Guthrie, Arlo 82

Hardy, Thomas 27
Hawkes, J. G. 85
Hegel, G. W. F. 68
Heim, Michael Henry 25
Hernandez, Gilbert: *Heartbreak Soup,
    Duck Feet* 146–50
Hernandez, Jaime 147
Herrick, Sir James 57
Hogarth, William 176
Hollywood Anecdotes 135, 136, 137

Homer 1, 20, 103
Hopkins, Kenneth 52, 56

Irish Folk Tales 21

Jack, Ian: *Before the Oil Ran Out* 112–5
Jarrell, Randall 178
Jarry, Alfred 45, 68
Jolas, Maria 193
John, Augustus 204
Johnson, Dr Samuel 125
Joyce, James 5, 54, 178, 207–13:
    Finnegans Wake 21, 207, 213;
    Ulysses 207, 209–10, 211, 212, 213

Kafka, Franz 4, 13, 54
Keats, John 99
Kerouac, Jack 119
Kerr, Deborah 114
Kierkegaard, Soren 201
Kis, Danilo: *The Encyclopedia of the
    Dead* 24–6; *The Protocols of the
    Elders of Zion* 26
Koestler, Arthur: *Darkness at Noon*
    190
Kunzle, David: *Fashion and Fetishisms*
    173–6
Kureishi, Hanif: *The Buddha of
    Suburbia* 109–11; *My Beautiful
    Launderette* 111

Lamb, Lady Caroline 169
Langland, William: *Piers Plowman* 87
Lautréamont 68
Lawrence, D. H. 3, 54, 80–1, 178:
    Women in Love 163
Leavis, F. R. 9, 80
Le Corbusier 194
Leigh, Janet 135
Lessing, Doris 172: *The Golden
    Notebook* 177
Lévi-Strauss, Claude 74, 79
Levy, Paul 82 *see also* Barr, Ann and
    Levy, Paul
Lively, Penelope 10
London, Jack 114, 208: *People of the
    Abysses* 79, 124
Lovecraft, H. P. 122

MacColl, Ewan 112
MacDonald, George: *The Princess and
    the Goblin* 54

Index

Marie Antoinette 86
Marquez, Gabriel García 149: *One Hundred Years of Solitude* 149, 152
Marvell, Andrew 59
Marx, Karl 28, 68, 114
Masefield, John 52
Mature, Victor 136
Middleton Murry, J. 52
Miller, Karl 5
Miller, Lee 101
Miller, Max 86
Milton, John 20
Minton, John 93
Mitchell, Peter Todd 81
Mitford, Nancy 81
Monroe, Marilyn 137
Montaigne, Michel Eyquem de 80
Moorcock, Michael 46: *Mother London* 116–8
Morris, William 11
Morrison, Blake 5
Morrison, Toni 151
Munch, Edvard: *The Scream* 206
Murasaki Shikibu: *The Tale of Genji* 196–9
Murdoch, Iris 46
Mussolini, Benito 70

Neurgroschel, Joachim 38
Noll, Marcel 72

Official Foodie Handbook, The 78
Official Preppy Handbook, The 78
Official Sloane Ranger's Handbook, The 78
Official Young Aspiring Professionals Fast-Track Handbook, The 78
Orwell, George 113–14: *The Road to Wigan Pier* 113; *Nineteen Eighty Four* 190

Paley, Grace: *Enormous Changes at the Last Minute* 155–8; *The Little Disturbances of Man* 155–8
Pavic, Milorad: *Dictionary of the Khazars* 9–16; *Landscape Painted with Tea* 17–9
Peary, Danny: *Close-Ups* 137
Pepys, Samuel 1
Perelman, S. J. 82
Peret, Benjamin 37, 72
Plato 61

Plummer, Christopher 137
Porter, Cole 91
Pound, Ezra 70, 140
Powell, Anthony 46
Priestley, J. B. 52
Pritchett, V. S. 44
Privicevic-Zoric, Christina 14
Propp, Vladimir: *Morphology of the Folk-Tale* 10, 14
Pynchon, Thomas 152

Queneau, Raymond 72

Ray, Man 101
Reagan, Ronald 78, 151
Reeves, Maud Pember: *Round About a Pound a Week* 97
Raleigh, Sir Walter 86
Renoir, Jean 175–6
Rhode, Eric: *On Birth and Madness* 200–8
Rhys, Jean: *Wide Sargasso Sea* 163
Rigby, Elizabeth 162
Rimbaud, Arthur 68
Rose, Phyllis: *Jazz Cleopatra* 193–5
Rossetti, Christina: *Goblin Market* 55
Rushdie, Salman 6

Sackville-West, Vita 52
Sade, Marquis de 179
Salaman, Redcliffe: *The History and Social Influence of the Potato* 85–9
Salinger, J. D.: *Catcher in the Rye* 149
Sand, Georges 169
Sartre, Jean-Paul 81
Schulz, Bruno 12
Scott, Sir Walter 80
Seidensticker, Edward 196
Seymour-Smith, Martin 13
Shakespeare, William 106, 201
Shearer, Norma 136
Shelley, Mary: *Frankenstein* 162, 163
Shelley, Percy Bysshe 56, 169
Simenon, Georges 194
Sinclair, Iain 4: *Downriver* 119–127
Sinclair, Upton 114
Smith, Adam 28
Sontag, Susan 37, 38
Sophocles: *Oedipus the King* 201–3
Sound of Music, The 137
Soupoult, Philippe 70
Spielberg, Steven 149

Index

Stead, Christina 4, 177–8, 188–9: *The Beauties and the Furies* 179, 180, 181, 182, 183, 186; *Cotter's England* 177, 178, 179, 180, 183; *For Love Alone* 172, 178, 179, 180, 186–7; *House of All Nations* 182; *I'm Dying Laughing* 189, 189–91; *Letty Fox: Her Luck* 178, 179, 183–4, 187, 189; *A Little Tea, A Little Chat* 178, 180, 184, 187, 188, 189; *The Man Who Loved Children* 178, 179, 180, 181, 182, 183; *Miss Herbert* 177, 185–6; *The People with the Dogs* 187–8, 189; *The Salzburg Tales* 181–2, 183; *Seven Poor Men of Sydney* 179
Stendhal 196
Stevens, Wallace 13
Stoker, Bram: *Dracula* 162, 163
Stopes, Marie 52
Stoppard, Miriam 95
Suskind, Patrick: *Perfume* 12
Synge, John Millington 21

Taylor, Elizabeth 136
Thackeray, William Makepeace 169
Thalberg, Irving 136
Thatcher, Margaret 4, 78, 112, 115, 123, 126
Theroux, Paul: *My Secret History* 143–5
Thorne, John 84
Thucydides 1
Top Hat 132
Traeger, Tess 93
Traherne, Thomas 56, 99
Trevelyan, Sir Charles 87–8

Trevor, William 44
Tribute to Walter de la Mare on his Seventy Fifth Birthday 52
Triolet, Elsa 72–3
Truffaut, François 137
Tzara, Tristan 71–2

Vache, Jacques 71
Vogue see Food in Vogue
Vaughan, Henry 56
Vaughan, Keith 93
Vaughan Williams, Ralph 54
Victoria, Queen 53

Waley, Arthur 197; *The Secret History of the Mongols* 143
Walter: *My Secret Life* 143
Ward, Donald 33
Ward, John 82, 83, 101
Waters, Alice: *Chez Panisse Menu Cookbook* 81–2
Waugh, Evelyn 190
Welch, Denton 45
Whistler, Laurence 52
White, Edmund: *The Beautiful Room is Empty* 139–42; *A Boy's Own Story* 139
White, George: *Scandals* 90
White, Gilbert 101
White, Patrick 120
Williams, William Carlos 128, 151
Woolf, Virginia 80, 98

Voltaire: *Candide* 109

Yeats, W. B. 21
Yuppie Handbook, The 78